Contents

Acknowledgments

I WOULD LIKE TO OFFER MY THANKS to those people who assisted me in the completion of this book. Thanks to Harlan and Helen Fick for their never-ending support and fine eye for detail. Judith McDougall was tireless in her efforts to help me meet all deadlines. The support of Don and Colleen McGregor was most appreciated. Vicky Heatley's encouragement and research efforts were also helpful. Thanks are also due to Diko Melconian and Cal Boyington. Bert German Dickey III, Joseph Purvis, attorney-at-law, and Cpl. David Donham were kind to give of their time and offer their knowledge about President Clinton. Thanks to Michael Meyers, M.D., for granting me the interview that produced a medical perspective.

Two individuals were particularly instrumental in ensuring that the American people had an opportunity to consider the information in this book. My literary agent, Gregory Boylan of Otitis Media, was superb, and I enjoyed working with him. Hillel Black, editorial director of Carol Publishing Group, refined the book to help me state my message clearly. I am most grateful to him and his associates at Carol Publishing Group.

The Lewinsky Affair

SINCE THE 1996 EDITION of *The Dysfunctional President*, new allegations of serious sexual misconduct by President Clinton have come to light that reinforce the book's original thesis. In January 1998, there emerged stunning allegations that the president had had an affair with Monica Lewinsky, a White House intern, and then encouraged her to lie about it. Ms. Lewinsky's testimony was being sought by Paula Jones in connection with her sexual harassment suit against the president. In the affidavit Lewinsky said she had not had an affair, but in conversations with a friend, Linda Tripp, she had said she had. The friend taped the conversations and turned them over to legal authorities.

This bombshell, coming as the date neared for trial of the Paula Jones charges, finally spurred the media to take seriously allegations that the president has been leading a very active extramarital sex life that could compromise his ability to govern the country. Almost overnight, the president's personal weaknesses, which were self-evident and detailed several years ago in this book, ceased to be under a media taboo.

Attention to the president's sexual misconduct by mainstream newspapers and television networks was long overdue, and is certainly welcome, though it is tempting to respond to the current media fervor with a passive-aggressive retort, "Where were you when *The Dysfunctional President* was initially released? Why did you elect to stonewall information prior to the 1996 election?" However, what is truly important is that the impact of the president's psychology and sexual compulsion can now be subject to reasoned discussion.

The Lewinsky affair has to be evaluated in light of what I have called a sexual compulsion. This is discussed in chapter 13 in detail. Here I address specific aspects of the new evidence of flaws in President Clinton's character.

The Lewinsky matter made headlines because it was being investigated by the Office of the Independent Counsel, Kenneth Starr, and the alleged misbehavior occurred while Clinton was president. There were reports that Lewinsky's affidavit in the Paula Jones case may have been influenced by the president or his adviser Vernon Jordan. Such stories could not be ignored by the press. The president denied the allegations both that he had had an affair, and that he had sought to have Lewinsky lie about it.

Now that the topic has been deemed acceptable for public consumption, an examination of the impact of sexual compulsion as a public policy issue is warranted. According to opinion polls, President Clinton's approval ratings following the initial Lewinsky allegations have remained high. The simultaneous high interest in the story and the high approval ratings seemed inconsistent. Several explanations are possible.

The public's high interest in this scandal in comparison with prior Clinton administration legal and ethical lapses correlates with the ravenous appetite for daytime tabloid television. Bill Clinton, Monica Lewinsky, William Ginsburg, and Kenneth Starr would be a dream lineup for Jerry Springer and his kind. The imagination runs wild when one considers the questions that an audience could raise.

A second reason is that the information as originally presented was quite easy to follow. The public, seemingly uninterested in learning the intricacies of Whitewater, cattle futures trading, the misuse of FBI files, the firing of the White House travel office employees, White House "fund-raisers" in the form of coffees and Lincoln bedroom overnights, Buddhist temple campaign contributions, and other similar scars on the administration, found the sexual allegations easier to understand.

Possibly, too, the administration's prior legal and ethical lapses had a cumulative effect. After five years of questionable presidential behavior, the public perhaps recognized at last that the newest allegation, despite the president's denials, might have merit. The president's extensive sexual history, having become known to a wider population, lent plausibility to the allegations. In 1992, most voters were unaware of that history. Many knew only of Gennifer Flowers and may have concluded that the president and his wife had resolved that issue to their satisfaction. The Flowers episode was set in ambiguity for many voters because the president and the First Lady, most notably during a *60 Minutes* interview, never admitted the affair directly. In fact, that interview is a classic example of Clinton's ability to meet an interviewer's questions without providing direct answers.

The White House response to the Lewinsky allegation has been skilled but of dubious value. First, the president issued denials but then refused to discuss the matter further. Then major counterattacks were launched. The First Lady responded to the crisis in characteristic fashion, as she did in the gubernatorial years, coming to the rescue whenever Clinton created chaotic circumstances. Now the president was basically mute, whereas the First Lady took the offensive, charging that a "vast right-wing conspiracy" was responsible for the president's current dilemma. She failed to identify the individuals or groups in the conspiracy, but the First Lady's charge diverted attention from the allegation.

Some members of the media then began to speculate about the possibility of a conspiracy. The "vast right-wing conspiracy" theory advanced by the First Lady certainly had an effect. The media shifted attention from the true problem and began to question their role in scrutinizing the president's personal life.

The First Lady's response also merits attention in another respect. In response to a question about whether she was hurt by the Lewinsky allegation she said that she was not hurt because she has faced this type of problem many times in the past. She associated the history of sexual allegations to people who have wanted to hurt the president over the years. Taking her comments at face value, I believe she is seriously misguided. The reason that sexual allegations have surrounded the president for years is that he has had numerous affairs. In fact, it is quite amazing that the president's political opponents have acted in such a restrained manner about his sexual history. For example, rumors abounded in Republican camps during the late summer of 1992 that the Bush campaign was poised for an October revelation that the president had an illegitimate child. For whatever reason, lack of substantive proof or prudence, the October surprise never occurred and Clinton won the presidency. Contrary to the First Lady's claim, Clinton's political opponents have been very restrained about the president's sexual life. Though one must grant that the allegations in the Lewinsky affair have not been proven, the pattern of the president's sexual behavior lends them credence and will demonstrate, in my opinion, that they are factual.

The second counterattack directed powerful attacks against the independent counsel, Kenneth Starr. This shifted media attention from the president and portrayed him as a victim. One prong of the attack on the independent counsel accused him of having overstepped the bounds of the Whitewater investigation. In fact, Starr had sought out and obtained appropriate legal authority from the attorney general, Janet Reno. This attack served to bolster previous charges made by the administration that Starr was on a personal vendetta against the president. The preposterous nature of this argument should be self-evident. It was Tripp who approached Starr with information permitting the inference that the president had engaged in illegal activity, a by-product of a sexual liaison. Obviously, having learned of possible illegalities, Starr had a responsibility to act.

Additional smokescreens about Starr's investigation included the rehashing of the duration and cost of the Whitewater investigation. Without question, that investigation has been lengthy and expensive. Ironically, Starr's failure to complete a report on Whitewater and related matters has frustrated many of the president's political opponents, who, according to the First Lady, are supposed to be colluding with the independent counsel. The charge that Starr has been lackadaisical in completing his assignment overlooks two important points: The administration has acted to thwart Starr's investigation by delay in providing documents; and the chaotic nature of the administration has resulted in an expansion of the investigation. Despite claims by the White House that it is cooperating fully with the independent counsel's investigation, the administration has been adept at providing information in a measured form. Even Starr's investigation into the Lewinsky matter has resulted in consideration by the White House of seeking executive privilege so that White House staff may be reticent to provide full disclosure. Whether executive privilege is warranted in this case or not, the fact remains that such tactics serve to delay and disrupt the investigation.

Starr has been criticized roundly for leaks to the press. Supporters of the administration and Lewinsky's attorney have claimed that the leaks from sources inside his office are evidence of an abusive independent counsel. Clinton's attorney, David Kendall, denounced Starr for allowing leaks in order to further his objectives. If leaks are indeed coming from the independent counsel's office, the problem requires immediate remedy. The irony of the administration's claims is alarming, however. The president's staff and spouse attacked the media for reporting inaccuracies and "rushing to judgment." Yet they also accept at face value media reports that the information leaks came from the independent counsel's office.

The net result of the White House counterattacks of claiming a "vast right-wing conspiracy" and demonizing Starr has been a reduction in public focus on Clinton and increased support for him. The administration's response here is similar to that after the Republican congressional victory in 1994. That response was to demonize the opponent and portray the president as a victim who is upholding what is "right." The president's current popularity shows that this tactic is working with a gullible public once again.

Some of the gullibility is the direct result of Clinton's effective miscommunication campaign. This miscommunication is not part of a "vast *left*-wing conspiracy." Instead, the miscommunication parallels the communication patterns that existed in Clinton's childhood home. One method utilized by the president is called "double message." The double message transmits two contradictory verbal messages. The president used the double message pattern in his prior statement that he did not have an affair with Gennifer Flowers and his January 1998 admission that he did have an affair with her. White House spokesman Mike McCurry, when asked about the double message, claimed there was no inconsistency: "The president believes that what he said before was true and what he said now is true." McCurry was attempting to validate contradictory statements, a typical double-message technique. In addition, his response possibly provided additional insight into Clinton's cognitive process. Given the communication pattern of the president's childhood family, it is entirely likely that he believes both statements to be true. The president himself has stated that being an adult child of an alcoholic resulted in his sending mixed signals. A further result of being an adult child of an alcoholic is that he also received many double-message communications. It is likely that he learned to accept contradictory messages as truthful as a means to cope with an untenable situation.

The second miscommunication style used by the president in response to the Flowers matter is that of double-bind messages. Double binds occur when a verbal message contradicts a nonverbal message. Double binds are common in the homes of alcoholics. As a child Clinton likely experienced this double bind: his stepfather, Roger Clinton Sr., said that he loved Bill and his mother (verbal) but battered her and emotionally abused him (nonverbal). It is exceedingly confusing to experience a double bind. This, in part, explains why Clinton was able to characterize his childhood home as "generally happy."

The double-bind message is part of Clinton's communication style, professionally and personally. The president's denials regarding Lewinsky do not appear to match the situation; that is, what is known about his sexual behavior, her audiotaped statements, and her postemployment visits to the White House. The double bind forces people to try to make sense out of the incongruity. This is true of the American citizen, too. A large number of Americans choose to support the president's words while discounting the contradictory nature of his behavior. In order to resolve this double bind, people discount the significance of the allegations. Even as the majority of the people believed Clinton had sexual relations with Lewinsky and lied about it, they approved of his performance as president. Therefore, many concluded what really mattered was the economy, jobs, and education, not the president's "personal life." Clinton managed to create a high level of dissonance for many Americans. Out of a desire to continue to view the president favorably, they once more chose to ignore serious behavioral problems.

It is the contention of *The Dysfunctional President* that the behavioral problems are far more reflective of Clinton than the state of the economy is. Since the Lewinsky matter has serious implications for Clinton, speculation about the outcome is valid. The president could be removed from office, remain in office but be damaged politically, or remain in office and maintain or increase his popularity.

Despite the effective attacks on the independent counsel, Starr continues to investigate the case with vigor. If the investigation results in irrefutable evidence that Clinton engaged in a serious crime, lied under oath, or encouraged others to lie, most likely he will be removed from office, even if the public continues to support him for a short duration. His removal from office would depend on the response of congressmen, particularly those of his own party. Fellow Democrats could find it difficult to provide strong support for Clinton with their own elections looming in November. I also think that public support for Clinton could wane just as it increased after the allegation. Recall that an element to the increased popularity was based on the double-bind communication of contradictory behavior and the president's statements. With strong evidence to establish the behavioral side of the equation, the presidential denials would lack strength.

If Starr's investigation should prove limited, for example, such as finding evidence that Clinton had an affair with Lewinsky but failing to find evidence of criminal wrongdoing, then Clinton could survive as president.

The third possibility is that Starr would fail to provide significant evidence of either a sexual relationship or criminal wrongdoing. In that case, the administration would maximize its political gain. The "vast right-wing conspiracy," although unproved, would take root, and the president could be protected from similar situations for the rest of his presidency. There is but one flaw in this positive position: Clinton's inherent desire to sabotage himself would remain.

If the public fails to hold the president accountable for his behavior, the outcome is relatively easy to predict. President Clinton will remain an individual with a serious sexual compulsion in a highly stressful position with access to many women, and the public will have provided reinforcement for his behavior. This combination would result in an increased need to exhibit even more risky sexual behavior. Clinton's need for self-derailment, which derives from overachievement and anger toward himself, has not changed. The only difference will be that the public has sent a message to him: his sexual behavior has to be extreme in order to provoke public outrage.

Very likely, the president will comply with that message.

Part One

CHAPTER ONE

What Others Have Said

THE PRESIDENT OF THE UNITED STATES, William Jefferson Clinton, is in trouble. Clinton's problem-plagued presidency is the topic of daily news. His problems are not the result of right-wing demagoguery or a grid-locked Congress, as Clinton has claimed, but of the actions of the president himself. Judging from the number of comments made by political observers about Clinton's behavior, it is time they are explained.

Two articles in particular typify the media's interest in Bill Clinton's behavior. The first, "Please Tell the Truth, Mr. President," was written by Robert J. Samuelson and was published in the June 9, 1993, issue of the *Washington Post.* The second article was published in the *New York Times Magazine* on July 31, 1994. Written by Michael Kelly it was entitled "Why the President Is in Trouble." Both articles were subsequently condensed and published in issues of the *Reader's Digest.*

Robert J. Samuelson's critique of Clinton in "Please Tell the Truth, Mr. President" is both startling and accurate. At the time that Samuelson wrote the article, David Gergen had already been appointed to a position in the administration as counsel to the president. Samuelson wrote that Gergen's advice to the president should be to "tell the truth" and was necessitated by Clinton's tendency to lie.

Samuelson encapsulated one of the primary reasons why President Clinton is in trouble when he wrote, "Clinton lies. I could put it more delicately, but that would miss the point. Sometimes the lies are blatant untruths. Sometimes they are artful distortions, technically true but misleading. But the effect is the same. They destroy public trust in the President and his Administration. We see this pattern constantly." Samuelson was describing a characteristic exhibited by Clinton which exceeds a typical politician's penchant for hyperbole and unrealistic promises. Samuelson wrote, "His distortions are brazen, unrelenting and unusually specific."

Samuelson identified several specific distortions which evidence his claims. He cited Clinton's adamantly rejecting the charge that he had supported more stringent regulations on automobile fuel efficiency. Clinton's denial contradicted his support of federal regulations as outlined in his book, *Putting People First*. Samuelson also cited incongruities between Clinton's claims and the true effectiveness of his proposal for national service as a means for students to repay their student loans; reneging on campaign promises for the middle-class tax cut; waffling on acceptance of responsibility for the incident in Waco, Texas, involving the David Koresh cult; and vacillating on acceptance of responsibility for the firings of the White House travel staff.

Those examples and others Samuelson cited, considered individually, would not merit much attention. But as he wrote, "The cumulative impression forms of a man who must forever explain himself because he's temperamentally incapable of starting with the unvarnished truth. The President thinks he can talk his way around almost any problem or inconsistency. Believing this, he often says one thing and does another. Sooner or later the inconsistencies are discovered and turned against him. He retreats, and no one is sure what he stands for." As this book will detail, Samuelson's assertion that Clinton lacks the temperamental capability to render the truth is true.

The second article, "Why the President Is in Trouble," by Michael Kelly, was published a little more than one year after Samuelson's article appeared. Michael Kelly's article details the threat to Clinton's presidency. It is found in "an abiding public doubt about his character. In mainstream journalism and even more so in popular entertainment, President Clinton is routinely depicted as a liar, a fraud, an indecisive man who can't be trusted to stand for anything or anyone."

Like Samuelson, Kelly identified a number of examples of Clinton's behavior which makes understandable the "public doubt about his character." Kelly wrote about Clinton's belief that his political striving for the presidency at times exceeded his adherence to principles. Clinton sought to avoid the draft and made a commitment with R.O.T.C. Commander Col. Eugene J. Holmes to enter the Reserve Officers' Training Corps (R.O.T.C.) program at the University of Arkansas and in exchange obtain a four-year deferment from the draft. According to Kelly, Clinton later was reclassified 1-A, eligible for the draft. Clinton misrepresented his action by stating he thought he had an obligation to his fellow men to be reclassified when in fact he took the action only after President Nixon was reducing the forces in Vietnam and after the threat of his being drafted diminished. Clinton subsequently received a high draft number, then broke his promise in a letter to Colonel Holmes dated December 3, 1969, to the R.O.T.C. at the University of Arkansas and applied to Yale University. According to Kelly, the letter which Clinton wrote "captures with shattering clarity a young man learning to rationalize acts of deception and compromise as necessary in the pursuit of doing good—which Clinton now regarded as inseparable from his political advancement." Clinton wrote in the letter that his decision to accept the draft was made in opposition to his beliefs but was done "to maintain my political viability within the system."

Kelly's analysis of Clinton's handling of the draft issues and his broken R.O.T.C. commitment was: "Here, astonishing in its hubris, is the idea expressed in its all-excusing force. Other young men might justify their actions regarding Vietnam on the ground of simple self-interest; they did not want to lose their lives to a stupid war. Clinton decided that his self-interest was the same as his country's. He was acting for the sake of the nation's future."

Kelly cited other examples of Clinton's tendency to break promises, contending that a pattern of such behavior existed throughout his governorship. As Samuelson had pointed out, the individual broken promises are not noteworthy unless viewed in the context of what the pattern evidences about Clinton's character. Kelly wrote that the net effect of Clinton's broken promises was that Clinton "quickly earned a reputation as someone who didn't understand that a handshake deal was inviolable" and that "jokes about Clinton's honesty, his predilection for saying whatever his listener of the moment wanted to hear, his willingness to reverse himself, grew steadily."

Kelly suggested that the pattern Clinton demonstrated as a youth and as governor also is reflected in his presidency. Kelly recounted Clinton's famous "I didn't inhale" statement, Whitewater, Paula Jones, Haiti, Bosnia, Somalia, and China as examples of issues in which Clinton's character has been questioned. Kelly wrote, "The episodes of rationalization and compromise from Clinton's Arkansas past are the progenitors of the indecision and betrayal that damage the White House present." He added, "The conventional diplomatic wisdom is that the pledges of the President of the United States are to be regarded more as well-meaning sentiments than actual commitments."

The articles by Samuelson and Kelly demonstrate that President Clinton is besieged by a significant problem. Bill Clinton is in trouble because of Bill Clinton. This book will explain why that statement is true. Kelly wrote, "Bill Clinton's problem isn't that his past haunts him. It is that his past has made him what he is today." This book will explain how his past has made him *The Dysfunctional President*.

CHAPTER TWO

Initial Insights

THE PRESIDENTIAL CAMPAIGN was heating up in the summer of 1992, and Bill Clinton was increasing his lead in the polls over the incumbent, George Bush. My knowledge of the Democratic challenger was limited, and I, like many Americans, began to attend more closely to the message of the candidates. I observed that Clinton was an extremely effective orator who engaged his audience. I also noticed something else about him that caused me great concern.

The consternation I felt was based on my observation of Clinton from my professional experience as a clinical psychologist. It alarmed me that his significant behavioral characteristics mirrored so closely a particular clinical population which frequented my practice since I began serving as a psychotherapist in 1983. The more I observed Clinton, the more confident I became that my diagnosis was correct.

What caught my eye about Clinton was the following: He had a roller-coaster candidacy with many highs and potential campaign destroying lows; he was faced with repeated embarrassing disclosures about his personal life; he responded to those disclosures with a glaring tendency to lie; he appeared indecisive and waffled on significant issues; and he was energized by the self-created chaos.

Recall for a moment some of the events of the presidential campaign. Revelations of Clinton's alleged affair with Gennifer Flowers surfaced prior to the New Hampshire primary. The allegation was muted by an appearance by Clinton and his wife, Hillary Rodham Clinton, on the television program *60 Minutes*. During the interview, Clinton was not asked specifically whether he had ever engaged in sexual relations with Flowers. Instead, he was asked if he had had a twelve-year affair with her. Clinton adeptly avoided direct answers to the charges. He simply denied having carried on a twelve-year affair with her. Meredith L. Oakley, political reporter for the *Arkansas-Democrat Gazette* and author of *On the Make— The Rise of Bill Clinton*, provided this analysis regarding Clinton's response that he did not have a twelve-year affair: "By that statement, Clinton did not deny having had an affair with Flowers, he merely denied having had an affair of twelve years' duration."

Flowers later revealed that she had audiotapes of telephone conversations with Clinton. On one of the tapes the voice she claimed is Clinton's clearly encourages her to "just deny it." The audiotapes were offered for sale.

A second stumbling block for the Clinton campaign was the question of his marijuana usage. This question had been raised at various points during Clinton's tenure as governor. Oakley wrote that marijuana usage was "a dalliance he would go to great lengths to avoid admitting during his years as governor of Arkansas." Clinton has said that he has not "broken any drug law" and also that he has "never broken a state law." (If the allegations about campaign financing practices, money laundering, and dollars for votes reported later in this book are determined to be meritorious, Clinton may have to amend this last statement as well.) With both of these statements, Clinton again was being evasive, since he later revealed that he had smoked marijuana while in England. The consensus seems to be that his famous "I didn't inhale" statement is, to put it mildly, implausible.

The tendency to lie also was revealed during the campaign when questions about Clinton's Vietnam War protest activities and the manner in which he was not drafted into service were raised. Inconsistencies in his presentation of the facts were apparent. In December 1991, Clinton claimed that he never received a draft notice. In August 1992 he told an American Legion audience, "In 1969, while studying at Oxford, I received a draft notice." In December 1991 he emphatically denied requesting assistance of anyone in Sen. William Fulbright's office to avoid being drafted. When the issue was brought to a head in September 1992, Dee Dee Myers, then serving as a campaign spokeswoman for Clinton, said that he had "talked to the Fulbright people about what his options were." It was readily apparent that, contrary to Clinton's earlier contention that he had put himself "in a position to be drafted," the truth was that he, like many other young Americans at the time, had sought a means to avoid being drafted.

The issue of Whitewater also surfaced during the campaign. Whitewater refers to a number of financial dealings conducted by the Clintons and their acquaintances. Clinton's defense of the financial dealings has revealed additional inconsistencies. Martin L. Gross, author of *The Great Whitewater Fiasco*, serves as a reference source for those interested in a detailed summary of Whitewater to date. Gross recorded some of the inconsistencies.

Another issue is Hillary's cattle-futures trading. Referring to the president's comments, Gross wrote, "Even her [Hillary's] husband couldn't get his story on the cattle futures straight. At a town meeting, he declared that Hillary had stopped trading during her pregnancy because of the stress (which became the 'operative' tale) and also because she got 'cold feet' when the brokers gave her a margin call.

"The White House quickly put out an updated operative story. No, she had never received a margin call, and Hillary had traded right up through the birth of Chelsea. In fact, in the very week of the birth, she had made three trades, raking in $10,000 more in profits!"

Gross also points out a disparity between what Clinton claims to have been their role in Whitewater and what was the reality of their involvement. Gross wrote, "The Clinton claim to innocence in Whitewater and its involved tributaries is that they were 'passive' investors. If Hillary had been any more passive, she would have been frenetic. The tale is one of *active* personal involvement by Hillary, and later Bill, that sets up legal and financial complications that have not yet been fully unraveled, even by astute federal investigators."

Gross also reported claims by Judge David Hale. Hale administered the Small Business Administration loans to minority-oriented companies. Hale contends that one of the loans for $300,000 to Susan McDougal (Clinton's friend and the spouse of James McDougal, co-owner of Whitewater with the Clintons) was made not only with Clinton's knowledge, "but on more than one occasion Clinton had personally pressured him [Hale] to make the loan. In addition, Hale claimed, $110,000 of the $300,000 had found its way into the Whitewater bank account." President Clinton "has flatly denied that he ever spoke to Hale about this and has accused Hale of talking a 'bunch of bull.' "

Attorney General Janet Reno appointed a Republican, Robert B. Fiske Jr., to the position of special counsel. Fiske took the oath of office on January 20, 1994, and began an investigation into Whitewater matters. His report, released on June 30, 1994, found no evidence of obstruction of justice by White House employees. Limited Senate hearings were held between July 26, 1994, and August 5, 1994. The hearings revealed some apparent conflicting testimony. Roger Altman, deputy secretary of the Treasury, lost his position as a result. Fiske was criticized for his investigation, particularly by Republican members of the Senate Banking Committee. An independent counsel, Kenneth Starr, was named by a panel of three judges to continue the investigation. The veracity of Clinton's remarks undoubtedly will be tested by Starr. Arkansas state trooper, L. D. Brown's testimony contrasts sharply. Brown has said that he was present when Clinton spoke with Hale about obtaining money. Brown did not recall the word "loan" being used. At any rate, the statements of Hale and Brown are divergent from the president's denial.

The investigation of Whitewater will be a test of the president's tendency to lie and to make statements that are difficult to believe.

A more direct statement was attributed by Gross to "the former *Arkansas-Democrat Gazette* editor," who labeled "Bill Clinton 'that lying son of a bitch.'"

The marital-infidelity issue, the Vietnam-era behavior, and the use of marijuana may not seem to go beyond the norm for individuals of Clinton's age group. That clearly does not condone the behavior but gives him the benefit of the doubt that he was a product of his times. None of those situations, per se, is what caused me concern when I began to consider who Bill Clinton is.

What troubled me was the multitude of chaotic circumstances and, most important, his response to them. It has been said of Clinton that he had had his sights on the presidency since he was a youth. It also has been said that he is an extremely intelligent man. My dilemma was in reconciling these facts with the reality that he had made errors in judgment and then skirted the truth or was inconsistent in his responses. A man who was on the brink of meeting his lifelong goal and who knew that all these issues probably would be raised in the campaign should have been prepared to confront them directly and forthrightly. Clinton knew where the land mines were planted, and yet he plowed through the field seemingly unaware. It also is significant that although he repeatedly was bloodied, he was never felled.

If I had been considering Clinton's behavior from a political standpoint, I would have been appalled by his missteps while lauding his ability to survive. He truly fit the political nickname of "the Comeback Kid." But as a psychologist, I was more observant of the personality style and what his behavioral characteristics revealed. Here was a future president who developed his own chaos, as the examples show, and yet thrived upon the very chaos he had created. He openly distorted the truth, denied that he distorted the truth, yet epitomized sincerity at all times. And he waffled on issues of national interest. His behaviors went beyond the typical political maneuvering; this behavior was at the core of his character. The realization struck me that instead of becoming the next president of the United States, William Jefferson Clinton could just as well have been any of the hundreds of adult children of alcoholics (ACOA) I have treated in the hospital or in my outpatient office. I knew that the dysfunction which Clinton displayed during the campaign would typify his presidency. His would be a presidency that evidenced a continued trend toward chaotic administration, indecisiveness, and a tendency to lie. I was, and am, concerned that if the emotional factors underlying his behavioral characteristics remain untreated, deleterious effects upon the country will likely result.

I want to state clearly that I am not interested in causing harm to the Clinton presidency. If Clinton had been one of the hundreds of patients I have treated for this particular problem, I would have been bound by confidentiality laws and would not have written this book. After some soul-searching, I concluded that this book needed to be presented to the American people. I have compassion for the president and the fact that his psychological laundry is being aired publicly. I have no quarrel with him and sympathize with the fact that he must know that what is in this book is true.

Studies indicate that some, not all, individuals who grow up in what has become commonly termed dysfunctional homes exhibit exactly the type of behavioral characteristics that I mentioned earlier and will describe in detail in later chapters. These individuals have been termed adult children of alcoholics (ACOA). One of the factors which influence the effects of the childhood experiences is the severity of the alcoholism. Another is the freedom that the child has to express his pain openly. Other factors include whether violence occurred in the home, the degree of chaos present as a result of the alcoholic behavior, and the family members' responses to the disorder. Clearly, it is through no fault of one's own that one or both parents are alcoholics. It is a sad state of affairs that such conditions are so prevalent. While it is not the child's fault that he is relegated to such a family life during his formative years, that child must take responsibility for resolving problems he encountered during those early years. This becomes the unfortunate responsibility of that maturing child, because no one else will do it for him.

Our current president came from such a family system. For the purposes of this book I will use the term "adult child of an alcoholic," although technically Clinton is the adult child of a stepfather who was an alcoholic. Roger Clinton Sr. married Bill's mother before Bill was four years old. The stepfather was severely alcoholic, and at times he was violent. Life in Clinton's childhood home was chaotic. He did not discuss family problems with people outside the home. In other words, many of the factors that contribute to emotional complications for ACOAs were present in the young life of Clinton. (A more detailed description of Clinton's childhood will follow in a later chapter.)

It amazed me that little emphasis has been placed on the influence of Clinton's youth until now. I noted that the importance of Clinton's ACOA behavior exhibited during the campaign did not deter voters. Moreover, a limited amount of information about this problem was presented in the press, primarily for biographical input. Clinton did describe himself as an ACOA. However, the importance of that information was lost on the nation.

An article written by Garry Wills and published in *Time* magazine on June 8, 1992, details some of Clinton's childhood memories. Wills insightfully wrote in "Clinton's Forgotten Childhood" that while he is "quick to recall the tiniest detail on dozens of issues, the Democratic candidate for years suppressed memories of a violent stepfather. To understand his upbringing is to understand the man he is today." Some of the characteristics described in the article are complimentary, such as his being a "superachiever," "dutiful to a fault," and "disgustingly responsible." These characteristics are common among ACOAs. While Wills may have meant, by mentioning those characteristics, to accentuate the positive, the reality is that these characteristics work as a negative for the president. They all involve an overstatement of positive characteristics. It is positive to be an achiever, to be dutiful, and to be responsible. It serves as a negative characteristic, however, if those qualities are overstated or understated.

Wills correctly wrote that many factors must be considered when determining whether the impact of such a childhood is positive or negative. He argued that some children from such homes please others and that some are empathetic toward the unfortunate. What is of tremendous importance in this article is Clinton's personal revelation that many of his painful childhood experiences have been forgotten. Wills wrote, "Going back into his childhood is a form of emotional spelunking that Clinton has always avoided." Clinton was quoted in the article as saying, "People expect me to remember things I don't remember all of, or to share things I thought I was never supposed to share." He also described himself and his brother, Roger, as ". . . sort of the two prototypical kids of an alcoholic family."

Wills also offered insights that are helpful in understanding why Clinton exhibits this loss of memory. Clinton's mother, Virginia Kelley, told Wills, "Bill and I have always been able to do that. I know you people are amazed at this, but we would always put away anything unpleasant." Clinton echoed this pattern of household denial when he said, "Like most families of alcoholics, you do things by not confronting problems early, you wind up making things worse. I think that the house in which we grew up, because there was violence and trouble, and because my mother just put the best face on it she could—in later years a lot of the stuff was dealt with by silence."

Consider this description by Clinton and that by his mother. They are classic examples of how denial is utilized in the alcoholic family. The child is taught to maintain a silence about the family problems, to forget them. Unfortunately, despite the rudimentary attempt at self-help by denial and forgetting, the emotional pain is not alleviated by such behavior. The examples of Clinton's reactions to unpleasant personal situations during the campaign, as cited earlier in this chapter, reflect his mechanism of attempting to "put away anything unpleasant." His pattern of attempting to do so involves continued denial and the tendency to lie. As president of the United States, it is impossible to continue this pattern without Americans noticing.

A *U.S. News & World Report* article written by Matthew Cooper and published on July 20, 1992, is entitled "Bill Clinton's Hidden Life." In this article, Clinton described himself and his brother, Roger, as "archetypes of children of alcoholics." He revealed that he had learned in counseling that because of the family alcohol problem he was forced to mature early and become a peacemaker. Again, these qualities can result in positive characteristics.

Clinton's revelation that he had received counseling needs to be tempered. Cooper parenthetically included the phrase about the family counseling "which the Clinton family entered to help his brother." While I am pleased that the president has received some counseling for the ACOA problem, it concerns me when the focus for counseling was helping Roger. As a clinical psychologist, I am stating unequivocally that the president has not resolved these childhood problems and that his presidency has been negatively impacted as a result. He needs to seek treatment designed to help himself, not his brother.

The American people must understand the dysfunctional president that they have elected. They must also realize that Clinton's untreated childhood dysfunction is being reenacted in his presidency by chaotic administration and a tendency to lie.

CHAPTER THREE

The Pattern as Governor and President

FOR THE THESIS OF THIS BOOK to be credible, namely, that President Clinton's unresolved emotional status as an ACOA has resulted in behavioral characteristics which negatively impact his presidency, evidence of this pattern of behavior should be present prior to the campaign and during the presidency. A variety of sources, not only political opponents, should have raised issues about indecisiveness, a straying from the truth, and chaotic administration. That is the pattern.

The complications during Clinton's presidential candidacy arose from prior behavior. Many of those issues had been raised at one time or another during Clinton's Arkansas career and were responded to with avoidance or denial. Despite this legacy, Arkansans continued to return him to state office.

Arkansas-Democrat Gazette political reporter Meredith L. Oakley provided insight into why Clinton was able to find such success with Arkansas voters. She wrote in *On the Make—The Rise of Bill Clinton*: "The reporters and pundits who have watched Bill Clinton for years marvel at Clinton's uncanny ability to make himself over into whatever image appeals to voters." The ACOA exhibits what is known as the impostor syndrome. He creates an image of what he thinks others want him to be. It is as if the years of being hyperattentive to the inconsistent behavior of the alcoholic have

16

resulted in the development of an enhanced ability to "read" people. The resulting voter appeal would be at the expense of Clinton's
inner conviction.

Oakley cited examples of various promises broken by Clinton
during his Arkansas years. One of the broken promises is of particular interest because the "instant replay" occurred as president.
Oakley wrote, "Clinton could promise, as he did in three separate
elections, not to raise taxes and then do so, and still manage to get
reelected." While Clinton did not promise prior to his presidential
election not to raise taxes, he did promise a middle-class tax cut
that never materialized. In fact, Clinton's statements about lowering
taxes ranged from a clear utterance that his economic plan "starts
with a tax cut for the middle-class" to a claim that he would modify
but not abandon the middle-class tax cut to a denial of personal
responsibility ("the press and my political opponents always made
more of the middle-class tax cut than I ever did in my speeches") to
abandonment of tax reduction. Some politicians, including Dan
Quayle, believed that Clinton would revive the middle-class tax cut
prior to the 1996 election for political advantage.

Of further interest when considering the pattern exhibited by
Clinton in reneging on his tax promises in the 1986 gubernatorial
campaign and the 1992 presidential campaign is that on both occasions he claimed that he could not fulfill his commitment because
the severity of the financial condition was even worse than previously known. A pattern of false rationalizations follows Clinton.

Oakley offered another example of Clinton's promise-breaking
pattern. "He could face a statewide audience through the eye of a
camera that recorded his every word and declare that he would not
run for president if reelected, talk for months afterward about his
commitment to the voters of Arkansas, and still claim that he never
made such a declaration." This follows the pattern of denial that
was obvious during the presidential campaign. Clinton's decision to
run for president is hardly assailable, in my opinion, particularly
since he won the election. Demonstrated in Oakley's observation,
however, is the breaking of the promise and then the denial that the

promise was ever made. Remember Virginia Kelley's comment about Clinton's ability to "put away anything unpleasant." This ACOA characteristic erodes the credibility which is essential for effective leadership.

This behavioral characteristic exhibited during his governorship of Arkansas was not just a response to having boxed himself into a corner. According to Oakley, "Clinton officially broke his promise not to seek another office, a promise he had made in full knowledge that it would never be kept. But as Clinton had advised intimates, he had to tell the lie or he might not have been reelected, and he needed that reelection to enhance his viability as a presidential candidate."

Oakley reported that Clinton had lied to John R. Starr, who was the former managing editor of the *Arkansas-Democrat Gazette.* "Clinton 'confided' to Starr that he had once observed an antiwar demonstration in Washington while he was a student at Georgetown but had not taken part in the protest. That was the gist of his experience with antiwar activity, Clinton declared."

Edward P. Moser, author of *Willy Nilly: Bill Clinton Speaks Out*, collected a series of quotations by Clinton which demonstrate the extent of Clinton's contradictions. The author's collection evidences that Clinton is not beyond miscasting his accomplishments in Arkansas. For example, Moser cited Clinton's claim that "in my state, we've moved 17,000 people from welfare rolls to payrolls." Moser pointed out that "during the same period (1979–92) that 17,000 people in Arkansas left welfare, 51,000 people—three times as many—entered the state's welfare rolls."

Examples of how Clinton's ACOA background have impacted his presidency are plentiful. There are also many examples of people questioning Clinton's veracity, decisiveness, and administrative management. Moser's collection of quotes includes fellow Democrats raising such issues. Sen. Bob Kerrey said of Clinton, "I hope he's telling the truth, but I've got some doubts." Sen. Daniel Patrick Moynihan, in January 1993, described Clinton's tendency to renege on his campaign promises as "the clatter of campaign promises being tossed out the window." In June 1993, Cong. Kweisi Mfume described "the back-and-forth, up-and-down, in-and-out motion of this administration and of this president." Some Democratic members of Congress were shaken by Clinton's abandonment of the B.T.U. tax that he proposed and for which he sought their commitments of support. Cong. Charles Rangel said, "We were going to censure those that walked away from the President, and now it's reported that the President walked away from us." Cong. Patricia Schroeder epitomized the sentiment by saying, "We've been left hanging out on the plank."

Even one of Clinton's former cabinet members, U.S. Housing and Urban Development secretary Henry Cisneros, commented on Clinton's personal qualities. In a taped conversation with Linda Medlar, Cisneros's former mistress, he said: "There's a lot of personal qualities about Clinton that are troublesome for those of us who work with him. He just delays something terrible."

Thomas McArdle, writing for *Investor's Business Daily* in August 31, 1994, posed the question "Can Clinton Come Back Again? Or Has President's 'Trust Gap' Grown Too Large?" Democratic congressman Tim Penny from Minnesota, interviewed for the article, stated that "the president has worsened matters by failing to secure trust from Congress. I doubt that you could find many members of Congress who haven't been told something by the president that then was never honored. . . . It's the trust factor and there's a declining level of trust between Capitol Hill and the White House simply because the president tends to tell you what you want to hear. It's one thing to be upset with someone because you disagree with them. It's quite another to be led to believe that they get your point or they're on your side and then discover they aren't."

Harrison Rainie, in *U. S. News & World Report*, wrote that "they [Americans] are plagued by doubts about what kind of man he is." Michael Kramer in *Time* magazine, March 1, 1993, forgave Clinton for reneging on the middle class tax relief promise but questioned his truthfulness. "At a time when honesty is required, any perceived disingenuousness can be fatal—yet there has been too much of that already. Labeling Social Security tax increases as spending cuts invites ridicule, and mixing up gross and net deficit-reduction figures is similarly foolish. Correcting such lapses by demanding that the unvarnished truth be told should not be difficult, but getting the congressional Democrats in line is another matter."

Carl Bernstein wrote a column appearing in the *Los Angeles Times* on July 17, 1994, entitled "A Matter of Honesty: Bill Clinton and Whitewater." The column states that Clinton is headed for credibility problems. He wrote that the public was led to believe that "Clinton implicitly promised not only change for the country—but change in himself. . . . He appears not to have changed. The truth shaving, the lack of candor, that came to be known as the 'character' issue in the campaign are now attached to his presidency. . . . If Clinton succumbs to that part of himself that plays fast with the truth, that doesn't inhale—he is finished. If he thinks the lesson of the campaign is that he was helped by his equivocations, that he got away with it—on the draft, on his personal life—he is courting disaster . . . the truthfulness of the President—not the worthiness of his programs—will become the issue. . . . The fate of his presidency may be at stake."

What Bernstein and others were missing during the campaign is that people who have a tendency to lie are not concerned about implicit promises. They are concerned about meeting their objectives. It appears that Bernstein noted that a relationship does exist between a pattern of denial of truth about personal matters and professional matters. The change that Bernstein is asking the president to make is not one which Clinton can will into existence. It will require significant psychotherapy, just as it would for anyone else. I wonder how many times Clinton's stepfather made explicit or implicit promises to change.

Syndicated columnist Mona Charen wrote in an article entitled "The Draft-Dodgers' War" on September 16, 1994, "President Clinton says that U.S. credibility is at stake. He's confused. His own credibility is at stake—and for good reason. He is dishonest, and he changes course like a boomerang." Charen was referring to Clinton's decision to become militarily involved in Haiti.

An example of the media's description of Clinton's credibility problems is offered by Patrick J. Buchanan in an article dated March 25, 1994. Buchanan was referring to the apparent disparity between the Clintons' image as fighters for those left in the dust of the "greed of the 1980s" and their own accumulation of significant financial gain during that same time period. Buchanan wrote, "As a friend puts it, Bill and Hillary are going to end up as the Jim and Tammy Faye Baker of American liberalism . . . with the revelations of Madison, Whitewater, and Troopergate we learn that not only had the Clintons discarded the old morality, they felt unbound by the proscriptions of the new. It was all a sham. And the sudden savagery of the press commentary reflects the bitterness of Baby Boomers who discover they have been led up the garden path by two of their very own."

Clinton's tendency to lie is intertwined with his proclivity to waffle. As in the case of his shading of the truth, he has been assailed across the political spectrum for his indecisiveness. Recently, Gary Trudeau began depicting Clinton as a waffle in his syndicated cartoons. But this problem was evident to some prior to the election.

Thomas L. Friedman wrote an in-depth column in the *New York Times* on October 4, 1992, addressing Clinton's foreign policy agenda. Friedman claimed that "Mr. Clinton has repeatedly demonstrated a tendency to try to be all things to all people, and to avoid clear-cut decisions that could alienate constituencies. Such waffling in foreign policy can be deadly, literally." One of the examples of waffling was delineated by Friedman. He wrote, "Mr. Clinton now says he supported the use of force against Iraq in the Persian Gulf War. But in the weeks before Congress was scheduled to vote on a use of force resolution in January 1991, a group of hawkish Democrats approached Mr. Clinton about signing a full-page ad that would run in various newspapers around the country urging Congress to back the president. Mr. Clinton told them that he would consider it and get back to them. He never did.

"Later, after the vote, Mr. Clinton said, 'I guess I would have voted with the majority if it was a close vote. But I agree with the arguments the minority made.' "

To Clinton's credit, when the Iraqis increased their military strength on the border with Kuwait in October 1994, he responded swiftly by sending additional troops and military aircraft to the region. Ironically, in a speech delivered from the Oval Office on October 10, Clinton stated that one of his reasons for action was that Sadaam "cannot be trusted."

Shortly after the election victory in 1992, Walter Isaacson wrote a basically supportive article in *Time* magazine entitled "A Time for Courage." Isaacson sent out a warning to Clinton not to repeat the waffling errors of his campaign. "The resulting doubts about his trustworthiness produced enough near death experiences for his campaign to serve as warning that being all things to all people will not work. . . . Though hardly saintly in this regard, George Bush was not off base in charging that Clinton's tendency to waffle on tough issues was worrisome."

Clinton's behavior while in office has not resulted in a letup of claims that he waffles on difficult issues. Michael Barone wrote, "Once again, it's the 'vision thing,' " in *U.S. News & World Report* on January 31, 1994. Barone claimed that Clinton's waffling has been evident in both foreign policy and domestic agenda items. "On foreign policy and cultural issues, Clinton has wobbled from one narrative line to another. He has wobbled between multilateralist and humanitarian impulses on the one hand (Bosnia, Haiti, Somalia) and realpolitik on the other (Yeltsin, China). On cultural issues, he suggests the nation is moving toward ever more liberalization on abortion, feminism and gay rights, but he endorses more tradition or restraint on crime, religion, family. He is so conflicted on whether to head toward colorblindness or quotas that he can't fill key civil rights posts."

William F. Buckley Jr. also was direct in his article "A Foreign-

Policy Vacuum at the Top" on April 21, 1994. Buckley wrote that two schools of thought exist in terms of what American foreign policy should be in areas such as Somalia, Bosnia, North Korea, China, and Haiti. His claim that a foreign policy vacuum exists is that there "is the failure to enunciate a policy on the basis of which there can be a consolidation either of support or even of opposition. Clinton's emphatic declarations during the presidential campaign, to the effect that we needed to commit ourselves against the genocidal and disruptive war in Yugoslavia, were certainly persuasive, even though they were not dispositive: Many sophisticated strategists continue to resist U.S. involvement in that theater. But neither side is able to dig in, because digging in against a Clinton policy is on the order of nailing down quicksilver."

In May 1994, Clinton announced that he was renewing China's trade benefits. Thomas L. Friedman wrote in the *New York Times*, "Many foreign-policy experts think that President Clinton made the right decision. But, as always, look how he got there. During the campaign he denounced President Bush for his claim that engaging China rather than threatening it each year with trade sanctions was the best way to both promote human rights and protect America's myriad interests in Asia.

"Once in office, Clinton followed up his campaign speeches with a threat last May to withdraw China's 'most favored nation' trade benefits if it did not meet his human-rights conditions by June of this year. China fell short. The president, instead of imposing sanctions as promised, junked his threat and on Thursday gave what was surely the most eloquent defense of the Bush administration's China policy ever uttered at the White House, including by Bush."

Friedman's article sheds some light on Clinton's frequent claim that he and his administration do not receive due credit for successes they achieve in office. Note that Friedman acknowledged that many experts believe the decision was correct. That was not his problem with Clinton's handling of the China decision. The concern expressed by Friedman was based on Clinton's reversal of policy.

Clinton's handling of Haiti also involved many policy reversals that culminated with the Carter mission. Some, including Rep. Dana Rohrabacher, claimed that the development of a "crisis" in Haiti was Clinton's own doing. Rohrabacher said, "If there's a mess in Haiti, it was caused by Clinton running off at the mouth during the last election . . . by criticizing in an irresponsible manner President Bush's handling of the situation. It's too bad this political mess Clinton created will put American lives in jeopardy. In no way did he prove our interests are at stake."

While Rohrabacher's statement has a partisan ring to it, the fact is that prior to Carter's dealing with Cedras, Clinton did not have Democratic support for an invasion of Haiti. The *New York Times* reported on September 14, 1994, that "Democratic leaders tried Tuesday to find a way that Congress could vote on the issue next week without seriously embarrassing President Clinton. Democratic and Republican senators had separate meetings to discuss the situation. Afterward, almost everyone who spoke publicly expressed opposition to an invasion."

David S. Broder's editorial "Hostage to Haiti," published in the *Washington Post* on September 20, 1994, offered his perspective on Clinton's Haiti policy. He also echoed the fact that Clinton's support in Congress for his policy was lacking. "Amazingly, Clinton went to the United Nations for approval of military action inside our Western Hemisphere 'sphere of influence' but evaded Congress—because he knew support was lacking. . . . The president and his national security advisers are singularly lacking in any long-term policy perspective. Each step of Haitian policy from the initial offer of an American haven for refugees to the threat of force—was taken as if it would somehow resolve the problem by itself. No one in the inner circle was forceful enough to ask, 'Are we prepared to act out this threat if our bluff is called?'"

There certainly are those who will claim that Clinton's approach to Haiti eventually worked, since Cedras was ousted and

Aristide returned to power. But Broder's statement that "the president and his national security advisers are singularly lacking in any long-term policy perspective" is alarming. If that is true of the waffling evidenced in dealing with Haiti, what assurance is offered to Americans that the same lack of perspective is not present in foreign policy dealings of a grander scale?

Political observers were not particularly impressed with the manner in which Clinton and Carter arrived at the agreement with Cedras. William Safire wrote in the *New York Times* on September 22, 1994, "Jimmy reduces Bill to Carteresque stature." Safire called Clinton "the first U.S. president to permit an usurpation of his authority." The writer claimed that Carter's action had resulted in "a fiasco of wimpish indecision." He pointed out the disparity between Clinton's claim three days prior that Cedras was a "murderer and tyrant" and then "the thug became a man of honor, and worse, our partner in cracking skulls." Safire's summary of this reversal is that Clinton "does moral flip-flops with the greatest of ease." He also wrote that Clinton's "ultimatum means nothing" and that Clinton was significantly embarrassed by Carter's informing the world that he was ashamed of Clinton's policies toward Haiti. The conclusion that Safire draws is that "Clinton has lost control of his foreign policy."

Articles appearing in *Time* magazine and *U.S. News & World Report* on October 3, 1994, were similarly stinging in the face of what Clinton would have considered a foreign policy victory. Lance Morrow in *Time* magazine wrote of Clinton's last-minute shuffling. "What a performance—plates waveringly spinning on sticks balanced at the end of nose and chin and fingertips, a plate now and then wobbling and pinwheeling toward the stages only to be deftly rescued. . . . But those who, like me, voted for Clinton and have wished him well believe now that his multilayered, many dimensional reality, too slick by half, lacks a moral code."

Time magazine also ran an article by Michael Kramer entitled "The Carter Connection." Kramer wrote, "So why does Bill Clinton's Haitian success have that insistent scent of failure about it?

Was it only the stumbling way in which war was avoided?" He took on the Clinton waffle in the following manner: "It arises from the current President's breathtaking presumption that what is said with deep sincerity one day may be repealed with equal vigor the next. In the case of Haiti, the demonized dictators overnight became 'de facto leaders.' "

The lack of conviction that underscores the waffling appeared to be of particular concern to Kramer. "Bill Clinton at war has the disquieting countenance of Bill Clinton at peace: few principles seem inviolate; indiscipline and incoherence are the norm; careful planning falls to last-minute improvisation; steadfastness is only a tactic." Kramer compared this foreign policy behavior to Clinton's handling of Bosnia and Somalia. He quoted the presidents saying that America cannot sit idly by while people are exterminated in Bosnia, and yet "that of course is exactly what we have done."

Regarding Somalia, Clinton said that it will be "open season on Americans" if "aggressors, thugs, and terrorists . . . conclude that the best way to get us to change our policies is to kill our people." Kramer wrote, "But when eighteen U.S. troops were gunned down in Mogadishu, the President changed our policy. We left. Reasonable people may disagree about the wisdom of those policies. That is not the point. The point is that the President's words cannot be counted on for meaning."

U.S. News & World Report presented an article edited by Charles Fenyvesi. The commentary in this article encapsulates the significance of Clinton's waffling. "When military planners put together the aborted plan for invading Haiti, among the major factors taken into account: Bill Clinton's indecisiveness. The mission was constructed so that if—as happened—Clinton cancelled or postponed the invasion, all the units could be recalled right up to H-hour."

It is most unusual that one of the major factors needed to be considered in planning a military invasion is presidential waffling. It is not surprising, however, when considered in the context of an ACOA. In Clinton's own words, "If you live in that kind of constant environment where conflict is never resolved, you tend to repeat that pattern when you grow up. That was an early problem with me, so that I would let things fester too long and then try to deal with them in an emergency situation." It is my contention that herein lies the heart of Clinton's waffling.

Does Bill Clinton conduct an administration that functions in a chaotic manner? Many, including his former chief of staff, Leon Panetta, think so. Panetta was elevated to this position in an attempt to correct the administration's woes. Panetta believed that Clinton needed "tighter discipline, clearer lines of authority and a president more focused on his message," according to Joel Connelly of the *Seattle Post-Intelligencer.* When he assumed his position, Panetta described the administration as a "White House in which presidential aides 'roamed the halls' without knowing their authority and responsibility."

Panetta delivered what Connelly described as "a sharp critique of how the presidency was run during the first eighteen months of Clinton's term." Panetta said, "One [goal] was just better discipline within the White House. There tended to be a campaign mentality that went into the White House initially, rather than a governing mentality. That produced a situation where there was not really tight discipline in terms of individuals exercising their responsibilities and just the general operation of the Oval Office. . . . There were a number of people who did not have very clearly defined areas of authority that basically roamed the halls, so to speak. . . . It wasn't that they weren't talented or capable. It's just that they never had a clearly defined line of authority."

One of the tenets of the theory behind ACOA is that some people tend to grow up and re-create their childhood chaos in their personal and professional lives. I firmly believe that this is the situation with Clinton. Other shake-ups have taken place within the White House in attempts to correct the chaos problem. For example, David Gergen was brought on board, only later to be reassigned. What they need to understand is that chaos is inherent in Clinton as an untreated ACOA.

A *Time* magazine article, "Day of Reckoning," dated February 22, 1993, by Lance Morrow, begins, "Chaos theory likes to think that the beating of a butterfly's wings, say, in central Mexico may, in the complex interactions of nature, eventually stir up a typhoon in the western Pacific. The Clinton presidency seemed determined in its first three weeks to validate chaos theory."

Newsweek's June 7, 1993, cover pictures a worried Bill Clinton under the caption "What's Wrong? Ugh! A Mess in the White House." Joe Klein's "What's Wrong?" article states, "The big question began to bubble up: Had we, as a nation, done it again? Had we put another turkey in the Oval Office? He'd seemed a little slick, maybe, but smart and energetic—certainly not the sort to turn himself into a laughingstock before Memorial Day of his first year. Then again, Bill Clinton—a political Ferris wheel—had been a laughingstock, a national joke, last Memorial Day. (Remember: he was the one who didn't inhale.)" Klein wrote, "The disarray extended across the government—from the State Department . . . to Justice . . . to the military. . . . But the heart of the mess was in the White House. 'There is no chain of command,' said a Democrat close to the administration. 'Everyone is freelancing. Everyone is doing end runs; everyone is second-guessing.' " Klein revealed that such chaos is not new to Clinton since he became president. "Clinton had fallen into a chronic pattern, a management strategy derided as famously wrongheaded in all the texts: he had created a system where aides had responsibilities, but no authority. He had done the same during his first term as governor—and only corrected himself by hiring Betsey Wright, who trammeled him with a vengeance for a decade, after he lost his first re-election effort. . . . He had made the same mistake again in the presidential campaign, rectified when Carville was put in charge."

Chaos occurs when disorder is prevalent. A chaotic organization is one in which no one knows what might happen next. There is no steadiness to the wheel. In Clinton's childhood home he did not know what to expect when he came home from school. Everything might be all right. Dad might be drunk, or Dad might be drunk and violent. There was no way to predict how things would be on any given day or at any given hour of a particular day.

The same can be said of the Clinton presidency. Sometimes policies seem to work out quite well. When Clinton has a success, there is great excitement by some of the media as they wonder whether the president finally has mastered his role. Their excitement is tempered shortly thereafter by another presidential gaffe. It is important to understand that because Clinton is an ACOA does not negate the fact that he also is intelligent and will have some successes. As the hero of the family, he has a rather impressive resumé of successes; but also as the hero of the family he sabotages himself as a means of displaying his anger. If Clinton exhibited only successes or only failures all of the time, his administration would not be chaotic. His administration would be either a success or a failure. What makes Clinton and his administration chaotic is the uncertainty about what will occur. Even the successes in Haiti and North Korea for which Clinton has received credit are successes only in result. The processes involved were very chaotic, with Clinton changing course repeatedly.

Michael Nelson reviewed the president's chaotic nature during his first year in office. Nelson's article, "The Press and the President: How the Press Views the President," was published in the October 1994 issue of *Current*. Nelson is a professor of political science at Rhodes College in Memphis. Nelson wrote, "During Bill Clinton's first year, for example, he was described as, seriatim: Up (the inauguration), Down (Zoe Baird's failed nomination as attorney general, the controversy about gays and lesbians in the military), Up (his February economic address to Congress), Way Down (the defeat of his $200 million stimulus package, his $200 haircut, "travelgate," the Lani Guinier fiasco), Up (the appointments of David Gergen and Ruth Bader Ginsburg), Down (his unpopular budget), Up (the passage of NAFTA), and Down (Whitewater)."

The patterns exist. Clinton has a long history of a tendency to lie, waffle, and create chaos. Empathy abounds for him when one thinks of his traumatic youth. That empathy, however, conflicts with the knowledge that Clinton was aware of his ACOA behaviors and still chose to seek the White House.

CHAPTER FOUR

The Stepchild of an Alcoholic

BILL CLINTON IS THE PRESIDENT OF THE UNITED STATES as well as an adult child of an alcoholic parent, in this case a stepfather. This combination is destined to result in the continued dysfunction inherent in Clinton's upbringing. The initial months of the Clinton presidency were filled with evidence of miscommunication, denial, and lies. The falsehoods have resulted in an inordinate amount of wasted time and national interest directed at resolving the chaos brought about by the president.

It is hoped that this book will result in an increased understanding of alcoholism and ACOAs. The country has taken the leap by electing a president with identifiable dysfunctional behavior patterns. It is essential that the population view this behavior in a meaningful context. The belief that all presidents fudge the truth will not work with this president. Clinton lies to the public not only for political expediency but also because lying is what he knows. He cannot help but lie. For Bill Clinton, denial and lying are the result of learned behavior in childhood.

Spouses of ACOAs learn that they must view their mates' abnormal behavior in the context of their partners' past. If the dysfunction is not identified for what it is, it results in a dysfunctional marriage. The spouse who is unaware of the behavior of an ACOA becomes confused and distrusting. Often the spouse responds to such an individual's dysfunction by doubting him or herself.

The strained marital bond pales in comparison with the discordant bond that exists between a president and the people. The president serves as a guiding light through difficult times. Americans should recognize that Clinton's election to the presidency signals a dysfunctional marriage between the president and the people. Americans have been and will be lied to repeatedly by the president because of his background as an ACOA. Unless the denials and lies are identified for what they are, the people will develop a sense of national self-doubt. If Americans are lied to frequently without recognizing the lies, the country will experience a state of confusion which can immobilize the nation. The result in dysfunctional families is that children develop a strong dependent need. It is not surprising that part of Clinton's program is to enhance a national dependency on the federal government. It is essential for the American people to understand that they have elected as their beacon an ACOA who is filled with self-doubt, lies automatically, thrives upon chaos, and struggles with a feeling of loss.

I am not condemning children and adults who, through no fault of their own, grew up in homes in which one or both parents were alcoholics. As will be discussed, such children frequently are kind, loyal, and lovable people. But it is also true that common psychological and behavioral problems infuse the personality makeup of the ACOA. Furthermore, as Clinton did, children growing up in an alcoholic home frequently encounter episodes of violent behavior. The chaos and fear brought on by violence and encountered in a childhood home have long-lasting effects. One of these effects is a tendency toward peacemaking. Clinton has acknowledged that he needs to moderate this overstated characteristic. A third issue which is common to ACOAs, and Clinton, is that unresolved issues of abandonment plague a person until the issues are resolved.

Similarly, this should not be construed as a condemnation of Clinton himself. Clinton's behavior, like that of other ACOAs, merely reflects his chaotic upbringing. Despite the tremendous hurdles which he faced in his childhood, he must be commended for rising to the highest political office in the world.

David Viscott, in his book *Emotionally Free*, contends that our personalities are composites of three basic personality styles—dependent, controlling, and competitive. These three personality styles are developed during the early years of life. If one's home life is filled with love and encouragement, the child has a greater opportunity to move through these developmental stages effectively and to have an emotionally balanced personality. Individuals who do not enjoy stability or are affected by traumatic experiences are trapped in these developmental stages. The personality reflects the individual's reaction to events in the environment.

Throughout the presidential campaign the media mentioned that Clinton's stepfather was alcoholic. On occasion, Clinton the candidate would refer to that fact himself. However, the media and the public failed to grasp its importance and meaning. The Republican incumbent, George Bush, and the independent candidate, H. Ross Perot, failed to recognize the potential political gain to be had by clearly explaining why this information would predict a problem-ridden presidency. Vague stabs at "character issues" were deflected successfully by the Clinton campaign, which accused the opposition of not focusing on the real issues. Effective research by the Bush team would have revealed that what were ill defined as character issues were really evidence of Clinton's behavior as an ACOA.

With the enormous population of alcoholics in the United States, dwarfed further by the number of Americans who have grown up in alcoholic homes, Bush could have addressed thousands of people about an issue which would have touched their lives. If Bush had made the connection between Clinton's lies and his adult child of an alcoholic background, any spouse of an ACOA would have known exactly what he meant. That the media, the population, and the opposition parties were unable to focus on this issue demonstrates the high degree of national denial concerning ACOAs.

Research indicates that two former presidents of the United States have been ACOAs. One of the presidents, Franklin Pierce, who served from 1853 to 1857, also became an alcoholic himself. Pierce's mother was an alcoholic. She also suffered from depression. According to biographer Roy Franklin Nichols: "Pierce was open, congenial and pleasant. He mixed readily and won friends easily. However, he suffered from periodic bouts of depression. He also fought a longtime battle against alcoholism. Pierce found it hard to say no. He lacked a sustained feeling of self-confidence and was desirous of approbation, consequently he endeavored to be gracious and accommodating to all who sought [favors]. His graciousness was interpreted by many to mean approval of their requests."

This description demonstrates many of the characteristics of the ACOA personality. Pierce exhibited an outward appearance of pleasantness. He was able to win friends easily. At the same time he was undergoing an intense internal struggle which evidenced itself periodically by depression and repeatedly by alcoholism. Pierce, as an ACOA, had learned how to create a façade. He also had learned how to identify what others wanted and to offer them the appearance that he was in agreement. His low self-esteem and poor self-confidence made it difficult for him to take firm stands.

The second ACOA president was Ronald Reagan. Reagan and Richard G. Hubler, the authors of *Where's the Rest of Me?*, wrote of Reagan's father, "He was a man who might have made a brilliant career out of selling, but he lived in a time—and with a weakness [alcoholism]—that made him a frustrated man." Anne Edwards, in her book *Early Reagan: The Rise to Power*, described Reagan's father as having "a great thirst for Irish whiskey." Presidential biographer William A. DeGregorie provided information that might help explain why Reagan's character flaws were not as pronounced as Clinton's are. Reagan's mother was said to have taken "great care that her children realized that their father's alcoholism was a disease, for which they should not resent him."

In *An American Life: Ronald Reagan, the Autobiography*, Reagan expanded on the role that his mother, Nelle Wilson Reagan, played in forging his perception of his father. He also wrote about some experiences related to his father's alcoholism.

"When Nelle thought Neil and I were old enough to know, she

sat us down and explained why my father sometimes disappeared and told us the reason for these sudden unexpected trips from home. She said Jack had a sickness that he couldn't control—an addiction to alcohol. She said he fought it but sometimes lost control and we shouldn't love him any less because of it because it was something he couldn't control. If he ever embarrassed us, she said we should remember how kind and loving he was when he wasn't affected by drink."

Reagan described his father and their relationship. "Although he wasn't the kind of alcoholic who was abusive to his wife or children, he could be pretty surly. Still I always loved and always managed to maintain my respect for Jack, mostly I think because Nelle tried so hard to make it clear he had a sickness that he couldn't help and she constantly reminded us of how good he was to us when he wasn't drinking."

Reagan's recall of his father's alcoholism included one incident in which he displayed the ACOA's characteristic of trying to maintain the family secret and feeling embarrassed when others knew about the problem. He had a girlfriend named Margaret who brought up his father's drinking. "Of course, I'd never said anything to her about Jack's problem with alcohol and tried to keep it a secret. I tried to tell her what Nelle had told us about Jack's problem, that it was a sickness, but she'd never heard anything like that before and didn't buy it."

He was concerned that Margaret's discovery of his father's alcoholism would destroy his relationship with her. He told his mother that he didn't know how he would resolve the conflict but that "I'd probably disown him and never speak to him again." His mother responded in a sympathetic manner but encouraged Reagan to have additional patience. Fortunately for Reagan, his girlfriend elected to continue the relationship.

This reference affords an example of Reagan's freedom to discuss openly with his mother the conflict with his father's alcoholism and his relationship. It is also important to note that his recollection of his childhood was that it was devoid of family violence, one of the characteristics which is correlated with later emotional problems. Reagan recalled that his father would abstain from alcohol for periods of up to years at a time. But like many alcoholics, if he had one drink, he would return to compulsive drinking.

According to William A. DeGregorie, Reagan was "timid about asserting his authority, inept at personal confrontation. His impatience for detail and his willingness to delegate much authority to his staff came in for sharp criticism in the wake of the Iran-contra affair."

In contrast to the apparent functional communication that existed between Reagan and his mother, Clinton's mother, Virginia Kelley, has evidenced a different style of communication. Whereas Nelle Reagan discussed why his father "suddenly disappeared," Virginia Kelley, in her autobiography, described her response to Roger Clinton Sr.'s extended absences from the home as "a relief." One certainly can understand the strain of daily living with a violent alcoholic, but what a message to transmit directly or indirectly to your child: "It's a relief your father is gone."

Another difference in the manner that the alcoholism was handled in the Reagan and Clinton households is demonstrated by Virginia Kelley's quote that she and Bill had the amazing capacity to ignore anything unpleasant.

Further demonstration of the denial by Kelley and Clinton is seen in both of their vague memories. They both had limited recall of events which are documented, such as details about a deposition taken from Clinton at the time of his mother's divorce. His claim that he strongly confronted his stepfather to discontinue the abuse of his mother is not supported by his statements in the deposition.

As Meredith Oakley wrote in *On The Make—The Rise of Bill Clinton*, "Bill Clinton did not speak of those harrowing times publicly until thirty years later, when he became a contender for the Democratic nomination for president. When he did, he painted a heroic portrait of his dealings with his bullying stepfather. Nothing in his testimony indicates that young Bill was able, or even attempted, to stop Roger Clinton's beatings." Clinton himself said that the family difficulties were dealt with by silence.

Attempting to avoid confrontation and understating the importance of his personal involvement by being overly trusting are typical character traits of an ACOA. Reagan, however, seemed to have benefited from his mother's attempts at defusing any negative feelings that he might have otherwise felt toward his father. Interestingly, the pattern established by his mother's advice may have resulted in his style of interpersonal relationships which was nonconfrontational.

That we have had two previous presidents who were adult children of alcoholics directing the affairs of our country might offer hope to some that Clinton will manage as president. It is important to stress that a significant difference exists between Reagan and Clinton. Reagan did not repeatedly demonstrate the effects of his background as an ACOA. Clinton, on the other hand, does.

The discrepancies in Clinton's statements are the clearest examples of such behavior. Clinton frequently exhibits the process of denial and automatic lying. During the vice presidential debates, Dan Quayle referred to these occurrences as "pulling a Clinton." Following Clinton's election, the lies have become legendary. What is even more distressing than the lies is the chaotic nature of the administration, which has resulted in a loss of credibility. As a nation we are experiencing the replay of the dysfunction inherent in President Clinton's childhood.

CHAPTER FIVE

A Childhood of Abandonment and Violence

BILL CLINTON'S CHILDHOOD WOULD BECOME the blueprint for his adulthood and his difficulties as president. It was a childhood rife with abandonment, alcoholism in the home, and violence directed at his mother, his younger brother, and Clinton himself.

Clinton was born into tragedy. His biological father, William Jefferson Blythe III, died in an automobile accident three months prior to Bill's birth. He was thrown from the car and knocked unconscious, drowning in shallow water.

His widowed mother, Virginia Cassidy Blythe, was forced to further her nursing training as an anesthetist so that she could better provide for the family. Clinton's mother went to New Orleans, Louisiana, to further her education. She left young Bill with her parents in Hope, Arkansas, for the initial years of his life. It was fortunate for Clinton that he had grandparents to care for him; but, in reality, this young child had experienced the effects of growing up without his father and the loss of his mother at a critical time in his development.

Clinton's life took a significant turn when he was four years old. At this time, his mother married Roger Clinton, who was to have a traumatic influence on Clinton. The family subsequently moved to Hot Springs, Arkansas; and by the time Clinton was eight years old, his stepfather, Roger Clinton, had become increasingly violent. His stepfather was an alcoholic who periodically erupted in fierce outbursts of anger.

In *Bill Clinton: The Inside Story,* Robert E. Levin described Bill Clinton's family life: "There were frequent arguments between Virginia and Roger, who was an alcoholic. After drinking, he occasionally beat Virginia. He was usually calm, but when he drank, he became angry. During one episode, he fired a gun into a wall of the living room and was put in jail."

Charles F. Allen and Jonathan Portis wrote in *The Comeback Kid—The Life and Career of Bill Clinton:* "He was forced to come to grips with the stormy relationship between his mother and stepfather. Roger Clinton, Sr. was a heavy drinker with a mean streak. He and Virginia had a volatile relationship, frequently separating."

The commentary by Levin and Allen and Portis reveals several key points. First, Clinton's stepfather was unquestionably an alcoholic. Second, Clinton's childhood was chaotic and violent. Third, the violence peaked to such a point that Roger Clinton fired a gun inside the home. Fourth, Clinton saw his stepfather beat his mother. Fifth, his stepfather and mother frequently separated, adding to the already traumatic history of abandonment in Clinton's young life.

Allen and Portis's book also included an interesting quote by Clinton's mother, Virginia Kelley. The authors wrote, "Today, Kelley admits openly that Roger Clinton was an alcoholic—'a wonderful man, but alcoholic,' she says."

Compare this quote from Kelley with Ronald Reagan's mother's view of Reagan's father's alcoholism. Reagan's mother reminded Reagan during his youth that his father's alcoholism was a disease and that resentment for his behavior was therefore not necessary.

Kelley's remark is evidence of her denial years after the fact. Surely she admits that he was an alcoholic. No one could possibly deny that reality. It is her comments that describe Roger Clinton as "a wonderful man" that reflect her denial. This point is critical to understanding the different effects that alcoholism can have upon children.

In Reagan's case, the family dynamics included an open discussion between his mother and himself to assist Reagan in understanding the behavior and freeing him as an ACOA. In Clinton's case, there were obvious denial factors articulated by his mother which did not enable him to mobilize his emotions and free himself from the problems foisted on him by adults. This left Clinton with moderate to severe effects from his childhood as he became an adult, and later president.

Allen and Portis continued: "Because of his stepfather's troubles, young Bill Clinton experienced plenty of ugly incidents in his home when he was a young man. Once, Roger Clinton, Sr., even fired a gun inside the house." These acts of intermittent violence separated by periods of calm, continued until Bill Clinton confronted his stepfather during a violent incident between the stepfather and Clinton's mother and brother. Clinton had turned fourteen at the time. Reportedly, the violent acts ended then. However, his stepfather continued to drink.

Allen and Portis quoted Clinton's mother's description of his relationship with his stepfather, which included feelings of love as well as hatred of the alcoholic behavior. This is one of the factors which led to subsequent problems with intimacy. It is confusing as an adult to hold conflicting emotions for another person. As a child, there is less of an understanding of what feelings mean. A youngster growing up in a state of denial in an alcoholic home has little, if any, understanding of these feelings. The lack of resolution of this primary conflict in Clinton's life would later be replayed in intimate relationships as an adult.

Further supporting evidence that Clinton's childhood entailed extreme episodes of violence is provided by Levin, who wrote, "Roger's drinking led to a divorce when Bill was fourteen. In a deposition, Virginia said, 'He has continually tried to do bodily harm to myself and my son Billy.' "

In their book *Intimate Violence*, Richard J. Gelles and Murray A. Strauss offer an analysis of family and violence among relations. The authors reported:

Experiencing, and more importantly observing, violence as a child teaches three lessons:

1. Those who love you are also those who hit you, and those you love are people you can hit.

2. Seeing and experiencing violence in your home establishes the moral rightness of hitting those you love.

3. If other means of getting your way, dealing with stress, or expressing yourself don't work, violence is permissible.

The authors clarify that some children growing up in violent homes do not display behavioral signs of violence. They draw the conclusion that "in short, growing up in an abusive home can dramatically compromise the developmental and personal competence of the children. Many, if not most, maltreated children enter adolescence with severe personal defects."

These authors point out a number of important factors that could be applied to Clinton's childhood. By definition, Clinton would be characterized as an abused child. Unquestionably, if Clinton's family sought therapy, the therapist by law would have to report this abuse to appropriate authorities. There is no evidence that Bill Clinton ever directed his anger toward others as a result of these violent episodes. It is important to note that Gelles and Strauss stressed that observing violence in the home is particularly damaging to a child. This was something that Clinton experienced, in addition to the violence directed at him. It is important to note that just because Clinton did not outwardly display his anger does not mean that the anger disappeared. Clinton displays his anger today by a need for authority and by periodic outbursts. The feelings associated with a violent home life are substantial factors in the personality deficits inherent in his behavior.

The divorce did not end the relationship between Roger and Virginia. Over Clinton's objections, his mother remarried Roger one year after their divorce. Clinton was now fifteen. Levin reported Clinton's response to the remarriage: "When his mother remarried

Roger Clinton, Bill made the best of it: to make his mother happy, he changed his last name from Blythe to Clinton."

Imagine the feeling of loss of control when Clinton could not convince his mother not to remarry Roger Clinton. His mother brought back into her son's home a man who was abusive and an alcoholic when he promised to be better. What did this tell Clinton about his mother's dependency issues and his role in pleasing her? His belief that his stepfather would not stop drinking was correct, but his self-doubt and desire to please his mother took precedence over his belief. Note that Clinton did not just accept his stepfather's return; he went so far as to change his name. Clinton had been hurt once more, withheld his anger, and redirected it into guilt. This superresponsible boy overcompensated for his unacceptable guilt feelings by changing his name. "See, Mom, I am a good boy!" Clinton had to experience the chaos of feelings surrounding divorce and remarriage one year later.

Levin provided an interesting account of Clinton's perception of his childhood. Bill Clinton described himself as a child and his life as follows: "Overall I was a pretty happy kid. I had a normal childhood. I had a good normal life. But at times it was really tough. I had to learn to live with the darker side of life at a fairly early period. But I wouldn't say it was a tormented childhood. I had a good life."

This perception of self indicates Clinton's deeply ingrained denial of his youthful experience. Clinton certainly enjoyed happy times in his childhood. But one must grasp his deep-seated level of denial when he describes a childhood of repeated episodes of abandonment; parental alcoholism; marriage of his mother; divorce; remarriage; his stepfather's death; marriage of his mother; his second stepfather's death; violence directed at his mother, brother, and himself; and gunshots discharged in his home as a normal life. A true description of Clinton's childhood would be: chaotic and highly abnormal.

It is apparent that Clinton channeled his distress in what would be considered socially acceptable ways. He was successful academically and showed leadership ability. Allen and Portis wrote, "He had tried to be a mature adult when he was still a child in an effort to bring order to the chaos generated by his alcoholic, fearsome stepfather."

At home, he showed particular concern for his younger brother, Roger Clinton Jr. Carolyn Staley, a friend of Clinton's, was quoted by Allen and Portis in her description of Clinton's relationship with his brother: "Staley recalls that Clinton's relationship with his brother Roger was almost parental. 'Bill was forced into an independence early, which I think has bearing on his leadership.' "

Staley was correct in her analysis that Clinton's experiences affected his later leadership. In *Children of Alcoholism: A Survivor's Manual*, Judith S. Seixas and Geraldine Youcha consider the phenomenon of the Family Hero, a response to family alcoholism often exhibited by children. The Family Hero is basically the great kid in the family. He or she is the child who does everything right, repeatedly experiences success, exhibits leadership qualities, succeeds scholastically, athletically, or musically, and is praised by adults. This, in a nutshell, is Bill Clinton. The public views him as a wonder child. The psychotherapist understands that this family member is in a state of denial. He does not feel positive about himself but is searching for external validation for his worth. Clinton fits this model.

Roger Clinton Sr. died of cancer in 1967. At that time, Clinton was attending Georgetown University. For six weeks prior to his stepfather's death, Clinton made weekend journeys from Georgetown to Durham, North Carolina, where Roger Clinton Sr. was hospitalized. Clinton reportedly seized this opportunity to improve their relationship. Allen and Portis underscored the effect of the loss upon Clinton, noting: "But after only six weeks of this newfound closeness, Clinton had lost another father."

At this point, Clinton's abandonment included his biological father's death, his mother's departure to New Orleans, his parents' divorce, his stepfather's death following an attempt at repairing the relationship during his six-week hospitalization, and the emotional abandonment of living with an alcoholic. In 1974, he was to suffer a third parental death when his mother was widowed for a third time.

The effects of abandonment upon a child are tremendous. The abandonment just described involved actual physical and emotional loss. Clinton experienced the emotional abandonment inherent in a relationship with an alcoholic. Alcoholics are not emotionally available to their children for several reasons. When drunk, their awareness and expression of their emotions are flawed. In the case of Clinton's stepfather, the emotion that surfaced during the states of drunkenness was anger. Second, when an alcoholic is not drinking, he is thinking about drinking. Alcoholism has obsessive qualities in addition to the progressive nature of the disorder. The alcoholic, therefore, cannot connect emotionally with others. The intent of his drinking is to escape emotional pain and conflicts. Alcohol serves the purpose of "numbing" these emotions.

Clinton himself spoke of the effects upon his life of the death of his biological father. He said, "I should be in a hurry in life, because it gave me a real sense of mortality. I mean, most kids never think about when they're going to have to run out of time, when they might die. I thought about it all the time because my father died at twenty-nine, before I was born."

The above quotation indicates that part of Clinton's drive to accomplish things prematurely was based on the powerful feeling of abandonment resulting from his father's death. The other aspect of his drive to achieve consisted of his need to enhance his self-esteem and attain the approval of others, resulting from his stepfather's alcoholism and violent behavior. The denial of the pain from abandonment and the fallout from the alcoholism resulted in Clinton's taking on the role of Family Hero.

In contrast to the hero role which Clinton portrayed, his brother, Roger Clinton Jr., experienced some setbacks that would reveal the family dynamics and the personality of the future president. When Clinton was governor of Arkansas, he was alerted to the fact that his brother was involved in serious substance abuse. In August 1984, Roger Clinton Jr. was arrested and charged with five counts of distributing cocaine and one count of conspiracy to distribute cocaine. He served more than one year in prison for these offenses.

Allen and Portis described the effects of Roger's conviction upon Clinton: "His brother's arrest triggered all of the old doubts that he had worked so hard to keep behind the façade of supreme self-confidence. Intimates say that vacuum of a lost childhood finally drained him of his self-respect. He began to see himself as a failure. He hit a low in his moodswing and became self-destructive. Rumors of an extramarital affair again swept through state offices and newsrooms."

In this instance the intensity of the stress from Roger's arrest penetrated the wall which Clinton had erected to hide from his pain. Clinton as a child had taken on the responsibility of protecting Roger from the family pain. That Roger was a substance abuser and was in serious trouble meant to Clinton that he had failed. Clinton measures everything by performance and accomplishment, in a way typical of people having low self-esteem. This is a prime example of how something that was not in Clinton's control, his brother's drug usage, resulted in Clinton's overreaction. Overreactions occur when someone has built up negative feelings. The negative feelings spill out when a person is under stress. Clinton very likely took his brother's substance abuse as evidence of his own personal failure.

This event also demonstrated Clinton's failure to grasp the family dynamic of alcoholism. Roger was responding to the family pain, only in a different mode than Clinton had. Clinton controlled his feelings, in part, by being busy and compulsively organizing himself. While Clinton chose to numb his pain by seeking approval and through excellent performance, his brother numbed his pain by substance abuse.

Instead of being the Family Hero, Roger was engaging in behavior more characteristic of a Family Scapegoat. The scapegoat is the family member to whom others point as the person with the problems in the family. After all, certainly a governor of a state could not be troubled. Levin reported Clinton's comments to the press following Roger's sentencing: "I accept the judgment of the court with respect. Now all of us in my brother's family must do everything we can to help him free himself of his drug dependency." Clinton was focusing on his brother's symptomatology rather than the family pain.

The aftermath of Roger's arrest included some consideration given to the family disturbances. Allen and Portis wrote, "A period of intense family therapy began after Roger Clinton Jr. was released from prison a year later. Bill Clinton has said in several interviews that this therapy forced him to wrestle with the dark forces inside him."

This quotation reflects a startling revelation about Clinton when compared with another statement that he made. Recall how Clinton described his childhood: "I had to learn to live with the darker side of life at a fairly early period." In other words, Clinton had internalized the "darker side of life" and as an adult felt it when under stress as "the dark forces inside him." It was this internalization of darkness that attacked Clinton's self-esteem and left him feeling like a failure and a bad person.

According to Allen and Portis, in response to the family therapy undertaken after Roger's release from jail, "friends say he [President Clinton] still reads books and medical studies on children of alcoholics, searching for clues to his own behavior."

That quote seems to indicate that Clinton vaguely understands that his character flaws are due to the fact that he is an ACOA. Unfortunately, his failure to understand leaves him still "searching for clues." His behavior as president clearly shows that the search has not been completed.

In addition, great concern must be expressed about Clinton's emotional and behavioral response following Roger's arrest. According to Allen and Portis, Clinton became self-destructive. This behavior reflects Clinton's feeling of guilt about the family circumstances and his "failure" to have parented Roger effectively. His emotional response was to direct his anger inward. Clinton became angry with himself for his "dark forces." The intensity of the self-directed anger resulted in the need for self-punishment. The sabotage of himself was demonstrated behaviorally when the rumors about an affair surfaced. He felt undeserving and was setting himself up for a fall. His self-knowledge that he is undeserving of the presidency, being an impostor, has resulted in sabotage, or "self-created" problems, as David Gergen has written.

A description of how negative feelings develop is provided by Dr. David Viscott in *Emotionally Free*. Dr. Viscott created the Feeling Cycle, which clarifies the progression of negative feelings. The Feeling Cycle helps to explain what happened to Clinton. Dr. Viscott explained that the initial hurt that someone feels is dealt with effectively by releasing that feeling at the moment it occurs. Clinton's hurt involved pain from abandonment, domestic violence, and his stepfather's alcoholism. When the hurt is not released but held inside, it transforms into anger. Viscott identifies anger as old hurt. Clinton redirected the anger toward himself in the form of guilt. Clinton therefore has held himself responsible for the domestic pain which was out of his control. Viscott wrote that the transference of anger into guilt requires energy and that this depletion of energy is felt as depression.

When Clinton was faced with the heavy burden of stress, it was impossible for him to continue to withhold his pain without an obvious display of behavioral change. The pain is still present inside Clinton, and that is why we notice so many flaws in behavior and character.

One might even speculate that Clinton's domestic programs reflect his personal guilt about his domestic life as a child. Accomplishing what he believes to be positive goals would result in a symbolic cleansing of his failure to control the conflicts within his family of origin. It would offer him a freedom from responsibility for the heartache of others and an opportunity to remove the pain of his youth.

CHAPTER SIX

What We Know About Adult Children of Alcoholics

THE CONCEPT OF ADULT CHILDREN OF ALCOHOLICS was popularized in the 1980s. Therapeutic practitioners began to notice some common traits in behavior and character among patients who had one or more alcoholic parents.

Janet Geringer Woititz, Ed.D., was one of the pioneers who studied this phenomenon. Her book *Adult Children of Alcoholics* became very popular. It has served to spread the word about ACOAs and helped millions gain clearer understanding about themselves.

Another author, Dennis Wholey, described the effect that alcohol has had on American culture and how many lives it has touched. He wrote: "If there are 20 million alcoholics in America, minimally 80 million Americans are directly affected by alcoholic behavior. This figure—which represents more than one-third of the entire population—includes the alcoholic themselves, and the husbands and wives, brothers and sisters, children and parents of alcoholics."

A review of the recent literature on this topic reflects the growing attention that ACOAs have been given. The professional psychological journals from 1974 through 1986 include only a handful of articles on this topic. From 1987 through the present, however, research articles and doctoral dissertations on the effects of alcohol on children in families are plentiful and revealing.

It must be noted that a number of researchers have found little or no significant differences between adult children of alcoholic groups and control groups in which those studied did not have alcoholic parents. Ronald W. Goodman studied characteristics of ACOAs. One of the author's conclusions was "that it should not be assumed that all ACOAs have been affected by their experience in the same way, that such effects are always negative, or that all ACOAs need counseling."

Acknowledging that all ACOAs have not experienced similar effects is consistent with the literature and serves to explain why some researchers find no differences between groups. The trauma of a child in an alcoholic setting can range from mild to severe. Many authors have found significant differences between groups of ACOAs and non-ACOAs. One should accept Goodman's cautionary remarks while applying ACOA characteristics to Clinton's character and behavior. This book will provide sufficient evidence based on Clinton's behavioral and characterologic history to conclude that Clinton's experiences as an ACOA are the overriding factors in his use of denial and lies.

Bernadette Mathews and Michael Halbrook, writing in the *Journal of Career Development,* found that ACOAs often reenact unresolved issues by replicating their family of origin at their work site. The authors isolated characteristics of ACOAs that are expressed by dependent attitudes and behaviors. They also found that ACOAs strive to become what others want, tending to avoid and placate others while striving for approval. Finally, the authors reported that ACOAs often distort the truth to avoid disappointing others.

When one's work site is the Oval Office, it is essential that any unresolved childhood issues which might affect performance be addressed. Clinton is using his "work site" as a forum to replicate the dysfunction in his family of origin. His character is one which manifests the dependent need to obtain approval and avoid conflict. As a result, he makes promises which are impossible to fulfill. This position leaves Clinton with nowhere to turn but to distort the truth. As of November 1994, Clinton's approval rating has dipped below the 47 percent mark. The midterm election was, in Nebraska senator Bob Kerrey's words, "a sharp, clear, and obvious repudiation of the president." Speculation exists that Kerrey may challenge Clinton for the Democratic nomination in 1996. Knowing that Clinton's weaknesses include dishonesty, one can safely predict that with his intense need for approval not being met, the president experiences increasing stress, which will result in further dishonesty. When we are under stress, our weaknesses become more pronounced.

In *Children of Alcoholism: A Survivor's Manual,* Judith S. Seixas and Geraldine Youcha address the issue of ACOAs in the workplace. The authors identified factors which influence the ability of ACOAs to be good employees. The authors itemized the fear of success, feeling emotionally out of control, oversensitivity to criticism, self-doubt about abilities, and feeling not good enough as primary factors which inhibit the employment performance of ACOAs. Seixas and Youcha indicated that the fear of succeeding tends to undermine their own efforts. Also, oversensitivity to criticism results in a failure to ask others for help.

One of the ways that Clinton sabotages himself is by lack of perseverance. The glaring example of Clinton's failure to persevere is his diffusion of focus from economic matters. The campaign theme of "it's the economy, stupid!" enabled Clinton repeatedly to hammer away at one message. This focus was partially responsible for his ability to override references to "character issues." Once the candidate was in office, however, his focus began to blur.

Clinton turned his attention to other issues, such as gays in the military and rescinding the executive order to restrict disclosure about abortions. His immediate attention to these issues not only diffused his focus about the economy, it also resulted in the development of unnecessary conflict. Again, recall that for Clinton to function within a personal comfort zone, conflict is essential.

To be fair to Clinton, it must be emphasized that he was making good on campaign promises. Even in his attempt to do so he managed to raise the ire of his supporters for this agenda by seeming to back off from a tough stance on the "gays in the military" issue. Clinton once more was caught by surprise by the enormity of negative reaction to the position he had taken. Members of his own party, like Sen. Sam Nunn, surfaced in strong opposition to the recommended changes.

One perception evolved: Clinton could not close the deal. He was forced to do some political backpedaling, which would become his hallmark. Another perception that began to develop, even among his constituency, was that Clinton was not the New Democrat for whom they had voted. Indeed, those who had been swayed by Clinton's rhetoric about change and the economy had been led to believe that this "moderate" Democrat was going to Washington immediately to tackle some difficult fiscal issues. Instead, Clinton focused on typical liberal agenda issues, homosexuality and abortion rights.

When one considers that they were two of very few campaign promises on which Clinton followed through, it points out the importance of these issues to him. This has several ramifications. The populace soon began to discover that the New Democrat that they voted for was an impostor. Clinton, of course, has always known this, and research has indicated that he likely thought of himself as an impostor because of his upbringing. Because of his ability to campaign effectively, Clinton was able to disguise himself as something that he was not. Any objective analysis of his proposed economic package and his social concerns would place Clinton in the liberal camp. Yet by shrouding himself under the moderate image, Clinton was elected. Once Clinton became president, he was unable to appear as something that he was not.

A study by Sheryl L. Robinson and Shona K. Goodpaster, reported in *Current Psychology Research and Reviews*, compared a group of university students with a group of ACOAs. Statistical analysis comparing these groups revealed that ACOAs scored significantly higher than subjects with nonalcoholic parents on a measure for impostor phenomenon. The ACOAs felt that the image that they were portraying to others was false compared with what they believed about themselves. The study also showed that ACOAs believe that their lives are more controlled by external forces when compared with the control group. This significant factor, combined with the impostor phenomenon, demonstrates a false sense of self that leads to portraying an image as opposed to an honest reality.

Columnist Nat Hentoff began researching Clinton's gubernatorial record in the winter of 1992. His June 6, 1993, column, entitled "A President's Principles: 'There Is No Bill Clinton,' " describes the shell of the adult-child-of-an-alcoholic personality. Hentoff interviewed a Little Rock reporter who was on the political scene during the Clinton political years in Arkansas. The reporter told Hentoff, "There is no Bill Clinton. That is, he has no principles that he will stick to when the going gets rough. His great passion is to be popular."

Clinton seeks approval. Once the goal is reached, there is no substance to support it. Recall that the ACOA feels like an impostor. He or she has learned what to say to others. Clinton's learned behavior during childhood trained him to attend acutely to others and to tell them what he thinks they want to hear, which is radically different from holding a deep conviction and having others respond either positively or negatively to one's position.

Hentoff's research resulted in a series of articles on Clinton's gubernatorial years. He discovered that Clinton's record as governor was similarly marked with lies and broken promises. He wrote: "I noted that again and again he backed down on promises when keeping them might lose him larger public support or significant private support. He talked a good environmental game, for instance, but allowed an industry that gave him a lot of campaign funds to pollute the waters. He spoke in a forked tongue on abortion, leading both pro-choicers and pro-lifers to believe he was their champion."

Hentoff provides further substantiation that Clinton's woes as a new president are not due to external factors, such as the newness of the job or a difficult Congress. Clinton's dilemma is a long-standing personal issue that is easily identifiable as having its roots in his childhood trauma. One can safely say Clinton has psychological scars from his youth which affected his ability to govern the state of Arkansas and is affecting his ability to govern the nation. Clinton's personality conflict means that he will not magically be able to change given enough time, as some wistfully dream. Simply, Clinton cannot help himself!

Clinton's ability to win acclaim will be put to the test as his negative ratings continue to outdistance his approval ratings. For a person with a strong need for approval, these ratings can cause considerable inner turmoil. Clinton must temper his need for approval so that it will not be put ahead of the needs of the country.

It is perhaps difficult for people unfamiliar with ACOAs to accept that an intelligent, highly ambitious man has been affected by having an alcoholic parent and that those effects linger and pervade his adult life. Lisa D. Hinz wrote in the *Journal of Substance Abuse* about a group of ACOAs whom she studied in comparison to a group of non-ACOAs. The ACOAs reported more concern than the control group about interpersonal anxiety, depression, and family problems. Interestingly, the two groups did not differ in concern about academic skills. The author concluded that academic achievement did not appear to protect ACOAs from psychological problems.

Hinz serves notice that even an ACOA who appears to "have it all together" by obtaining academic success may still be experiencing the same internal conflicts as an ACOA whose life is in obvious disarray. No one would deny Clinton's academic achievements and abilities, which were apparent to his teachers even in elementary school. These academic achievements did not insulate Clinton from his childhood turmoil. It is not uncommon for someone with low self-esteem developed in his childhood to attempt to obtain a sense of worth and approval through academic achievement.

Other authors, including Sandra H. Tweed and Carol D. Ryff, found similar results in that ACOAs scored significantly higher for anxiety and depression than did adults from nonalcoholic families. The authors stressed in their article in the *Journal of Studies on*

Alcohol that further research in this area is important to explain the variability in psychological functioning of ACOAs.

Howard Protinsky and Steven Ecker described in *Family Therapy* the effect of parental alcoholism on later relationships between parents and offspring. The ACOAs reflected a more dependent relationship with their children than non-ACOAs. When one considers that previous studies demonstrated that the ACOA relives his dysfunctional childhood family through his work, it is understood that the relationships established through work will be dependent in nature. It is clear that Clinton favors an increasingly dependent relationship between the government and the citizenry. It is as if the president has assumed the father role by establishing a dependent relationship with his "children."

There are two main purposes for this action. Clinton gains political benefit by developing a growing number of voters dependent on him. The psychological component involved is that the person who seeks to be in a position of overcontrol has an underlying fear of abandonment. When people are afflicted with low self-worth, as is typical of ACOAs, they fear that others will come to the realization that they have been faking their competency and will reject them. This, of course, is painful in personal relationships but could prove politically devastating.

Research by L. G. Bradley and H. G. Schneider, reported in *Psychological Reports*, offers further support to the hypothesis that the effects of parental alcoholism persist into adulthood. Their study indicated that ACOAs exhibit a higher need for interpersonal control than do adults who did not have alcoholic parents. The need for control in relationships was found to be particularly strong in individuals whose father was the alcoholic, as was Clinton's stepfather. While being in control is a strength which serves a president well, becoming a controlling person is a weakness which is an overstatement of the strength of being in command. This need to control, again, evidences itself by establishing a dependent constituency. Just as dependency is dysfunctional within interpersonal relationships, it is dysfunctional on a national scale. At a national level the dysfunction can have grave societal and financial implications.

In another study, conducted by Tarpley M. Richards and presented in the *Alcoholism Treatment Quarterly*, the author found that ACOAs exhibit many emotional and behavioral problems. The effects identified by the author may be mild, moderate, or severe. Three categories of problems were discovered—an impairment of self-esteem, failure to establish reasonable concepts of personal responsibility, and difficulty in appropriately regulating sexual and aggressive drives.

This study is of interest in that these three problems are attributable to Clinton. Two of the categories, in particular, are issues that have been raised in the media regarding President Clinton. Clinton's denial of personal responsibility has been assailed by the public and the media. Examples of this are plentiful. Readers will recall Clinton's handling of the fallout from the Waco, Texas, affair; the so-called Travelgate scandal; and the haircut on the tarmac at Los Angeles International Airport as cursory examples. In each instance Clinton's initial response was a denial of personal responsibility. This is his gut-level reaction to conflict. It is obvious to everyone that Clinton played a role in each of the aforementioned incidents. Even still, he maintained an initial denial which was followed by a series of miscommunications by White House staff designed to offer damage control and to suggest that, while not responsible for the mishaps, Clinton is aware and in control. Clinton's advisers were then dispatched to various press and television outlets to provide a "corrected response." Even the corrected responses issued by the staff are frequently at odds with one another. This is because it is impossible to recover from a lie without acknowledging that the lie occurred.

The second point, difficulty in appropriately regulating sexual and aggressive drives, also has been considered publicly. During the campaign, Gennifer Flowers alleged that Clinton had a twelve-year affair with her. She provided an audiotape which purportedly indicates Clinton encouraged her to deny that their relationship had occurred and that she received favored status in obtaining a job. Clinton's response was to deny personal responsibility.

In *The Comeback Kid*, Charles F. Allen and Jonathan Portis reported that rumors about Clinton's having an affair were common after two separate stressful events. After Clinton was defeated for reelection following his first term as governor of Arkansas, "rumors began filtering into the newsrooms and throughout state offices that Clinton was having an affair with another woman. Clinton was known to have said, 'What am I supposed to do about these women who throw themselves at me?' "

Following his brother Roger Clinton's arrest for distributing cocaine, "rumors of an extramarital affair again swept through state offices and newsrooms." Whether the affair occurred, or whether it is an issue determining the outcome of an election is of little importance at this point. That rumors circulated at times of personal distress coupled with the fact that research indicates that ACOAs have difficulty in appropriately regulating their sexual drives and use denial of personal responsibility offers further credence to Ms. Flowers's claims.

Also, of greater importance, Clinton's denial was ultimately accepted as an effective means of making this a nonissue in the election. In fact, the Comeback Kid skillfully used this and other relevant issues related to his character to his advantage. He convinced a large segment of the population that his character was unimportant. What mattered, according to Clinton, was the economy and not superfluous issues. Unfortunately, the "character issues" could have tremendous negative impacts upon the economy because of the need for control, the development of dependency, denial of personal responsibility, and the tendency to lie.

A further indication of Clinton's difficulty with forming appropriate intimacy boundaries occurred with his selection of his wife, Hillary Rodham Clinton, to serve as chairperson of the commission for health-care reform. Regardless of her educational and other qualifications, her selection raised a number of issues.

Hillary's appointment also related to the issue that ACOAs have difficulty with intimate relationships. Part of the reason is a lack of awareness of typical boundaries to be established within a relationship. If Clinton had become dissatisfied with the action of the commission, would he have fired his wife? Did members of the health reform commission have complete freedom to express their opinions knowing that the chairperson shares a bed with the president?

Even if these freedoms exist, such a decision reshapes the role of a nonelected spouse, which leaves many Americans uncomfortable. Recall that your discomfort means increased comfort for the president, as discomfort is what is familiar to him.

When the president was governor of Arkansas, Hillary Clinton also served as chairperson on an important committee reforming educational standards. Clinton's comment at the time was: "This guarantees that I will have a person who is closer to me than anyone else overseeing a project that is more important to me than anything else."

It is unusual for any president to have involved himself in as many conflicts as Clinton has. The president seems to misfire several times a week. His desire to please others, an ACOA characteristic, contributes to this problem. Clinton said in a television interview that each morning he hopes he won't make any stupid mistakes.

The reason for the frequent "stupid mistakes" is supplied, in part, by a study conducted by Elizabeth Stark which appeared in *Psychology Today*. Stark's article addressed the emotional effects on children growing up in alcoholic homes. She reported that the children feel anxious and guilty, are self-blaming, and defend themselves from their pain with denial. The author also found that these emotional scars are carried into adult life. Stark wrote that ACOAs look for external solutions to feel good about themselves. They often reveal some type of addictive behavior and often create trouble for themselves because they feel more comfortable when there is a crisis.

David Gergen, writing about the president in *U.S. News & World Report*, said, "A good chunk of Clinton's problem is self-made . . .

he began dealing with a bewildering array of issues. . . ." Gergen's comments tie in with Stark's research. No wonder President Clinton seems to move from one self-created crisis to the next or that complaints about his inability to stay focused upon one issue surface. When one grows up in conflict and with each day arrives a new crisis, one perpetuates those situations. Providing the American people with repeated crises enables an "impostor" president to continue in office. While the citizens are uncomfortable, the adult-child-of-an-alcoholic president is more comfortable. Do not be fooled by an apparent air of self-confidence. Clinton's underlying personality is one of low self-esteem and poor self-confidence.

The harsh self-judgment is signaled by his needs for power and approval. At age thirty-two, Clinton became the second-youngest governor in U.S. history. His ascendancy to the presidency as a relatively young man is the culmination of a constant striving for power underscored with an intense competitive drive. While self-criticism for some serves to be an insurmountable hindrance, it has spurred Clinton on to great achievement.

It is common among children growing up in an alcoholic home, particularly those who encountered violence to the other parent or themselves, to be self-effacing. The negativity and criticism which were leveled at them was great. Several factors affect the emotionality of the child. The child is being berated or physically mishandled by someone he or she is supposed to love. The resulting intrapsychic conflict pits positive feelings in opposition to negative ones. Since it would be at great physical or emotional risk to address these feelings to the family, the child tends to withhold the emotions. The painful feelings, when withheld, turn into anger. Some children act out the anger, usually outside the family environment or with younger siblings. Other children, and this appears to be the case with Clinton, redirect the anger toward themselves. The turning of anger on oneself results in guilt.

Children frequently vacillate between having angry thoughts toward others and feeling guilty for having those thoughts. Imagine the thoughts that run through a child's mind while encountering a ritual of parental alcoholism, violent actions toward his mother, and violence directed at himself. Some children mature, receive assistance for their conflicted childhood, and find release from the pain and the emotional bondage related to it. Others become emotionally incapacitated and imprisoned by their anger and guilt. Still other children deny the painful emotions withheld from these experiences and reexperience them in their relationships and work sites.

Clinton's denial of the painful realities and his odd description of his childhood as a happy one are the links between his youth and his aberrant personality issues as an adult. Any psychotherapist who had a client with a childhood history similar to Clinton's and heard the client describe his youth as a happy childhood would recognize the denial and emotional control that the client was using to defend himself from his pain. It is critical to understand that controlling this emotional distress greatly affects a person's ability to function. If one denies an objective reality of his life, one is easily able to deny other conflicts as they arise.

The withholding of the pain is at times impossible to accomplish. Outbursts of rage occur when a person is under stress. The realization that one is an angry person adds to lowered feelings of self-esteem. Clinton's self-esteem has always been buoyed by accomplishment. His competitiveness enables him to pick himself off the floor whenever there is a political setback. His response to personal conflicts will be shown to be less resilient. Being labeled "the Comeback Kid" indicates that Clinton rebounds when necessary and manages the political ups and downs. His resiliency in such situations is a testament to his riding the waves of tumult within his childhood home. He grew up in a home of periodic upheaval, and he was a survivor. Clinton's experience with chaos makes that his comfort zone, while others marvel at his ability to make comebacks.

Bick Wanck, in the *Carrier Foundation Letter*, described the dynamics and characteristics of ACOAs. He found that the behavior of ACOAs is characterized by a struggle to maintain control, a tendency to distrust one's feelings and perceptions, and a drive toward constantly seeking approval. When someone has low self-esteem, he frequently seeks external means to gain an increased sense of worth.

Clinton's election with 43 percent of the vote certainly indicated that enough people approved of him to elect him. However, his victory was hardly the mandate for change that he sought. If his approval ratings slide, Clinton's need for validation will increase and cause him stress, resulting in more aberrant behavior and an increase in the defense mechanism of denial.

"Adult Children of Alcoholics," an article appearing in the journal *Hospital and Community Psychiatry*, by Barry S. Tuchfeld, also found problematic behaviors associated with ACOAs. They included low self-esteem, inability to process and evaluate experiences (cognitive abilities), lack of adult models, and overreaction to change.

President Clinton sought to address his low self-esteem at a rather odd time. Perhaps the first hint after his election that this presidency would be different from those of his predecessors occurred at a meeting of his cabinet. Clinton had his cabinet take an early morning bus trip to meet him for an organizational retreat. Each member had been asked to reveal something personal to help develop cohesiveness of the group.

Clinton reportedly cited as his example how children used to make fun of him about his weight. It would seem that someone whose father had died before his birth, his mother's marriage to an alcoholic, their divorce and remarriage, violence in his home, the death of his stepfather, and the subsequent death of his third father might have produced more substantial information to "share" with his encounter group. Clinton either avoided revealing these personal conflicts to the group for fear of their rejection, sought to reduce the tension from group members, or he failed to identify them as the overriding unresolved issues of his life. In fact this failure to resolve personal problems from his childhood and to seek treatment in an appropriate setting has led Clinton to this behavior.

The accumulation of emotional scarring from such traumatic

experiences can be overwhelming. Perhaps the most revealing element of this "exercise" is that it demonstrates that at some level Clinton is aware of unresolved life issues. A person who entered the presidency free of past emotional scarring would not have selected an organizational cabinet meeting as a place for psychological growth. The "damage control" efforts of the White House staff included references to Clinton's desire to run his presidency like a business. Businesses were said to engage in this type of group work. The staff either intentionally or unintentionally missed the point. The point is that this type of behavior is not normal, since the cabinet is not designed to function as a personal growth group.

It is important to stress that processing and evaluating information is not necessarily an exercise in intellectual ability. As mentioned previously, Clinton certainly has demonstrated academic achievement. Instead, the difficulty in processing and evaluating information is the outgrowth of his conflicted childhood.

The lack of an effective adult male role model in Clinton's family is also important. Clinton's mother identified Roger Clinton Sr., his alcoholic stepfather, as Bill Clinton's role model. This means he must continue to struggle to determine what is "normal" behavior.

It is ironic that one of the characteristics of an ACOA is overreaction to change. This president conducted an election campaign insisting it was time for a change. The reality is that Clinton has a built-in propensity to overreact to change.

Obviously, having a president who overreacts to change can have severe ramifications for the people. Domestically, the impulsive need to create chaotic change can result in major overhauls of systems, such as health care. Given the background of an ACOA, the mess that would result from such a president's actions would be more costly and chaotic than any potential benefits.

Consider further the consequences of a president who overreacts and changes his mind ill advisedly. Clinton's about-face on the Haitian immigrant issue resulted in a considerable loss of life.

Clinton the campaigner had promised that he would change the policy of the Bush administration relative to the immigration of Haitians. Clinton characterized the Bush plan as immoral. The Haitians took Clinton at his word and rejoiced at their apparent new opportunity to enter the United States. The man who manipulated his way into the presidency changed his position after taking office. The Haitians were duped by Clinton. A boatload of four hundred Haitians set off on a journey to freedom in the United States under the impression that Clinton would be true to his word. They died in the attempt. The suffering of these people and their families could have been avoided by less impulsive action and more consistent behavior.

Clinton's position on the war in Bosnia and Serbia further demonstrates his propensity to shift with the wind. One minute he indicates that the suffering in this war-torn region is so great that America must take a more active interventionist role. The next minute, the urgency to act is withdrawn. This erratic behavior is due in part to Clinton's failure to develop support among the allies. When Clinton sought the support of the European community, European diplomats stated that they would not support Clinton's interventionist strategies because they weren't certain what he would do from one day to the next. Clinton as an unknown commodity was viewed with intense skepticism by the seasoned diplomats. Clinton's impulsive waffling undermines American prestige and could have devastating effects on our foreign policy making.

Ironically, after the years of concern about a president "having his finger on the nuclear button," a former war protester enters the Oval Office with a proclivity toward overreaction. With an issue as potentially grave as nuclear war, I am not implying that Clinton would misuse such authority. The concern about overreaction is mentioned just to underscore the need to elect an emotionally balanced president.

Remember: ACOAs thrive on chaos, and crises produce a feeling of comfort. The citizenry's acceptance of Clinton's concept of change means more chaos, since chaos is his comfort zone. Unfortunately, Clinton's ability to arrive at change resulting in a more comfortable existence for Americans will be difficult given his history as an adult child of an alcoholic.

CHAPTER SEVEN

Lies, Deceit, and Chaos

AMERICANS HAVE COME TO EXPECT and begrudgingly have accepted the fact that during a political campaign the candidates frequently fudge the truth or outright lie. During the presidential campaign between George Bush and Michael Dukakis in 1988, Vice President Bush declared that he would not raise taxes if elected with the pledge "Read my lips." This pledge was politically expedient and helped elect Bush president. It would also work against him in his bid for reelection in 1992. Bush's failure to make good on his campaign promise by compromising with Congress on a tax increase in 1990 at the outset of a recession resulted in a deepening of the economic problems that the country faced. The downward turn of the economy, coupled with the perception that Bush was not attentive enough to domestic affairs, made him vulnerable in his attempt to be reelected.

Clinton and his campaign staff exploited Bush's "Read my lips" promise. Bush lost, in large part because he had lied to the American people. It is probable that this lie would have been overlooked and Bush would have been reelected if the economy had not worsened. Following the Gulf War, his popularity was at the highest point ever for a president. The ultimate irony and one that will have lasting effects is that President Bush in part was defeated for lying by an individual who, because of his childhood background as an ACOA, has the same tendency to lie. The lies which President Clinton has and will put forth are automatic in nature.

In an alcoholic home, truth is of little value. The alcoholic parent frequently makes promises that fall by the wayside. Whether it is a promise to attend the Little League game or to quit drinking, the promise is of little consequence. Clinton's mother remarried the stepfather on the pledge that he would not drink anymore. That pledge was not honored by Roger Clinton.

For a time, a child in the home believes the word of the alcoholic parent, only to be hurt and disappointed repeatedly. The hurt resides inside the child because in the alcoholic home there is not an effective communication structure to express the pain. The hurt turns into anger over time. Withholding the anger results in a lowering of the child's self-worth. The child ultimately learns that telling the truth is not only of no value in the home but also that lying is acceptable.

It becomes easier to go along with the dysfunction rather than to fight against it. Since Dad seemed to be telling the truth when he made his promise to stop drinking, that seemed to be all that mattered. That he never followed through did not seem to have consequences. Every time he promised and displayed a sense of guilt, Mom stayed with him and figured that he "really means it this time." For Clinton, the lesson to be learned was that while one is supposed to tell the truth, in reality appearance is all that matters.

It also was of little practical value to tell the truth in an alcoholic home. An alcoholic's behavior is unpredictable. Clinton's stepfather would go on violent sprees when he was under the influence of alcohol. On other occasions, his stepfather would appear calm. The disparity in behavior from violence to calmness teaches one to be constantly attentive to other people's actions. One learns to react to them rather than to take action for oneself. To take a risk by exposing some truth that could result in harmful consequences would be foolhardy. The child in the alcoholic home learns to lie automatically without any sense of guilt. It is the thing to do within the dysfunctional system. The child learns not only to lie but also to distort reality in such a fashion that at times he even deceives himself. The child begins to believe his own lies. In addition, since lying does not have negative consequences, the child learns that there is no true purpose in following through with projects.

The child growing up in an alcoholic home experiences a dysfunctional communication pattern within the family in which one "seems" to be telling the truth while actually telling lies. The child also displays this dysfunctional communication outside the confines of the home. Maturing in such conditions leaves one with a feeling of shamefulness about what is occurring at home. The biggest lie of all is the cover-up of the parent's alcoholism. This takes many forms, including utilizing denial to defend against the realities. The child with a sense of shame becomes a participant in the denial as an attempt to protect the parent and himself from being exposed to peers or neighbors.

The work of Bernadette Mathews and Michael Halbrook informs us that ACOAs transfer their childhood dysfunction into the workplace. A child's "work site" is the school, where deceit, denial, and lies occur. The fear of others discovering what is taking place at home far outweighs any desire to expose the truth. After all, in the home the child has learned to lie guilt-free. The lies might leave others with a sense that something does not quite add up, for it becomes increasingly difficult to keep the lies straight over time.

The child does not realize that other children are not nearly as interested in what is occurring in his home as he believes, which might be a possible explanation as to why Clinton's childhood friends did not emphasize such concerns in previous books about his life. The goal of the child from the alcoholic home is to keep others at a distance while appearing to be close to them. The distance may be created interpersonally by lying or by physically not allowing others into the home. Keeping others at bay also requires inventing a variety of "excuses." One of Clinton's mechanisms of lying to his classmates was to deny his feelings and strive for their approval.

Just as it is difficult for the child to maintain accurate recall of the deceptions, excuses, and lies, the adult in the public spotlight finds it extremely difficult to maintain the image. Clinton's actions and words are under a microscope. Unfortunately, the results of a test on veracity demonstrate that Clinton fails miserably. Clinton's upbringing taught him to lie automatically, with no guilt, and to present excuses spontaneously. However, Clinton is no longer dealing with schoolhouse chums.

It is critical to understand that the concern about President Clinton's lies is not based on the doublespeak associated with the political world. A column by D. R. Segal which appeared in the *Orange County Register* on April 11, 1993, addressed this issue. Apparently, Mr. Segal received a bumper sticker that alluded to our current president. The bumper sticker read Impeach the Liar. Mr. Segal noted that it would be difficult to ascertain to which administration the bumper sticker referred. Indeed, lies, deception, and dishonesty are nothing new to the political world. D. R. Segal continued: "I am not much worried about Mr. Clinton's truthfulness because no American beyond the grade of imbecile expects a president of the United States to be foolishly honest when it is not absolutely necessary, any more than we expect him to tap dance or recite *Finnegans Wake* from memory."

William F. Buckley Jr. wrote in his February 26, 1993, column: "The con man in Clinton slowly emerges." Buckley described the political personality of Clinton as "the most salable political personality since John F. Kennedy." He discussed Clinton's capacity to leave the impression that he is completely involved in the problems of almost everyone. The columnist proceeded: "There is, of course, the difficulty that more and more observers are pointing to, however reluctantly. It is the encroaching sense of the con man; the sense, also, that all of those people around him have become shills."

Buckley's analysis of Clinton as a con man appears accurate and entirely consistent with literature on ACOAs. Dr. Janet Geringer Woititz commented in *Adult Children of Alcoholics:* "The con artist can generally get away with it for a while. This, too, is what he learned at home. The highly manipulative behavior of the alcoholic for a while reaps reward in terms of achieving the ends that he thinks are desirable. But manipulation doesn't work forever, others stop being fooled. . . . Having a distorted sense of his own power, he doesn't quite know what hit him when he is finally caught."

An ACOA often charms because he has learned to manipulate and say what he thinks others want to hear. After analyzing why he went down to defeat after his first term in office in Arkansas, Clinton said: "I simply didn't communicate to the people that I genuinely cared about them. . . . I gave the appearance of trying to do too many things and not involving the people as I should." Clinton learned his lesson that even if you are not sincere, you must put forth the appearance of caring. The shills are necessary to attempt to cover Clinton on his gaffes. While the automatic lie has initial "utility," it does not offer the substance to fend off the press.

Clinton's use of shills demonstrates that the dysfunction has reached some of the highest positions within the administration. James Risen of the *Los Angeles Times* wrote a column which appeared in the *Sacramento Bee Final* on February 27, 1993. Risen began his column by writing: "The Clinton administration has decided not to propose any more spending cuts to offset proposed tax increases in its economic plan—even though the president vowed earlier this week that more cuts were coming, senior administrator officials said Friday."

Leon Panetta, then White House budget director, was reported to have said that "the administration will stick with its original plan and not draw up a more extensive list of specific cuts." The article also quoted Labor secretary Robert Reich as stating that the president and the economic team spent "weeks squeezing as hard as we possibly could on defense, non-defense and entitlement programs" and that the decisions would remain. Risen wrote, "Clinton left a very different impression Tuesday, when he told a meeting of the U.S. Chamber of Commerce, 'I'm looking for more cuts.'"

Ross Perot, who had hoped to be a factor in the presidential election in 1996, did not ignore Clinton's handling of the truth. An article by Charles Green of Knight-Ridder Newspapers was printed in the April 3, 1993, edition of the *Orange County Register*. Green reported that "Clinton lashed out at Perot. He suggested Perot had been 'rumor-mongering' on the issue, criticized Perot for not supporting the administration's economic plan and knocked him for slighting his chief of staff." Green wrote, "Perot quickly fired back, suggesting that Clinton was a liar."

The *Orange County Register*, a newspaper that has a definitely conservative bent, in an editorial preceding the Republican National Convention, had encouraged President Bush not to seek reelection. Clinton skillfully utilized the editorial and cited dissatisfaction within the Republican ranks even in that conservative California county. Clinton's failure to acknowledge that the newspaper was far from satisfied with *his* policies is a mere sidelight. It serves as an example of political deception which is deemed acceptable by the general populace. What is of interest in the discussion of Clinton as an inveterate liar is that the *Orange County Register* has printed caricatures of Clinton with a Pinocchio-type nose under the caption "The Clintonometer." The Clintonometer measures Clinton's lies and provides a quote from Clinton underscored with the truth. The length of Clinton's nose is measured by the determined seriousness of the lie. The lie might be scored "Whopper," "Baloney," "Fish Story," "Half-truth," or "Little White Lie."

Questions about Clinton's truthfulness have come not just from traditional opponents of the Democratic party. Fellow liberal Patricia Schroeder, congresswoman from Colorado, expressed displeasure with Clinton's misstatements and behavior. She was miffed by Clinton for her support of Clinton's B.T.U. gas tax plan. When Clinton caved in to opposition to the plan, Schroeder felt she had been abandoned. She could have expected Clinton's action, since it was not the first time that he had amended a similar gas-tax proposal. While governor, Clinton had proposed a series of substantial tax increases to pay for educational reform. He had proposed raising the severance tax on natural gas; it was blocked by gas lobbyists and was defeated. Of his many tax proposals, only an increase in sales tax remained.

For those who believe that Clinton is not a heavy taxer but have accepted his impostor role, Clinton reflected upon his actions as governor in relation to his tax proposals. In his review of the year, his "biggest disappointment had been the failure of the legislature to pass his entire tax program during the special session." Patricia Schroeder can take heart, knowing that she is not alone, because, as Allen and Portis wrote, "critics said he was not willing to push the lawmakers to force them to drop their own self-interests long enough to vote for a tax on business and industry."

Clinton's use of deception and lies should have been apparent to all during the election campaign. When issues central to Clinton's character were raised, his drive to achieve his political ends superseded his truthfulness. Remarkably, Clinton was able to overcome such minefields as the Gennifer Flowers affair, marijuana usage, and his avoidance of the draft. Clinton responded to each of these instances either by deception or lying. The Flowers affair, as discussed previously, provides an example of Clinton's gut-level ability to lie guilt-free. William F. Buckley Jr.'s column of June 9, 1993, quoted "liberal journalist and author Mickey Kaus" as saying, "The press saved Clinton during the campaign. I should think he'd be permanently grateful to reporters simply for ignoring the Gennifer Flowers tape."

This comment by Kaus, described by Buckley as a liberal, indicates that the press willingly overlooked Clinton's lies and did not delve too deeply into the Flowers affair. Since Clinton has managed to alienate the press along with the American public, the press is taking a closer look at Clinton's behavior and lies. Part of the reason for this, according to Buckley's column, is that "Clinton is just plain inconsiderate."

Kaus provides further analysis of what causes the intensity of dissatisfaction with Clinton. He referred to Clinton's staff as not knowing "the difference between truth and lies." The reason that the staff appears to be untruthful is because the dysfunctional president heads the staff. As one expert put it, "A person not involved in active recovery is probably part of the problem." Again, the press is beginning to realize that no distinction exists between truth and lies within this administration. That is solely rooted in Clinton's guilt-free automatic lying. As Buckley had indicated in previous commentary, "All of those people around him have become shills."

Clinton had similarly skirted the truth regarding his smoking marijuana when he was asked if he had ever violated any laws. His response that he had not violated any U.S. laws provided him with a veil of deceit over the fact that he had smoked marijuana while in England. To push the issue to even more fanciful levels after it was discovered that in fact he had smoked marijuana, the future president claimed that he had not inhaled. As with most lies, there is a remote possibility the person is telling the truth. Few people could believe such a statement. If the *Orange County Register* had been using the Clintonometer at the time, it would surely have scored a "Whopper."

What is significant about Clinton's denial of marijuana use, followed by a denial of inhaling, is that it follows the pattern established from his youth of denying the significance of substance abuse. Perhaps his stepfather wasn't drunk but "had been drinking." Similarly, Clinton wasn't stoned: he had smoked "but not inhaled."

Clinton's attempt at avoidance of the draft-evasion issue was classic ACOA behavior. A former acquaintance of Clinton's claimed that he had reneged on a promise to fulfill an R.O.T.C. obligation. Questions were raised by Cliff Jackson, Clinton's former classmate at Oxford, working in conjunction with the *Los Angeles Times*, about Clinton's use of the staff in Senator Fulbright's office to obtain his deferment and travel to England on a Rhodes Scholarship. Despite potentially damaging documents, Clinton denied that there was any wrongdoing on his part. The focus on his veracity became diluted when it was reported that during his education at Oxford, he participated in war protests. Clinton denied that his involvement was extensive despite the recollection of others who were present that he was an active organizer of the events.

A letter written by Clinton in 1969 confirms his deception. Clinton wrote, "I have written and spoken and marched against the war.

After I left Arkansas last summer, I went to Washington to work in the national headquarters of the Moratorium, then to England to organize the Americans for demonstrations October 15 and November 16." These are hardly the words of someone who was passively involved in the protests.

It was further revealed that Clinton had traveled to the Soviet Union during his Oxford years. Clinton denied any wrongdoing and stated that he was vacationing. In fact, no evidence to the contrary surfaced despite a questionable search of Clinton's file by the State Department. Ironically, that Clinton was not completely forthcoming may have saved him at the time from devastating political injury. With each new layer of deception uncovered, the chaos surrounding the situation increased. The chaos came to an end with the improper use of the State Department. The focus was shifted away from questions surrounding Clinton's character and directed at the State Department.

Following the election, a State Department official was forced to leave office because of this flap. On November 16, 1992, Clinton reveled in the fact that the official had been forced to quit six weeks prior to the end of the Bush administration. He then vowed that if such a misuse of power occurred during his administration, the action he would take would be swift.

Clinton not only lies and deceives, it has also been reported that he has made statements which would indicate a projection of his weakness. An article by Bob Deans of the Cox News Service on April 6, 1993, was printed under the heading "Remarks by Clinton Put White House on Defensive." Deans wrote that the White House staff "scurried Monday to quell a diplomatic tiff after President Clinton suggested that the Japanese sometimes say one thing and mean another." Clinton was reported to have told Boris Yeltsin during their summit in Vancouver that "when the Japanese say 'yes' to us, they often mean 'no.'" Then White House spokesman George Stephanopoulos was quoted, "This was a casual comment [by Clinton] about Japanese courtesy and etiquette."

Part Two

CHAPTER EIGHT

Denial

PRESIDENT CLINTON HAS ACKNOWLEDGED that memory of his childhood is hampered by forgetfulness. This revelation would not be of particular significance except that Clinton's dysfunctional childhood shaped his adulthood and is shaping his presidency. It would not be of significance to me, as a psychologist, except that Clinton's childhood was fraught with extreme violence and his stepfather's alcoholic behavior. The temptation would be to compare Clinton's failure to recall with a limited memory of a normal, happy childhood. Such a temptation would not be clinically acceptable. Most people believe that other people think as they do.

This view is not correct. The truth is that children from difficult upbringings, such as an alcoholic home, frequently "forget" the traumas as a means of functioning and coping with stressful displeasure of an extreme nature. Memories from their childhood experiences seldom are brought into awareness without some external stimulation that triggers the recall. This is not to say that the memory is not available to the individual. It is that an ACOA has learned to employ forgetfulness as a form of denial to prevent the emotional pain from the experiences from overtaking his daily living.

Denial is a term which has been grossly overused in today's nomenclature. "Denial," as is used in this context, is a clinical term that describes a defensive technique employed to protect the individual from emotional pain. In an interview with *Time* magazine,

Clinton said that he has forgotten a large portion of his childhood completely. A correct description of what Clinton is referencing is the form of denial known as blocking. Blocking occurs when large segments of awareness cannot be recalled. Forgetfulness refers to an inability to recall specific memories.

Clinton acknowledged that much of his awareness about his childhood trauma was only brought to his attention by others during the 1992 campaign—an important point for several reasons. First, clinically blocking and forgetting are symptomatic of children from traumatic upbringings, such as those an ACOA experiences. Second, it serves to explain Clinton's misrepresentation of his childhood as a happy one. Third, and most importantly, it offers the clinician and all citizens an insight into Clinton's cognitive functioning.

It is essential to understand that the way a child responds to emotional events will tailor the way that child will respond to stressful circumstances in his adult life. When one considers that Clinton's response techniques to stressful situations was to utilize denial—blocking and forgetfulness—one then can understand Clinton's functioning under similarly stressful occurrences as an adult. Those who have been deeply troubled by Clinton's tendency to lie as president have good cause for their concern. Clinton has identified himself as a classic ACOA who engages in overachieving behavior. For the overachiever with fragile self-esteem and the need to prove his worth to others and gain their approval, admitting failure and errors is virtually incomprehensible. When the ACOA overachiever is confronted by circumstances that test his worth, he responds the way he did in his childhood. For Clinton, that often means lying and denying.

Interviewers seeking information about Clinton's youth are unable to find credible friends or neighbors who have information about the disturbed family life. This is a classic situation with the ACOA and is also representative of an aspect of the denial in which Clinton engaged. The humiliation and shame of revealing the actual events of his home life to his childhood friends would have been extreme. To protect himself from such negative feelings, Clinton denied the family problems to his friends. He did not deny them by commission; he did so by omission. He failed to tell even his closest friends about the painful life he led behind his front door.

Insight into why Clinton engaged in such denial is obtained by considering the coping strategies his mother employed. In her autobiography she described her approach to the difficult marriage with Roger Clinton. This approach was the epitome of denial. She claimed that she was basically unconcerned about Roger Clinton's whereabouts when he would be away on extended drinking bouts. It is certainly understandable that the absence of his alcoholic behavior for several days would create feelings of relief. It is, however, unbelievable that she was unconcerned. Also, what does that teach one's child about marriage and adult relationships? Assuming that Clinton's mother was being truthful that she was unconcerned about Roger Clinton's whereabouts, it is hardly the formula for modeling a loving marriage for her children.

An even clearer example of the denial employed by Clinton's mother is her remarriage to Roger Clinton. Coming to the conclusion that it would be a good decision to remarry Roger Clinton required a tremendous amount of denial on her part. The emotional pain of years of living with an abusive alcoholic is significant. To have taken the step to seek and obtain a divorce, only to remarry the abusive alcoholic on a promise of change, is startling. Clinton's mother displayed a naïveté and denial of her own feelings.

Another factor which describes the denial employed by Clinton's mother is that it is not only the president who has memory failure regarding occurrences in his childhood. His mother forgot many of the abusive details herself. This is important because it characterizes the emotional support available to Clinton supplied by his mother. Her defensive strategy was to deny the existence of problems by ignoring and forgetting them when they occurred. This does not enable the child in the abusive home to enjoy a free outlet to express his own pain. Obviously, Clinton was unable to approach his out-of-control stepfather with his emotional concerns, since he was the source of many of them. His mother, living in her own denial about the alcoholic behavior, was not someone Clinton could approach for help. Her shield of denial meant that she was partaking in the same rudimentary defense mechanism as her child.

The commentary about Clinton's mother is not designed to disparage her personally. The circumstances described by her behavior and denial are characteristic of many homes of an alcoholic. The description of his mother's response to the family problems is given in order to clarify Clinton's dilemma. He believed there was no one with whom he could discuss his family problems. Clinton's affidavit written for the court stating the incidences of abuse in his home is one of the items which he completely forgot until it was presented to him in the 1992 campaign. He did not remember that the abuse was ongoing at that time.

The reality for Clinton was that he was trapped in a painful family life with no one to turn to for release of his emotional pain. The result was that he was left to manage the pain by himself. Children are not equipped emotionally to process these harsh feelings effectively. What happens to the hurt that is withheld? The emotional pain results in feelings of anger and guilt. The guilt that is experienced is the anger redirected toward oneself. When one withholds such feelings, he tends to see himself as a bad person.

This self-characterization may be displayed in a variety of behavioral fashions. As Clinton has stated, he characterizes his experiences as an ACOA as classic overachieving. It becomes clearer to see why he chose the path of overachievement when it is realized that such behavior is underscored by a feeling of unworthiness. Overachievement becomes the behavior designed to prove that a person is good and worthy. Goodness and worth, therefore, rest on a fragile precipice. They must constantly be tested and retested. This is necessary, since the feelings of being good and worthwhile are artificial, based on the reactions of others to one's achievements. It also is one of the reasons for the roller-coaster approach in which Clinton conducts his personal life and his presidency.

Understanding Clinton means that one must accept that his

youth defines his adulthood. For all intents and purposes, he still is functioning as he did as a youth. Clinton is still forgetting, blocking, and lying about his traumatic childhood. While this is a harsh assessment of the president, it also is an honest appraisal of his behavior. Clinton will continue to malfunction in this way until he resolves his childhood conflicts. This is true of Clinton as it would be of anyone who has chosen to overlook his emotional debt. Clinton is frozen into responding to stressful circumstances by denial and lying. He is stuck in this mode of operation until he chooses to free himself from his emotional pain. It is true that Clinton received some counseling following his brother's cocaine arrest. This counseling made him aware of his identification as an ACOA. It also obviously is true that the problem persists. The obviousness of that belief can be defended as follows:

An objective appraisal of Clinton's response to questions of his goodness or worth leads to an unmistakable conclusion that a process unfolds over time. An immediate denial of any impropriety is Clinton's first line of defense. This initial denial is followed either by Clinton's—or, more typically, his staffers'—changing the denial slightly. The reshaping of the truth continues with further revelations until, in the end, the initial defense can only be characterized as a lie. This analysis can be tested vis-à-vis any of a number of Clinton's responses about his financial difficulties in respect to Whitewater and his personal indiscretions, which are now generally accepted as having occurred.

Another rationale for easily defending Clinton's failure to resolve the ACOA issues is the number of chaotic occurrences which have sprung up during the relatively short duration of his administration. It is startling to make an accounting of self-created problems inherent in this administration. Some of the more notable chaos that has developed include: Travelgate; Lani Guinier; the tarmac haircut; the handling of Whitewater; the Arkansas troopers' revelations of sexual finagling; dismissals or resignations of key counsellors with close connections to the First Lady; and the Paula

Jones story. It is safe to state that this incomplete list represents an extraordinary number of difficulties for a new administration.

Most of the items mentioned as early problems for the Clinton administration involve situations in which the average person simply would have said no. Stop for a moment to consider the allegations by Paula Jones. Without judging the truthfulness of her allegations, what is phenomenal is that polls indicate that many Americans believe that what she alleges has validity. It was stated previously that Clinton functions on the precipice between good and worth and badness and unworthiness. The American people, if it can be so construed from the polls, clearly see that Clinton teeters on this precipice.

It is difficult to imagine a president of this country being sued for sexual misconduct. This is an example of the characteristic of ACOAs with unresolved issues to perpetuate their dysfunction in their personal lives and workplaces. Furthermore, it is remarkable that many Americans find merit in such a lawsuit. Compare this view as a possibility with any other American president who comes to mind. Americans would be rushing to the defense of their president. With Clinton, however, Americans may find the lawsuit unsavory; but they do not think that the character of the president is such that it would rule out the distinct possibility that the lawsuit is meritorious.

Additional interest regarding that particular matter is in Clinton's response to the allegation. Based on his response profile, he would deny not only that he had ever met Ms. Jones but also that he was not even at the hotel where the alleged incident occurred. As is typically the case with Clinton, his response suggests either forgetfulness or lying. True to form, his staff has begun the reshaping process by releasing statements which place Clinton at the hotel at the time of the alleged incident. The reshaping process followed the statements by third parties who confirmed Clinton's presence at the hotel.

In October 1994, Clinton issued a statement through his attorney acknowledging that he may have met Ms. Jones and that Ms.

Jones did nothing inappropriate. Clinton's statement was designed to address Ms. Jones's concern that a false impression may have been given in a magazine article that indicated she was a willing sexual partner. Her contention was that she had never engaged in sex with Clinton and that she certainly was not willingly accepting his advances. Her response to Clinton's statement was that she would drop her lawsuit, including the financial claim, if Clinton would present the information publicly within one week. When Clinton did not comply with her offer, she held a press conference and stated that she would continue to pursue her legal action.

Once more Clinton's response profile to a stressful situation followed the expected pattern so characteristic of him as an ACOA. What is notable about the Jones lawsuit is that because of the seriousness of the allegation, Clinton has obtained counsel for his defense. For this particular situation it was impossible to rely solely upon denial to protect himself. Obtaining effective counsel was a logical response and is characteristic of adult functioning.

Unfortunately, even in that action, Clinton offered a bizarre twist. Not only for the first time has a president been sued for personal issues which preceded his presidency, but Clinton also has sought to establish a legal defense fund, asking the general public for donations.

A tenet of the psychological process of an ACOA is that he fails to grasp what is normal. While one can empathize with the president that legal costs can be quite a burden, the propriety of a sitting president establishing a legal defense fund is outside the bounds of normality. Of course, given the bizarre nature of Clinton's recurrent chaos, such a defense fund would not be an issue for other presidents. For some, Clinton's request for a defense fund might not seem unusual. Such a belief can best be understood in light of the expansion of what is normal during this administration.

One of the concepts which psychologists employ when analyzing the level of functioning within a family is to consider what the family members consider normal or acceptable behavior. As has been presented, Clinton's family had an extremely wide range of acceptability of what others would consider abnormal behavior. A child maturing in such a household lacks an understanding of just what normal is. Is it normal to have a father who physically abuses a mother? The emotional reaction tells the child that such behavior is not acceptable, but the reality of the child's circumstances indicates that such behavior is acceptable. For Clinton, his reality was that his mother did allow for such behavior to occur repeatedly. Her responsibility for the problem was not that Roger Clinton was abusive; it was in her allowing the behavior to persist. Clinton was caught in a family life that made abnormality normal.

Alcoholic behavior is laden with chaotic actions which exceed normality. Metaphorically, think of behaviors which occur in a family similar to a thermostat. A temperature range exists in which all inhabitants are comfortable. Outside that particular range, the inhabitants become either too warm or too cool. Now compare the thermostat concept to that of a normal household. In the normal household, all family members are made aware of what is considered acceptable behavior and what is considered unacceptable. When a family member strays from the limits of acceptability, he is reprimanded for his unacceptable behavior and learns the limitations of his behavior.

Contrast such an approach with what occurs in an alcoholic home. The limits of acceptable or unacceptable behavior are ill defined. No one discusses these limits, for they are changeable at the whim of the out-of-control alcoholic. One day it may be permissible to engage in a particular behavior, while the next day it is unacceptable. There is no clear identification of normality, and there is no effective response to a child's engaging in abnormal behavior. Similarly, normal behavior is not even consistently well received. The behavior of the alcoholic himself is erratic and outside what most people would consider normal. As a result, the child maturing under such conditions lacks the knowledge of normality; fails to learn to self-regulate himself away from what others define to be abnormal behavior; and has an immature knowledge of how to respond to someone who questions his behavior. Clinton's training did not teach him what is normal and how to avert abnormality. Instead, true to his upbringing, abnormality is embraced and, in fact, sought out.

In addition to the abnormality of Clinton's behavior, an aspect of his denial may be described as duplicity. An example of duplicitous behavior can be found in Clinton's financial dealings. During the 1992 campaign, Clinton expended considerable effort characterizing the twelve years of Reagan-Bush as a time manifested by greed. The depiction of the 1980s as the decade of greed has been disputed by other authors. Of importance to this topic is that implicit in Clinton's characterization of the 1980s is the assumption that his behavior and his policies would exemplify something other than greed.

A problem arises for the president when one compares his personal financial dealings with his rhetoric. It has been unequivocally demonstrated that the president and the First Lady benefited substantially from various financial "investments" during the 1980s. Most people would have no quarrel with their right to do so, assuming that the financial gain was obtained by legal means. What is duplicitous about the financial gain compared with his rhetoric is that the president and his wife engaged in the exact behavior he decried as a candidate.

Perhaps the president's duplicity related to his financial dealings can be excused in a candidate seeking election—a means to an end. This might be acceptable to most people except for the reality that there are so many areas in which the president has failed to be truthful. Assuming that the president and the First Lady followed the letter of the law in all their financial dealings, it would be refreshing to hear him acknowledge his duplicity rather than deny the obvious. His forgetfulness in the financial area is reminiscent of other situations forgotten and denied.

CHAPTER NINE

Personal Responsibility

THE PSYCHOLOGICAL COMMUNITY has been attacked justifiably for failing to foster personal responsibility among its clients. In fact, many forms of psychotherapy do just the opposite; they foster a sense of victimization. In recent years Americans have grown increasingly weary of such psychological excuse making for behavior that is grossly wrong. There is a growing sense of unease about the guilty who are found innocent, in part because of the testimony of "experts" in the fields of psychology or psychiatry. To the reasoning observer there appears to be something questionable when the expert for the defense arrives at a position diametrically opposed to that of the expert for the plaintiff.

The response to the caning of Michael Fay in Singapore provides an example of the attitude of many Americans toward personal responsibility. The Fay case also demonstrates the growing dissatisfaction of Americans regarding the input of psychotherapists in explaining away delinquent behavior. Therapists who presented information claiming that Fay experienced attention deficit disorder (ADD) did not intend to exonerate Fay of any behavior based on that diagnosis. The public generally thought that the diagnosis was beside the point. It was as if Americans were collectively stating, If he did the crime, ADD or not, he is responsible and should receive the punishment, even though the punishment seemed excessive.

The reason that it is important to discuss personal responsibility in this book is that I want there to be no mistaking my position in this matter. That President Clinton grew up in an alcoholic and violent home is indeed unfortunate. He serves as an example of millions of other Americans who grew up in similar homes. Despite the empathy felt for Clinton's upbringing, the issue of victimization and personal responsibility should be examined.

Clinton *was* a victim; he is not a victim now. The president exhibits unmistakable behaviors consistent with those of an ACOA. He is fully aware that his clinical profile reflects that of the ACOA. He reads materials on the subject. Clinton has attended some psychotherapy sessions familiarizing himself with this topic. But he has failed to seek a resolution of his problem. For that, President Clinton must be held fully accountable.

Clinton sought out the oval office and was victorious. A fair question to raise is: should he have run for the presidency knowing that he had personal problems that impaired the way he functioned? Furthermore, with his knowledge that this problem impacts his behavior and cognition, why has he not been straightforward with the American people about it? To do so would require an acceptance of personal responsibility which the president repeatedly has shown that he is unwilling to do.

The key to assisting a client in accepting personal responsibility for his life lies in the therapist's ability to draw parallels between the responses employed by the child in the alcoholic home and the responses utilized as an ACOA in present-day situations. This connection enables the client to recognize the association between his childhood and the present.

It is important for the client to go beyond a mere recognition of such parallels in behavior. The client must accept that while he should not be blamed for what happened to him as a child, he is completely accountable regarding his response to the abuse and chaos. When the client accepts that burden, it greatly aids in his capacity to accept responsibility for his present-day misguided behavior. This acceptance of responsibility for responses to childhood abuse frequently does not come easily. The ACOA functions for years under the guise of not being responsible for himself. But the truth is that whether we admit it or not, we are accountable for our actions. If we do not accept responsibility for ourselves, who will?

The ACOA is being asked to admit that while he was a child he behaved in dysfunctional ways. Too often, however, therapists pose the following questions: "Who hurt you?" "How were you hurt?" Unfortunately, the therapist fails to delve much deeper. Once the pain is revealed and the perpetrator of the pain is identified, a "poor baby" attitude develops that leads to further victimization of the client.

The necessary question to be asked following the first two questions is: "And what did you do in response to being hurt?" Even in circumstances in which the client thought as a child that there was nothing that he could do about being abused other than remain silent, he is responsible for his silence. If the client is unwilling to accept responsibility for his silence, he will perpetuate his dysfunction as an adult. Individuals who remain silent while being hurt repeatedly as adults will continue to feel helpless in the process. They will fail to consider alternatives in responding because they have elected to limit responsibility for their responses. They will act as victims and blame others for their pitiful lives.

As an alternative, an effective therapist enables the client to accept his personal role in his childhood by accepting his responses as his responsibility. The effective therapist helps the client explore what alternatives existed at the time of the abuse. The therapist enables the client to identify that some emotions he experiences as an adult handicap him unless he identifies them as feelings from his past; the choice is now his to respond in new, functional ways. Effective therapy enables the client to release his long-held feelings of anger and guilt by forgiving both the alcoholic parent and himself for electing to withhold his anger for so many years. An effective therapist assists the client in identifying areas in the client's personal life or workplace in which his prior unwillingness to accept personal responsibility was harmful. Effective therapy occurs when atypical events of childhood can be considered coherently and free from emotional distress.

Mention of these therapeutic truths is made so that the president's behavior can be considered in this light. The president, by virtue of an analysis of his behavior, has not accepted personal responsibility for his role in his childhood experiences. Quite the contrary, Clinton repeatedly has engaged in behavior which intentionally denies personal responsibility. Lying is a way of refusing personal responsibility. Clinton frequently has been forgetful and has denied the obvious. He has accepted responsibility for being an overachiever. This is a convenient admission, akin to the job applicant's responding to an employment interviewer, "I have one weakness: I tend to work too hard."

The president must accept responsibility for his youthful responses to the abuse and chaos he experienced as a child. Those responses involve denial of responsibility and lying. Until the president is willing to admit his unresolved problems and to forgive his parents and himself, his behavior will persist. We will continue to be led by a man lacking direction.

President Clinton has a golden opportunity to come clean to the American citizenry. It is a time when the public has lost its patience for those refusing to be accountable personally. The example set by the holder of the highest office in the land to engage in personal responsibility would represent a model of behavior to the countless others who similarly lack such discipline. Unfortunately, to do so not only would run contrary to Clinton's history but also would alienate a large segment of the constituency which gravitates toward him.

CHAPTER TEN

Credibility and Foreign Policy

THE PRESIDENT HAS RECEIVED FREQUENT CRITICISM for his handling of foreign policy issues. Many contend that his approach is confused, lacking direction, and devoid of consistency. None of this is surprising when considered in the context of Clinton as an ACOA, since all of the attacks on his foreign policy approach also describe the inner workings of an ACOA. Clinton's foreign policy approach mirrors who he is.

Clinton's response to these criticisms of his foreign policy missteps is not particularly surprising. Clinton reacted strongly to the criticism, but also in a manner that only makes sense, in terms of reasoning, to other ACOAs. Clinton stated on May 20, 1994, "The administration acted with remarkable consistency. When one thing doesn't work, you leave to go on to another."

An individual who considers that foreign policy is necessarily clear and directed would question his remark. However, Clinton is exhibiting his propensity to react rather than to act. Decision making for the ACOA is not an inner-developed process; it is an outer-developed process. Decisions are not arrived at by analyzing and weighing alternatives and pairing them with one's convictions. Instead, the decision-making process evolves as a form of response to the actions of others. This was true of Clinton when he was a child reacting to the crazy behaviors that were ongoing, and it is true of him as the president reacting to incidents, leaders of nations, and political winds that blow this way and that. To have a clear, consistent foreign policy, Clinton would have to be capable of conducting his thought process in such a fashion. The ACOA does not think in such a fashion.

The genesis of the current foreign policy debacle rests in the childhood experiences of the president and, more important, in his failure to resolve those conflicts. Clinton reacts to world events in the same way that he reacted as a child to the pain, confusion, and sadness of his home. Bear in mind that if chaos is not present, President Clinton will create it. If a clear, consistent policy in the foreign arena would by some miraculous stroke appear, he would be at a loss to manage it. It would be asking him to conduct foreign policy in a style that is inconsistent with his thought process. Clinton would be out of his element in such a situation.

A further comment is warranted regarding the president's statement that foreign policy is being conducted with remarkable consistency. Please note the distancing in the words that he used. Clinton said that "the administration" acted in such a manner, as opposed to his accepting personal responsibility. This is a classic testament to the process of denying personal responsibility inherent in the ACOA. Much can be learned from his selection of words. It reasonably can be inferred from this statement that the ship is without a captain. What the president fails to realize is that the shift in responsibility from himself to the administration reflects one of the problems inherent in his foreign policy.

He has been criticized for his failure to provide effective foreign policy leadership. Without leadership, foreign policy runs aground. If the direction of foreign policy is to be conducted by "the administration" as opposed to the president, there is no true leader to look to for direction. It offers the president, however, an escape that is always sought. The escape is "Don't blame me; they did it." If Clinton truly believed that foreign policy was being conducted in a remarkably consistent fashion, he would have accepted personal accolades for his endeavors. Any politician would do so.

Think of the response to former president Bush following the Gulf War. While he praised the warriors and civilians who helped ensure success, the emphasis was placed on President Bush's coalition-building capability. The result was a tremendous upsurge in popularity. If, in fact, Clinton truly believed that foreign policy was being conducted in the manner that he claimed, would he not go out of his way to obtain personal reward and political benefit? Clinton has managed to deflect obvious failure onto an impersonal "administration." This is another example of the ACOA's lack of leadership.

The second sentence in Clinton's reaction to the criticism also is quite revealing when viewed from the perspective of a president who is an ACOA. Clinton revealed his lack of conviction. It is true that it is a weakness to be inflexible and a strength to be flexible. Do not be fooled, however, that Clinton is showing flexibility in his statement. It is the reactive process of a man without inner conviction. Recall the concept that the president knows that he is an impostor. The impostor syndrome is perhaps nowhere clearer than in Clinton's foreign policy dealings.

One of the more outspoken critics of the president's foreign policy approach is former vice president Dan Quayle. Quayle declared in a lecture at the Richard Nixon Library on May 19, 1994, that a president must lead the nation's foreign policy in a manner that projects America's respect and credibility. His analysis of Clinton's leadership in this regard was that Clinton demonstrates a "confused response" and conducts "leadership by consensus." Clinton's foreign policy could be summarized as containing three basic elements: first, to utilize confusion to develop self-created chaos or to further existing chaos; second, always to react as opposed to acting (because of a lack of personal conviction); and third, to utilize consensus rather than personal thought (thus providing an escape hatch of personal responsibility). Substantiation of Quayle's analysis appeared in Bob Woodward's book describing the chaotic processes within the Clinton administration and Clinton's failure to take hold of the reins.

Quayle further expounded upon Clinton's foreign policy by describing it as a policy of "misjudgments and mistakes." In particular, he attacked Clinton's approach to seeking NATO consensus as opposed to formulating effective policy in the best interests of the United States in relation to Bosnia. Quayle assailed Clinton by saying, "You don't ask what the consensus is. You form the consensus. You lead."

It is essential to note, however, that foreign policy under Clinton's leadership is not primarily devised to obtain that goal unless it includes a mechanism of deniability. Quayle's foreign policy model is that of a dog wagging its tail; the president assumes full responsibility for both foreign policy successes and failures. Clinton's foreign policy model is that of the tail wagging the dog. He still can claim credit when successes in foreign policy are stumbled upon by reaction or NATO consensus, but he also can deny responsibility for foreign policy failures. Unfortunately, it is a model which decreases the level of eminence of the United States and places the country in a role of subservience to NATO decision making.

The former vice president alluded to Clinton's Haitian policy by stating that the "president is conducting foreign policy by hunger strike." Quayle was referencing an example of Clinton's reactive foreign policy approach when he altered his course in response to an activist's hunger strike. Of course, Clinton's policy toward Haiti had demonstrated particular instability on previous occasions when he had criticized Bush's policy toward the Haitians and later adopted it as his own. As previously noted, hundreds of Haitians who mistakenly took Clinton at his word died in their attempts to gain freedom in the United States.

The publication of Quayle's book *Standing Firm* and his candor in assessing the Clinton presidency are the first steps toward announcing his candidacy to oppose President Clinton or another Democratic nominee should Clinton not be the candidate. He attacked Clinton on other matters, such as domestic affairs, as well. For the purpose of this work, only those issues that strike at the core of the president's ACOA character will be mentioned. Quayle stated, "He is for everything," and then cautioned, "Watch what they do rather than what they say—they have a very radical left-wing agenda." Once more Clinton's role of impostor is observed. There may be some political benefit in being able to stand before any group and function as a chameleon, but a toll is taken on the individual's integrity. Standing for everything means being for nothing. It is a reactive effort to please this group or that group for personal gain.

I asked Quayle, "How does Clinton's reputation for lying affect his ability to conduct effective foreign policy?" Quayle's response was informative and strikes at the heart of Clinton's foreign policy difficulties. He responded, "It diminishes credibility and has affected his ability to direct national and international affairs. When you aren't completely forthcoming about national or international issues, you lose credibility, and then you lose leverage in foreign affairs."

The president's inability to be truthful has dealt a serious blow to his credibility. The decreased credibility has hurt his ability to direct national and international affairs. Americans accept that he is disingenuous. That is not to imply that they accept it as all right. Rather, they accept it as being true. The decreased credibility undoubtedly is reflected in Clinton's sharply declining approval ratings. Without credibility and support, a president loses control of the destiny of his policy, as is happening with health care legislation.

Similarly, the decreased credibility hurts the president's effectiveness as a world leader. When allies cannot count on the president to keep a steady course, they understandably become hesitant to follow his direction, particularly if it is likely to be unpopular in their nation. Today many United States allies do not stand with him on policy issues ranging from Bosnia to North Korea. Why should they commit to supporting a Clinton policy when that policy may change tomorrow or the day after? Furthermore, such a decline in credibility reduces the power or leverage of the United States while increasing the stature of other nations. When a nation such as North Korea or Serbia hears numerous empty threats coming from

President Clinton, it simply turns its back on him and the United States, aware that no retribution will occur.

A treaty has been signed between North Korea and the United States which provides for inspection of North Korean nuclear facilities. It remains to be seen whether the North Koreans will live up to the treaty agreement. Presidential credibility helps to ensure that foreign powers follow the agreements.

In some areas perhaps the truth shading does only limited damage to the presidency. In the area of foreign policy, however, such damage is extreme and enduring. Quayle said that the domestic damage can be solved rather easily by voting Clinton out in 1996 and replacing him with someone with conviction and effective policy. Foreign affairs, however, are being hurt to such an extent, according to the former vice president, that it will require significant time and effort to repair the damage.

In a lecture given at the Richard Nixon Library on July 20, 1994, Henry Kissinger offered his thoughts regarding the current foreign policy situation for the United States. He identified three primary problems:

> 1. With the passing of the Cold War, the United States conducting its policy in the absence of clearly defined ideological and political differences between powers;
> 2. A change in the mental formation of the generations currently in political offices throughout the world;
> 3. The particular approach of the Clinton administration to foreign policy.

According to Kissinger, the post–Cold War world has five or six nations of "more or less equal strength," with the United States having the strongest military force among the world leaders. He stated that in such a world, in which the ideological differences are not as clearly defined as they once were, America must operate from a position of defined national interest. He cited Haiti and Somalia as two examples of confused policy in which the national interest was not clearly established. He said, "I do not support a military invasion of Haiti because I cannot explain the threat that Haiti poses to America . . . I think it's a dangerous precedent."

Regarding Somalia, Kissinger contrasted the Bush policy of a humanitarian approach seeking to achieve an alleviation of starvation while not engaging in civil war with the Clinton policy, which included military engagement in the civil conflict. He said, "President Clinton took the second course and got involved in the civil war, and quit after eighteen casualties." Kissinger stressed that "before we commit American forces we have to know the outcome we want and what is in the nation's interest."

Kissinger also pointed out that the attitude of the generation of the current administration differs from that of his generation. According to Kissinger, the older generation honed their mental abilities by reading books, while the newer generation has been more greatly influenced by television. "The TV generation is brought up on pictures, and they react to sentiment and emotion. . . . It becomes very difficult to develop long-range policies." He also stated that there is a difference that has developed in political approach between the politicians of the two generations in part because of this difference in mental formation: "The modern politicians ask you what they should say." The older politicians asked "what they should think or do."

With those insightful elements as a background, Kissinger continued with an analysis of the present conduct of foreign policy by the Clinton administration. He cited the policy as being influenced by two factors: "By the age of television and by the radicalism of the early seventies." The radicalism of that era was one "which resented the use of power, which raised questions about the fitness of America to conduct foreign policy." With these dual influences, the administration "therefore finds it very difficult to deal with the world as it is."

Kissinger pointed out that the Clinton foreign policy has inadequately addressed the reformulation of Europe following the reunification of Germany and the withdrawal of Soviet troops. He said that three basic questions exist regarding Europe: first, "What is the role of NATO?" second, "What is Europe?" and finally, "What is the relationship of Europe to Russia and of all of this to the United States?" Kissinger asserted that the "administration has not answered any of these questions."

He described Clinton's proposed Partnership for Peace as a "scheme that undermines, in the long-term, any specific purpose of NATO." The proposal fails because "no distinction is made between historic victims of Russian aggression and the Russians." He further derided the administration's handling of Europe. "In the two years . . . it has yet to describe what the role of the Atlantic Alliance is." He summed up the Clinton approach to Europe as "an invitation to further turmoil."

His comments about Clinton's handling of Asia were just as negative and, in fact, predicted it might have even more disastrous effects. He established the need to consider the relationships between Japan, China, Russia, Korea, and, possibly, India. He described the relationships as "like eighteenth- and nineteenth-century Europe." As a result of the unstable relationships, "arms races have a high potential for getting out of hand." He sharply criticized the Clinton administration by stating, "In this administration we have had the 'masterpiece' of quarreling simultaneously with Japan and China and now sliding into a position with Korea where it is very difficult to know what we want." He warned that North Korea's nuclear development will "almost guarantee" a spread of the development of nuclear weapons in other Asian countries. He expressed concern "that the American public has not been told (*a*) the danger and (*b*) what we want." The recent treaty agreement between North Korea and the United States may represent the beginning of Clinton's response to such criticism.

He further added, "We have to come up with some concrete proposal that puts an end to that weapons program." Such a proposal would require "very careful thinking." Chiding the administration's ability in this area, he said, "We'll never be able to decide with wishy washy diplomacy." An example of Clinton's lack of conviction in diplomatic matters was noted. "One day we ask for sanctions, and three days later we leave the countries that supported it with egg on their faces."

Kissinger concluded his remarks with some interesting comments about the policy makers within the administration and of the need for credibility. He said, "We cannot keep trying to relive the slogans of the radical movement of the seventies in a world in which it has no relevance—not that they had any then."

When questioned about the use of bluffing in diplomatic relationships, Kissinger was very clear that it is poor policy. He declared, "It is very important to establish your credibility. Never threaten anything you aren't willing to do. After you have done several things that you have threatened, then the threats may become indistinguishable from a bluff." Compare his approach with Clinton's response to Haitian leaders. Clinton said, "I won't be outbluffed." Yet there is no reason for Haitians or any world leaders to believe what Clinton says. In the absence of a willingness to back up the threats, Clinton is considered to be merely crying "Wolf."

In addition to failed policies and a lack of conviction, Clinton also suffers in the area of diplomatic integrity. Kissinger pointed out that when conducting diplomacy, you repeatedly interact with the same world leaders. It is essential to be straightforward and tell the truth. He does not believe that diplomacy is aided by "telling white lies." In fact, it is hampered because of a further erosion of credibility. "The only thing that works is if you tell everybody virtually the same story."

Quayle and Kissinger have years of experience in conducting foreign policy. Both honed in on Clinton's failure to achieve credibility and how such a failure erodes his capacity to be effective in the diplomatic arena. It is a problem that goes deeper than Clinton's lack of foreign policy experience. The lack of credibility has its genesis in his childhood.

In the fall of 1994, Clinton managed what were considered to be foreign policy successes by avoiding armed conflict in Haiti, responding militarily to Iraq's possible aggression, and obtaining a treaty with North Korea. Even with the apparent successes, some critics pointed out that mismanagement of foreign affairs led to some of the problems and that some of the solutions which Clinton claimed as successes were less than stellar.

Syndicated columnist Georgie Anne Geyer wrote a column in the *Orange County Register* on October 25, 1994, entitled "Clinton's Dangerous 'Pay-Off' Foreign Policy." Geyer reflected upon the foreign policy action taken by the Clinton administration within the two-week period prior to her column. She lamented the apparent new policy direction in which "we pay off the 'murderous' (President Clinton's word) Haitian generals so they will leave the country, and we give 'rogue nation' (ditto) North Korea $4 billion so it will not nuclear-blackmail us and the world."

Geyer wrote that a part of the agreement to remove Gen. Raoul Cedras from Haiti included the provision that Cedras become the United States' landlord. The United States agreed to rent Cedras's property for $5,000 per month in addition to unfreezing millions of dollars which he held in banking institutions.

Geyer also considered the Clinton agreement with North Korea. She described the pact as one "the very study of which is enough to send even the most persnickety researcher into shock." What is most troublesome to Geyer is that the pact is extended for a term of at least ten years. During that term, Geyer wrote, the United States "will essentially have no control at all over the fuel rods that have been at the crux of the controversy (and from which, experts say, probably five bombs could be constructed). But the administration insists that the deal can stop hundreds of bombs from being made."

Geyer noted that the Haiti and North Korea agreements resulted in the loss of no American lives. She contemplated why such agreements then left her so unsettled. Her conclusion: "The sad truth is that, underneath, it is woefully unprincipled. It rewards alike blackmail on the part of thugs like Cedras and of dangerously but predictably Byzantine regimes like North Korea's."

The true result of the pacts, according to Geyer, is that Haitian attachés remain in Haiti and can cause peril at any time and that the initiative for action rests with the North Koreans as opposed to the

Americans. The conclusion that Geyer drew is bleak. She wrote, "We appear to the world like a nation wrapped tightly in a straitjacket of its own fears about any involvements where we might get hurt. And, in such cases, everybody pays."

Michael Elliott, in "Something to Salute," an article published in *Newsweek* on October 24, 1994, offered his insight into Clinton's foreign policy successes. He wrote that even the administration was seeking to temper the perception of the successes out of concern that the public's level of expectation for future policy would be heightened, only to be met with additional foreign policy bungles. Elliott's thoughts on the successes were: "Two swallows do not a summer make, nor two foreign-policy successes erase a long perception of incompetence."

Elliott also noted that the deals were largely due to Carter's efforts, as opposed to being generated by the administration. He mentioned that Carter completed the final deal, which included the real estate agreement described by Geyer. Elliott did write that Clinton seemed to be more attentive to foreign policy matters, citing his penchant for telephoning foreign dignitaries.

Similar commentary appeared in the *National Review* on November 7, 1994, in a column entitled "Foreign Policy, Stupid." The review gives credit to Clinton for his action against Saddam Hussein's apparent aggressive action and for movement toward peace by Jordan and Israel.

The commentary is also critical of Clinton's handling of foreign affairs and, in part, blames Clinton for events precipitating the Iraqi confrontation. The contention was that Clinton's prior performances in Haiti and North Korea gave Hussein the impression that the United States would avoid a military response. Instead, the author's contention is that Hussein likely assumed that President Carter would be sent to Iraq and make concessions. "Mr. Clinton stumbled into success—misleading his adversary by weakness beforehand. More important, the Iraq affair dramatizes the weakness of the Clinton defense policy."

Like Geyer, the *National Review* article indicates that it is important to reserve judgment on apparent successes in Haiti and North Korea. The Haitian policy was compared with previous attempts at keeping the peace in Somalia and Lebanon. Both instances resulted in American soldiers' deaths. The North Korean agreement was criticized for the delay in the United States' inspection capability. The article concluded: "The message sent loud and clear to other thugs is that it pays to go nuclear—you'll end up with either the Bomb, or Western largesse, or both."

David C. Hendrickson is an associate professor of political science at Colorado College. He wrote an article, "The Recovery of Internationalism," which was published in the September-October 1994 issue of *Foreign Affairs*. Much of the article is beyond the scope of this book, but it does comment on how Clinton's foreign policy record is viewed by policy experts.

Hendrickson's observation: "That American foreign policy stands in disarray and confusion is one of the few propositions on which a consensus exists in the country today. The flips and flops of policy toward Bosnia, Somalia, Haiti, North Korea, and China, to mention only the more prominent examples, have elicited ridicule from all points of the political spectrum."

Hendrickson's contention was that Clinton's foreign policy debacle was due, in part, to his responding to special interest groups. The greater measure of the foreign policy problems, according to Hendrickson, was: "Clinton's strategy in the game of political poker he played with Bush was to see all bets the incumbent had placed and then raise him." Hendrickson believed that Clinton's one-upsmanship during the campaign resulted in two relatively unsavory choices for the president. If the president did not follow through with his campaign promises, he would lose credibility. Or if he did make good on his promises, he would be altering American policy radically. According to Hendrickson, "the administration retreated from its stated aims in area after area of policy."

Hendrickson wrote that the pattern established by Clinton and the administration resulted in decreased international prestige "stemming from the realization in foreign capitals that American policy cannot be taken at face value or need not be taken seriously." The second negative effect was that American public opinion became one of disillusionment. "The likely effect of an administration that repeatedly fails its own litmus tests is a further deepening of the insularity of the American people and its propensity for international disengagement."

It is important to consider the perception of the international community toward the president and his handling of foreign affairs. On the one hand, Hendrickson contended that Clinton's foreign policy making resulted in an erosion in American prestige overseas. On the other hand, when President Clinton returned to the United States from his European D-day trip, he claimed that the press overseas was glowing in its praise for him.

I reviewed some articles to determine how Clinton's credibility is perceived by the international press. The *World Press Review* is a magazine that includes an analysis of press from around the world. The August 1994 issue provided a review of the international press's commentary about Clinton at the time of his D-day comment. The article in the *World Press Review* offered a different picture of the international communities' perception of Clinton than his comment indicated.

According to the article " 'No' to Clinton's Foreign Policy," "As Clinton returned from his D-Day celebration trip to Europe, the *World Press Review* Opinion Index found that of the 50 leading daily papers, 74 percent disapproved of his policies. The harshest criticism came on U.S. action and inaction in Bosnia, Haiti, and Somalia and on trade issues. The general approval rating was 22 percent. Only 3 of 50 gave unequivocal approval for Clinton's foreign policy. Clinton's critics focused on what they called his indecisiveness, his lack of principles, and his willingness to tailor policy to domestic political opinion polls."

Examples of some of the commentary found in the foreign press are given in the magazine. Brazil's *Folha de S. Paulo*, a liberal newspaper, stated that the United States' foreign policy problems were due to "the president himself, who does not like the subject and prefers to avoid it whenever possible."

The perception of Toronto's *Globe and Mail*, a conservative newspaper, was that "Clinton is endlessly flexible. He is Winston Churchill one minute, Neville Chamberlin the next." South Korea's conservative newspaper *Chosun Ilbo* of Seoul, said, "His policy just drifts." The liberal *Gazeta Wyborcza* of Warsaw, Poland, described Clinton's foreign policy as "incompetent, ineffective, and lost in a moral wilderness."

Similar concerns expressed by the international media were found in the July 1994 issue of *World Press Review*. The liberal *La Repubblica* of Rome reported: "The idea that the U.S. does not intend to be the policeman of the world turned into the implicit announcement that the UN will not be able to count on the U.S. when there are new international peacekeeping missions. We can call this crisis 'American absence from the world.' It is a serious crisis. No U.S. president, in war or in peace, has been important in his country if he has not been important for the world."

Trybuna, a leftist periodical from Warsaw, contributed the following comments about Clinton's foreign policy: "Does Clinton's America have its own thoughtful, consistent foreign policy? Such questions are being asked more frequently and persistently not only by America's European allies but also by Americans. Career diplomats are increasingly worried that the Clinton administration's foreign policy may lead to loss of world leadership and a collapse of America's prestige, as well as to international conflicts or even wars with unpredictable outcomes." The *Times*, a conservative London newspaper, included an article that not only identified some of Clinton's struggles with foreign policy in July 1994 but also foretold the outcome of his Haitian policy. According to the *Times*, "The Clinton administration's failure to follow through on its threats has not been lost on Haiti's military regime. It is in Haiti, however, that Clinton could least painfully reestablish his battered credibility."

The president's policy shift toward China did not go unnoticed by several Asian newspapers. The *Hong Kong Standard* attacked him for his handling of China. "President Bill Clinton has whipped away the silk handkerchief and pulled a collection of white rabbits out of the administrative hat in the form of watered-down measures to combat human-rights violations in China. We applaud the renewal of Beijing's 'most favored nation' (MFN) trading status. But honesty compels the acknowledgment that there have been few changes in China's human-rights situation since Clinton's landmark announcement last year that he would not renew MFN unless there had been 'overall improvements in human rights.' The truth is that Clinton has done a backflip by denouncing his own policy of linking human-rights improvements with trade."

The independent newspaper *Joong Ang Ilbo* of Seoul considered the policy shift a foreign policy triumph for China. The commentary also reflected the viewpoint of Clinton's credibility problem overseas. "The [U.S.] administration's renewal will be harshly criticized as another inconsistency in the Clinton foreign policy [His] administration will be at a great disadvantage when it encounters China on other difficult issues."

An article entitled "Clinton's Sanctimonious Diplomacy" by Swapan Dasgupta, published in the liberal *Indian Express* of New Delhi, reported on the Clinton policy in an area of the world that is often overlooked in the national media. According to Dasgupta, relations between India and the United States have become increasingly strained as the result of the Clinton administration's policy. Dasgupta's assessment of the dilemma is that the problem stems from the dogmatic position of the administration;

"Just as the Kennedy era was marked by a burning desire to establish an idealistic alternative to communism in the Third World, the '60s generation that now rules the White House is anxious to impose its civilizing agenda on the rest of the world. Under presidents Ronald Reagan and George Bush, there was a counter-establishment of right-wing ideologues bent on asserting the supremacy of the free market and traditional values. This has now been substituted with an amateurish fringe, untutored in *Realpolitik*, that imagines a brave new world crafted on moral sanctimoniousness."

The *Economist*, a magazine published in London, has also been very attentive to President Clinton. In the January 15, 1994, issue, in an article entitled "Clinton's First Year," the conclusion was that the president's initial year in office yielded mixed results. The contention was that part of Clinton's problems stem from his overwhelming desire to be liked and to make people happy. The article cautions: "He would probably do better all round if he worried less about opinion polls and more about leadership." Clinton's chaotic administration was not overlooked in the article. "It has been a rollercoaster ride, carrying his administration from exhilaration to near-disaster and back again. Mr. Clinton has been written off as an incompetent and then hailed soon afterwards as a conquering hero."

Clinton's successes and failures during his initial year in office were recited in the article. The question was then posed as to why Americans are not overly pleased with Clinton, and the answer given to the question is Clinton's personality. "Their reservations have a lot to do with the other side of his personality. Enter Clinton-the-wobbler. No one doubts that Mr. Clinton is a hyperactive president whose head fizzes with knowledge and ideas. The worry about his wobbliness has nothing to do with the quantity of effort, and everything to do with the quality of decisions. On that score Mr. Clinton still has a lot to prove, beginning with his style of government."

The *Economist* article includes comments that Clinton's style of governing leads to general confusion and a lack of direction. It was also noted in the article that Clinton has been contradictory about various campaign policies. This was considered to be related to his desire to please everyone.

The article detailed foreign policy procedures that have resulted in the decline of credibility. "A pattern has been repeating itself. First, America signals bold intentions: it will do something about the butchery in Bosnia, make a stand on human rights in China, hunt down Somali warlords, restore Jean-Bertrand Aristide to power in Haiti, stop North Korea from becoming a nuclear power. Then each time, it backs down. A message of American weakness is sent to the world."

That Clinton has been embroiled in sexual and financial legal issues did not go unnoticed in the article. In fact, the contention was that such legal problems will make it more difficult for Clinton to improve in the area of leadership. The scorecard by the *Economist* provided the president with high marks for effort and mediocre marks for instilling confidence.

The June 4, 1994 issue of the *Economist* included an article, "Cornered by His Past," that further addressed the Paula Jones lawsuit and Whitewater matters. The commentary was a quite harsh assessment of the president. "It is not hard to list the traits that disturb voters, translating into approval ratings of a mere 40 percent. Mr. Clinton is inconsistent. He appears to breeze into subjects, gulp them down, speak before he thinks, and retreat at the first complaint. He seems casual even on things he professes to believe in. He let Congress kick his health-care plan around until it is virtually dead, and is bundled into a Supreme Court appointment he does not much care for. On foreign policy he is simply embarrassing."

The issue of Clinton's dishonesty was also addressed in the article. "Americans want their president to lead them and to stand for something, just as they want their country to stand for something. So they snap at him, ridicule him, call him a liar, all to his face. No layer of authority separates Mr. Everyman Clinton from the ordinary citizen. Many voters do not respect him because they do not trust him, or think him honest."

About foreign policy issues, the contention in the article is that Clinton has an extremely difficult task to renew credibility. "He needs to show that he is in charge, has some backbone and can take decisions. But the difficulty goes deeper. His undisguised disinterest in foreign policy, together with his administration's utter absence of a framework for thinking about America's place in the world, have convinced many of America's friends that their worst nightmare may be coming true: a one-superpower world in which the superpower does not have the faintest idea how to perform its central role of preserving peace through preserving the balance of power."

Without a doubt, the concerns expressed by Vice President Quayle and Secretary Kissinger seem to have a strong factual basis. America's credibility in the foreign policy arena is eroding because of the president's credibility problems. The press from every corner of the world has made such claims. The voices of the foreign press are not often heard in the United States. They obviously conflict with the president's description of the positive press that he receives overseas.

CHAPTER ELEVEN

What the Liberal Press Has Said

THE NOVEMBER-DECEMBER 1994 ISSUE of *Mother Jones* magazine includes an interesting appraisal of the Clinton presidency. *Mother Jones* is a magazine whose political viewpoints have never been confused with that of the *American Spectator*. In this issue, Eric Alterman wrote an article entitled "So, Comeback, Kid." The author's appraisal of the state of affairs of the Democratic party under the guidance of President Clinton is that "1994 could mark the beginning of a political apocalypse."

The author's assessment of what ails the administration parallels that of this book. First, Clinton's lack of truthfulness, has produced negative results for his presidency. Alterman wrote: "The Democrats' own traditional constituencies, having spent two years watching campaign promises drop like timber in an Amazon rain forest, feel impotent and ignored, and lack the enthusiasm needed to fuel a successful election campaign."

Second, Alterman's comments are in accord with my contention that Clinton's problems are largely the result of self-created chaos. He wrote: "The Clintonians, meanwhile, are preoccupied with self-inflicted wounds ranging from lackluster appointments to Whitewater and Paula Jones, coupled with inept judgments on congressional matters. Strategically directionless, functionally disorganized, and psychologically dispirited, the White House is becoming a kind of titular party headquarters." This assessment of the White House mirrors what I consider to be Clinton's re-creation in the White House of his childhood dysfunction.

Alterman pointed out that while the presidency surely faces problems with a difficult international economy and a relentless media, his failures cannot be excused because of them. After noting some of Clinton's accomplishments, Alterman wrote, "Still, the administration's quasi-accomplishments pale before the fundamental fact of the Clinton presidency. Clinton has squandered the public's good will. In countless tiny ways, Clinton has proven himself a man not to be trusted. Voters had this feeling about Clinton during the election, but while judging him to be a flawed philanderer in his private life, they nonetheless believed he would fight for the 'people who play by the rules' as a populist president. Today, Clinton the non-inhaling, dissembling philanderer and Clinton the President seem all of a piece."

In the "Editor's Note" column of the same issue of *Mother Jones*, Jeffrey Klein concurred: "Many of his wounds are self-inflicted." Klein made the accurate connection between Clinton's behavior and the fact that he is an ACOA. The editor continued: "Clinton has invited this assault. Like many children of alcoholics, Clinton was a premature adult. He made peace. Although he felt primal abandonment, he developed his identity not by publicly expressing his rage, but by using it to drive forward, mediating ever-higher levels of conflict."

Klein's portrayal of Clinton reflects the president's need to sabotage himself. Clinton's role as peacemaker is more complex than just someone who doesn't like disagreement. As Klein pointed out, it is driven by rage. It might seem inconsistent to say that a peacemaker's motivation is his personal rage. However, that is exactly true in the case of Clinton. The anger has driven Clinton to a position in which he is responsible for the mediation of the highest level of conflict domestically and internationally. If the peacemaker role did not have a genesis in resentment from his youth, Clinton would be much more successful at obtaining his goals in conflict resolution. Instead, with the basis of the peacekeeping behavior one of anger, the result is an appearance of waffling and indecisiveness. The anger for having had to be a peacekeeper in the family against his will as a child results in the sometimes bumbling efforts as president. He did not want the role of peacekeeper as a child, and he does not want that role as an adult.

Another element of Klein's comment which deserves attention is his statement that Clinton did not develop his identity via a public expression of his anger. My contention is that Clinton did not overtly express his anger publicly, although reports of Clinton's private outbursts of anger are rife. Instead, Clinton showed his anger to the public in a covert fashion by self-sabotage. While less obvious, the behavior of sabotaging himself reflects an individual seething with anger in the same fashion as someone more forthright in expressing the anger. Clinton needs to discontinue dysfunctional forms of expression of his anger and resolve the hurt that is the basis for his rage.

Michale Krasny, also in the November-December 1994 issue of *Mother Jones*, published a series of interviews with prominent individuals. In an article entitled "Let's Talk Clinton," Krasny questioned these individuals about what Clinton ought to do in the remaining time of his term as president. Krasny found that the people with whom he spoke were interested in offering an assessment of Clinton as he has functioned to date.

One of the persons Krasny interviewed was Robert Jay Lifton, a psychiatrist. His comments relate to the perception that Clinton is indecisive. He said to Krasny, "His backing down encourages his enemies to stop anything he initiates and shows his weakness and exposes his jugular more than if he'd fought for something. Partial defeats out of strong convictions would leave him in better shape than compromising and backtracking. He comes out weaker, lesser."

Henry Louis Gates Jr. provided a similiar assessment to Krasny. Gates, a professor of humanitites, said, "Even people who hated Reagan miss his consistency. You knew where he stood. You never know where Clinton stands and he doesn't seem loyal to his own vision. He's a good guy and smart, and he has good instincts, but apparently wants to be loved."

Gates's comments reflect the difficulty that many people have with the president's inconsistent behavior. This concern is indicative of Clinton's re-creation of the inconsistency inherent in his childhood. Gates also drew an interesting parallel between President Reagan and President Clinton. It serves as an example of how two presidents, both ACOAs, can be perceived in strikingly different terms. It is my contention that the difference between the two exists because of the different ways alcoholism was addressed within each of their families. As has been noted, Reagan's mother dealt directly with his father's alcoholism. In the case of Clinton, denial of the problem and of anything unpleasant was the means by which the alcoholism was avoided. One cannot use the various forms of denial frequently without being perceived as inconsistent.

A final example from Krasny's interviews is the comments by Jerry Brown, the former governor of California who also sought the Democratic party's nomination for president in 1992. Brown was outspoken in his assessment of why Clinton's presidency has not been well received. He told Krasny, "Clinton was elected in a manner that made inevitable his failure. He ran a deceptive and hypocritical campaign, attacking Tsongas as a tool of Wall Street while he was collecting large amounts from the same people to pay for those ads. He's been abandoned and can't call upon people who want change because his pact with the devil has destroyed him. He sold out his constituents by abandoning single-payer health care. He's nowhere in campaign reform, having caved in to the same corrupt interests. His China policy is a complete betrayal."

The comments by former governor Brown and the other articles in this issue of *Mother Jones* demonstrate the need for Clinton to overcome his defensive posture, which is to blame others. Conservatives' criticisms of Clinton are to be expected, since they disagree with many of his policies. It is hoped that Clinton will realize that members of his own party are becoming disaffected as a result of his actions. As Brown said, it is his own constituents who feel abandoned by the president.

William Greider, national editor of *Rolling Stone* magazine, appears to be one of those who were a part of the Clinton constituency but have subsequently reevaluated their positions. Greider wrote a column "What Went Wrong?" in the November 3, 1994, edition of the magazine. The column is Greider's analysis of the Clinton presidency at midterm. It is a grim assessment indeed.

Greider wrote, "The presidency that looked so promising two years ago is now quite sodden. Bill Clinton has acquired a devastating reputation for unreliability. Some of this is manufactured—a malicious mixture of media second guessing and Republican scandal mongering—but much of it is earned." Greider's comments should be fair warning to Clinton to consider the causes of the erosion of his support. It is as if what Greider and others now believe to be true of Clinton were indistinguishable from the characterization of Clinton that they used to decry. Greider continued: "People are impressed at first (myself included). Over time however, we have learned not to take his words at full value because his actions so frequently betray them. When he tears up at some public gathering, people are now reflexively reminded of his inconstancy."

Such a characterization of the president from a former supporter is potentially devastating. It is an indication that people now not only are questioning the president's veracity but also his sincerity. Clinton has been considered to be a sincere person who was out to do good. If in fact his word lacks value and his emotional expression merely covers his fickleness, what is to be believed?

Greider attacked Clinton's handling of the health care agenda. He believed that Clinton entered into a policy matter which required a confrontational-style politician which, according to Greider, Clinton is not. Avoiding confrontation, coupled with the fact that Clinton did not even consider health care an issue of consequence until relatively late in his campaign, and then at the urging of campaign strategists, may be partially responsible for the administration's failure to succeed with the policy. Of course, there is also the consideration that a large segment of the population plainly did not want such a policy enacted. Regarding Clinton's failure in the health-care area, Greider commented, "As it is, he simply looks like a loser—compromised instead of principled, weak instead of valiant."

As Greider considered the near future of the Clinton presidency, he struck a familiar theme that the balance of Clinton's term will be greatly affected by his behavior during the first half of his term. Greider wrote, "It is also true that Clinton misled us with his own extravagant rhetoric, promising bold new directives when he really intended only to govern as a conscientious moderate. He is paying now for all the loose talk and paying for his straddles. After the November elections (1994), when Republicans expect to gain more strength in Congress, he is going to look even weaker."

Before concluding his article, Greider offered words of advice which he believed would help the Clinton presidency. He said Clinton should move to the right on issues such as welfare reform and immigration as a way to diminish Republican strength. He also called for Clinton to relinquish his indecisive policy style and take a strong, progressive stand. However, Greider does not believe that Clinton will do so.

The importance of dealing with the details of the *Mother Jones* and *Rolling Stone* articles is that the questions raised in conservative and moderate magazines and journals are also being raised in liberal publications. Clinton's problems are not a partisan issue.

CHAPTER TWELVE

The Midterm Election

MIDTERM ELECTIONS ARE NOTORIOUSLY DIFFICULT for the party occupying the White House. The president's party typically loses seats in Congress. During the 1980s, Republicans briefly held control of the Senate but lost it during a midterm election, even though President Reagan was popular personally.

The midterm election of 1994 held true to form. Voters sought significant change. The Republican party obtained control of both houses of Congress. This had not occurred since Eisenhower was president. In the Senate, Republicans gained eight seats and on the morning after the election, Sen. Richard Shelby of Alabama held a news conference and announced that he would be switching his party allegiance, yielding the Republicans a net gain of nine seats. In the House of Representatives, the Republicans gained fifty-two seats. Speaker of the House Thomas Foley became the first speaker to lose an election since 1860. Former Ways and Means Chairman Dan Rostenkowski was defeated in his reelection bid by a ten-point margin. No incumbent Republican senators or congressmen lost their seats.

The Republican Party was just as successful in gubernatorial elections. Republicans gained control of thirty-one governorships, the first time since 1970 that Republicans held so many state positions. Notably, New York governor Mario Cuomo was defeated despite the endorsement of New York City mayor Rudy Guliani and visits to the state by President Clinton and Mrs. Clinton. The Republican party now holds governorships in seven of the eight largest states, with Florida the lone exception.

Just how significant was this victory for the Republicans? According to Haley Barbour, Republican National Committee chairman, the margin of victory was the largest in this century. He pointed out that while numerous Democratic incumbents were defeated, no Republican congressional or gubernatorial incumbents lost.

What does this shift in power mean for President Clinton? When Clinton was elected president in 1992 with 43 percent of the popular vote, he claimed a mandate. Since his election, his victories in Congress (NAFTA, passage of his budget) have been by the narrowest of margins. His own party has taken a significant beating not only during the midterm elections but also in prior elections during his term. Many Democrats were hesitant to have Clinton campaign with them prior to the election. On the night of the midterm election, an ABC commentator noted that if our system was parliamentarian, Clinton would be removed from office within one week. "This election is essentially a vote of 'no confidence'." A CNN commentator questioned whether "Clinton would be dumped by the Democrats in 1996." Of course, he was not.

There obviously are many factors which contributed to the surprisingly wide margin of victory of Clinton's opposition party. The president's former spokespersons, George Stephanopolous, Dee Dee Myers, and Leon Panetta, presented the position that the results were a referendum on voter opinion of the way things have been done in Washington. Their position was that the results expressed voter's dissatisfaction with Congress. Stephanopolous, Myers, and Panetta were correct that voters felt such dissatisfaction. But their position failed to address the fact that while Democratic incumbents were dying on the vine, Republican incumbents won, and in most instances won handily. The disparity in party incumbent victories and losses must mean more than dissatisfaction with Congress.

Barbour contended that the election disparity indicated that the

American people were rejecting the "tax-and-spend liberal philosophy and big government for smaller, leaner government." Barbour's position undoubtedly tells part of the election tale. President Clinton, in the closing days of the election, had framed the voters' choice as "continuing to move forward [his way] or backwards [the Republican's way, the way of Ronald Reagan]."

The overall national vote tally presented a voting percentage of 53 percent for Republican nominees and 47 percent for Democratic nominees. Such a disparity leaning toward the Republicans is startling. Either Republicans voted in much larger numbers than the Democrats, or many Democrats voted for Republican candidates. Articles that appeared in liberal periodicals such as *Mother Jones* and *Rolling Stone* that were previously discussed pointed out that the dissatisfaction with Clinton within his own party was indeed significant. That certainly would result in a diminishing of enthusiasm for Democratic voters to get out and vote for their party's candidates. It does not speak well of President Clinton in light of his framing of the choice for the voters.

It is impossible to discuss the election results without considering how the public perception of President Clinton harmed his own party. I think that the president's negative personality qualities identified in this book have been perceived by the public. In 1992, despite some obvious examples that the president was less than honest, Americans chose to overlook those personality factors and elected him president. In the intervening years, with numerous additional examples of Clinton's enactment of his emotional problems into behavioral form, I think the public has seen enough.

One of the reasons I think that Clinton's personality flaws are an aspect of the midterm voter referendum is that already preceding the 1992 election, Republicans were aware that Clinton's vulnerability stemmed from issues of trust. This point is made clear by Mary Matalin, who was President Bush's campaign manager. Matalin also is host of the CNBC television program *Equal Time.* She is married to James Carville, who was President Clinton's campaign manager during the 1992 campaign. The couple wrote *All's*

Fair, which provided their insiders' viewpoint of the Clinton and Bush campaigns.

Matalin wrote in the book, "The unsolicited comments coming from our focus groups vis-à-vis Clinton all revolved around trust. And his negatives were increasing nightly. The trust side of the draft issue resurrected in people's minds all the amorphous things they didn't like about the man. We called answers to open-ended questions 'verbatims' and the verbatims re Clinton were 'You can't trust a guy who lies to his wife,' 'You can't trust a guy who says he didn't inhale.' Women in focus groups told me [Matalin], 'He's like that kind of boy in high school that you're attracted to that you just know is bad for you and is going to do you wrong. You can't trust him.' And everybody would go, 'Yeah, that's right!' "

Matalin wrote about the intangibility of the trust factor. She contended that the fact that people were unable really to put their finger on why they didn't trust Clinton added to their questions about his trustworthiness. Her point in the quotation is that people find Clinton appealing but that the appeal carries with it a sense of danger. I believe that the incongruity of his appeal is relevant to the analysis of the midterm elections. The growing distrust which people have of the president has consolidated. Men overwhelmingly cast their votes against Democratic candidates. In my view, the midterm elections, as they relate to Matalin's metaphor of attraction and danger, indicate that voters elected to have their date with Clinton and have come to realize that he is everything they feared.

Matalin also distinguished between public and private trust. She wrote that Bush was perceived by the public as a man they personally trusted. His breaking of his "Read my lips" pledge, according to Matalin, was perceived as a public-trust issue, not an example of Bush's being untrustworthy personally.

Clinton, on the other hand, is not perceived as being someone who can be trusted personally. This book details his tendency to lie, which certainly is the catalyst for the erosion of credibility. I think the lack of credibility which Clinton has demonstrated in the past two years personified for Americans their similar problem with the way Congress has been conducted. Clinton opened the umbrella of distrust, and its shadow was cast on many congressmen of his own party.

One point that is unmistakable is that the president placed a spotlight on Congress as he complained repeatedly about gridlock. Clinton's complaint that Congress was not being active paralleled one of the complaints about him. Clinton has been described as indecisive, a waffler, late for appointments, and a procrastinator. Again, Clinton personified what he claimed to be wrong with Congress. Interestingly, voters did not accept Clinton's contention that Republicans were to blame for his conflict with Congress. If voters had been in agreement with Clinton's policies, the midterm election would have been more favorable for the Democrats.

The comparison between Clinton's complaint of congressional mismanagement and his own mismanagement also reflected poorly upon both the president and congressional leaders of his own party. Two books, *The Agenda* by Bob Woodward and *On The Edge* by Elizabeth Drew, report on the inner workings of the Clinton White House. Both books provide many accounts of mismanagement and chaos under Clinton's leadership. The widespread dissemination of the information presented in these books offered Americans the opportunity to understand the extent of disarray within the White House.

Woodward writes about one of many outbursts of anger the president exhibited. On one such occasion, Clinton was angered by the difficulties that his budget resolution was experiencing in Congress. Clinton's anger lasted for hours and resulted in a tirade about a number of problems for the administration. One of the battles waged by Clinton was over health care. Notice his comment, as recorded by Woodward, which presaged (although underestimated) the midterm election. Woodward wrote: " 'There are so many Senate Democrats up in '94, we could lose the Senate that year,' Clinton said, returning to politics. 'People are ready for a huge deal on health care. We must convince people that our plan will improve

Bill Clinton as a young boy
GLOBE PHOTOS

Below   Bill Clinton (left) with his mother Virginia and his step-brother Roger in a 1959 portrait
ARCHIVE PHOTOS/Reuters/Family/ Jeff Mitchell

Defining moment: A teenage
Bill Clinton shakes hands
with his idol John F. Kennedy.
ARCHIVE PHOTOS/Arnie Sachs

Right Bill Clinton's step-
brother, Roger, with his
mother at the 1992
Democratic Convention
GLOBE PHOTOS/Adam Scull

The President and Mrs. Clinton celebrate daughter Chelsea's high school graduation, at Sidwell Friends School in Washington, D.C. GLOBE PHOTOS/Sharon Farmer/White House

Left Gennifer Flowers at a 1992 press conference. *Right* Paula Corbin Jones, who brought suit against President Clinton for sexual harassment, in 1997. The trial was set for May 1998. *(Left)* GLOBE PHOTOS/John Cordes *(Right)* ARCHIVE PHOTOS/Ron Sachs/CNP

Former White House intern Monica Lewinsky, in a 1994 file photo, who is alleged to have had an affair with President Clinton from 1995 to 1997

ARCHIVE PHOTOS/Reuters/FLS

Former White House aide Linda Tripp, who secretly taped conversations with former White House intern Monica Lewinsky

ARCHIVE PHOTOS/Richard Clement/ Reuters

Independent counsel Kenneth Starr addressing the press in January 1998, regarding new allegations against President Clinton

ARCHIVE PHOTOS/Arnold Sachs/CNP

Vernon Jordan, Bill Clinton's friend and adviser, speaks to reporters ARCHIVE PHOTOS/Rick Wilking/Reuters

every American's security. The only way they can beat us is by making people feel even less secure over our plan.' "

Clinton was right on both counts. His party lost the Senate, and his health-care proposal was not adopted by Congress. Woodward's conclusion of that account offered insight, however, into how Clinton perceived his role in the White House as it related with Congress. "Panetta had never seen Clinton so angry. Clinton, he concluded, must have naively thought he could implement his full agenda, according to his own timetable. But the spirit and enthusiasm of the presidential campaign just did not automatically or easily become a legislative program."

Another example of a breeding ground for chaos was reported in a later section of *The Agenda*. A chaotic atmosphere is bound to exist when the leader of the administration is inconsistent. Woodward wrote that even one of the president's closest advisers was well aware of this personal problem. "[George] Stephanopolous knew that it was a mistake to assume that any one moment with Clinton, any one conversation, day, or even week reflected Clinton's true feelings or unchanging fundamental attitude about something. With any single audience or person, Clinton was generally consistent and had mastered his rap. But he could articulate a totally different, even contradictory rap to the next audience with genuine sincerity."

Woodward also pointed out that the Travelgate and tarmac haircut incidents "exposed the lack of organization and discipline within the White House. Though neither story had long-term implications, they reflected basic management problems that Clinton did not insist be addressed."

The difficulty that Clinton had in passing the 1993 budget proposal had later implications in the midterm election for one first-term Democratic member of Congress in particular. Rep. Marjorie Margolies-Mezvinsky of Pennsylvania had been elected in 1992 from a district which typically elected Republicans. With the president desperate for votes in order to obtain passage of the budget, Margolies-Mezvinsky was contacted by administration officials to attempt to obtain her commitment of support. According to Woodward, Margolies-Mezvinsky told a teary-eyed Clinton that she would vote for the budget if it was necessary. "At 10:15 P.M., Margolies-Mezvinsky and Pat Williams of Montana finally filled out green cards, signifying a yes vote, and the count went over the top, to 218. The two remaining Democrats voted no for a 218–216 final tally. The house chamber filled with wild cheering from the Democrats, while Republicans chanted, 'Bye-bye, Marjorie!' "

In addition to the loss of Margolies-Mezvinsky's congressional seat, a description by Woodward of Clinton's reaction to the budget victory was given. Clinton, James Carville, Mark Gearan (White House communications director), and the White House photographer were present in the Oval Office when word was received that the budget resolution had passed. According to Woodward, Clinton said that Carville was the only one in the room making top-tax bracket money and that he would have to pay the big tax increase. Woodward wrote that Clinton reached over to pick Carville's back pocket. "Clinton finally released the wallet from Carville's back pocket. Some $80 in cash was inside. The president took it out and started throwing the $20 bills around the Oval Office, symbolically redistributing the wealth."

The type of attitude displayed by Clinton in the Oval Office scene has been available for people to read in Woodward's book throughout this past year. With the perception that Clinton was seeking to levy heavy taxes on the populace to fund his health-care program, such a scene does not evoke positive feelings in many Americans. That Democrats in Congress supported Clinton's budget resolution (albeit many against their better judgment, such as Margolies-Mezvinsky) contributed to the defeat of many of those congressmen.

Elizabeth Drew's book *On The Edge* opened with the following words, which depict the Clinton presidency's tendency toward chaos: "One of the most distinctive things about the Clinton Presidency in the crucial first eighteen months was the aura of danger. His Presidency was constantly on the edge—because of his past and what came to be called his 'character,' and because of the legislative gambles he took." Drew wrote that his presidential authority appeared to be jeopardized repeatedly as his personal strengths and flaws conflicted. She described the president and his presidency as "unusual."

Drew's insider's view of the first eighteen months of the Clinton presidency serves as further confirmation that significant problems are inherent in the administration. The reason the presidency is "unusual" is that the president is "unusual" as well. She described many of the conflicting characteristics of the president. On the one hand, Clinton was described as undisciplined and exhibiting contradictory behavior. At the same time, she reported his tremendous ability to recall names and to exude confidence. The following comment by Drew indicates how it would have been difficult for the Clinton presidency to have demonstrated anything but chaos. "But the truth was that as the confident new President took the oath of office, he, his wife, and his staff had no idea how unready they were to govern. Nor did the public."

Drew wrote that complications for Clinton ensued even before he took office. The selection of the various cabinet posts left the impression that Clinton could be persuaded to alter decisions. Another trait that Drew identified which had an impact upon the president supports the impression put forth by Bert Dickey in my interview with him (see chapter 16). Dickey was knowledgeable about Clinton and had been active in his campaigns. Dickey had said that Clinton had an extremely difficult time telling a person bad news; but if it were good news, Clinton would make the contact.

Drew noted that trait and recounted a situation at the highest level of government in which Clinton exhibited that propensity. She wrote, "Toward the end of the Vice Presidential search, with Gore about to be announced, Clinton had Senator Bob Kerrey meet with him in the governor's mansion late at night and told him, 'If it were up to me it would be you.' As a consequence, he could leave some people with the impression that they had a job when they didn't." This is the same Senator Kerrey whom Clinton later would chide for being responsible for the downfall of his presidency if the senator did not support his budget resolution.

Drew also commented on Clinton's indecisiveness as it related to the selection of candidates for administration posts. Drew wrote that after Clinton spoke with the candidates, they were then interviewed by Hillary. Clinton would ask for more names or more information. According to Drew, one adviser told her that Clinton's indecisiveness was due to the need for more knowledge. Drew's assessment, however, was that "sometimes Clinton's indecision stemmed from his own indecisiveness." Her appraisal is in accord with my position that Clinton's indecisiveness is a character trait not due to circumstances. Blaming the trait on situations is one of the defense mechanisms which Clinton has exhibited, but the number of times that he has been indecisive in varied circumstances begs the defense.

Drew identified instances in which Clinton was untruthful and situations in which he became defensive when his veracity was questioned. She wrote of Clinton's irritation even before he officially became president when pressed on the issue of his reneging on campaign promises concerning Haitian policy and the middle-class tax cut. After his inauguration, Clinton took up the legislative agenda of gays serving in the military. According to Drew, when Clinton was criticized for that early legislative issue, "Clinton blamed the Republicans for forcing the issue to come up when it did by threatening to add a rider to the pending family leave bill preserving and writing into law the existing Pentagon ban on gays in the military. This of course was untrue." While Republicans had made such a threat, it was, in fact, Clinton himself who initiated the subject. Drew cites this denial by the president as "perhaps the first example in his Presidency of his tendency to lay blame off on others."

The author wrote that after the first month in office there was doubt within the administration that Clinton could go one week without making a serious gaffe. The tone for such problems was partially established, again, by Clinton's promising more than he could deliver. Recall that Clinton had said that on the day that he was sworn into office he would have his economic program ready for presentation. Drew wrote that part of the reason the program was not ready was because of Clinton's propensity to delay decision making. Another reason, according to Drew, was that it had been overpromised. For example, the savings from health-care reform had been overinflated in Clinton's campaign rhetoric.

An example of the chaotic nature of the Clinton administration is found in Drew's description of the White House preceding Clinton's first major speech to Congress. "There was bedlam in the White House as the President and his advisers prepared for the big speech to Congress on Wednesday. Though this was a special speech for a special occasion, the way it was put together reflected some of the characteristics of the new administration."

Drew's use of the word "bedlam" provides an ample description of the Clinton White House. It is a word which also would serve to describe ably the nature of Clinton's childhood home. Bedlam evokes images of uproar, a madhouse. This description is interchangeable between his childhood home and his home as chief administrator. Note as well that Drew did not excuse the bedlam because of the special nature of the speech or situation. Instead, she believed that the situation served as a reflection of characteristics inherent in the administration. I think this is a clear example of how dysfunction infiltrates an organization when that organization is headed by a dysfunctional leader.

The crisis within the White House would worsen by April 1993, as Drew reported. She wrote that the administration held numerous meetings that were crisis oriented because of the dysfunctional administration. Concern was focused on the president's image, the problem with decision making or lack of decision making, Clinton's schedule, his mismanaged agenda, and the inability to get his message across to the public. Part of the problem was considered to be Clinton's sinking self-confidence. Drew described in her book Clinton's tendency to exhibit mood swings. Aides commented within the White House that he was inconsistent and indecisive.

Drew also described Clinton's anger. She wrote that the president, while appearing relaxed publicly, would exhibit intense anger privately. She described the physical action of his temper as he gestured with his arms, pointed fingers, and screamed. Drew also described his anger as petulant and strong. She provided some very insightful comments regarding the nature of his anger. "The real significance of Clinton's temper was what it said about his deeper nature. There was a self-indulgence in Clinton's tantrums, an immaturity, a part of him that never grew up." She also wrote of his anger: "There was in fact a kind of unmaturity about Clinton. There seemed to be something unfinished about him. Compared to many men his age, or even younger, he didn't seem quite grown up . . . he didn't come across a settled person, and the public seemed to sense that."

I think the reason Clinton seems unsettled, immature, and self-indulgent is that his anger is the result of childhood pain. Display of his anger as a mature man and as president seems distorted because it is not based on an emotional response in the present. Clinton emotionally lives in the past. The display of his anger is consistent with the tantrum of a child. The part of Clinton that never matured was the "part" of him that denied his pain. It is that central conflict which has resulted in the complications of the Clinton presidency.

The chaos in the White House was also evidenced in the handling of foreign affairs, such as Somalia and Bosnia, according to Drew. Policy decisions wavered, and meetings were directionless. The president gave conflicting public statements that confounded policy making further. Clinton frustrated his staff by making public policy statements before policy decisions had been formulated. Drew described the president in relation to Bosnia: "The President of the United States looked feckless. He had talked and talked about the moral imperative of doing something about Bosnia, and done nothing. He had said publicly that he would be coming up with a strong policy, one that could well involve military action, and had failed to do so. He had reacted to what he saw on television, and his mind seemed easily changed. He had also claimed, disingenuously, to be closer to an agreement with the Europeans than he was. Whatever the policy should have been, Clinton's way of making it didn't engender confidence."

Woodward had described the chaos that occurred in the White House when Travelgate and the tarmac haircut coincided in May 1993. Drew noted that when things went wrong, Clinton tended to deny responsibility. She wrote, "Clinton had a seemingly unshakable tendency to walk away from responsibility for things that had gone wrong: Waco, the travel office, LAX. And worse, to put these things in self-pitying terms: that people didn't understand him or that others [Republicans] did bad things to him. He threw out a blitz of excuses." According to Drew, such examples of denial rekindled Americans' memories of Clinton's other excuses for marijuana smoking and the draft record.

I think such further examples of Clinton's disingenousness played a role in the rejection of Democratic incumbents in the midterm election as the association between Clinton and the Democratic Congress solidified. After all, the Democrats have held the majority for most of the past forty years. While the zeitgeist has changed over the years, the single significant difference between this past election and prior elections was the Clinton presidency.

The dysfunction that is the Clinton presidency resulted in further bungling, such as mishandled appointments of Lani Guinier and Zoe Baird. Guinier, being a personal friend of the Clintons, provides yet another example of the president's reluctance to communicate bad news—in her case, that a decision had been reached to withdraw her appointment. Drew made the clear statement that the president didn't want to be the one to tell Guinier that her appointment nomination was being withdrawn. Clinton's tendency to avoid communicating unpleasant information is typical of a dysfunctional individual. Instead of being direct, a third party is used; or, worse yet, inaccurate information is disseminated, further confusing the matter.

In the case of the Guinier appointment, not only did the president fail in directly communicating with her, but "Clinton and his advisers put on an elaborate charade. The public was later told that [Vice President] Gore 'confronted' Clinton on Thursday morning and told him that he must read [Guinier's] writings. But as Clinton had said on more than one occasion, he was already familiar with her writings." Later, it was claimed that Clinton reviewed the writings and was uncomfortable with some of them. Even his words at the announcement of her withdrawal are marked with inconsistency. Clinton said of Guinier's writings that they "do not represent the views . . . that I hold very dearly, even though there is much in them with which I agree." According to Drew, Clinton made his statement while tearfully biting his lip.

When David Gergen was brought on board to counsel the president, he found a chaotic administration. Clinton frequently was late for appointments, decision making was still a problem, and the staff was inexperienced. These problems persisted. Drew wrote, "A source of confusion was the President. It could be difficult to know what he wanted done. Clinton gave his aides conflicting signals. He would tell one aide that he wanted more issues committed to paper and another that he did not. He would express frustration about the loose management of the White House and invite kibitzing by people inside and outside his administration. He complained about an overloaded schedule and urged that events be added. Confusion was also caused by Clinton's virtual incapacity to say no."

Adding David Gergen to the staff may or may not have been helpful to the White House management, just as the addition of Leon Panetta may or may not prove helpful. What the statement by Drew indicates and what is crucial to the thesis of this book is that minor improvements may be achieved but the inherent problem of the administration will not be resolved. This is because, as Drew's statement points out, the source of much of the dysfunction is the president. He is unwilling to disappoint others directly. He denies responsibility.

All of the dysfunctional characteristics just outlined are to be expected, given Clinton's dysfunctional youth and his failure to resolve it. Gergen submitted his resignation in November 1994 to pursue an opportunity at Duke University. Is there really that much change that the president has demonstrated since Gergen's arrival? Are things that much better? Panetta became chief of staff and sought to make some major changes in personnel within the administration. One of the reported changes he planned was to replace Dee Dee Myers. The word was leaked to the press. Myers, to her credit, did what she needed to do to arouse support for herself. Clinton, overriding Panetta's desires, not only kept Myers, but she was promoted and given a prestigious office. When the president behaves dysfunctionally, even his chief of staff is affected.

Bob Woodward and Elizabeth Drew describe the president as a man with a tremendous credibility problem, personal conflicts, and a chaotic leadership style. With the advent of direct media access to events and the dissemination of firsthand accounts of the president as presented by those authors, a president is unable to mask many of his flaws. Clinton's dysfunction is obvious to most close observers of the political process and to many who are only casually interested in current events. The result of his dysfunction, along with other political factors, was a devastating defeat for the Democratic party in the 1994 midterm elections. The president, in my belief, will be unable to turn the tide because the source of the dysfunction is the president himself.

CHAPTER THIRTEEN

Sexual Compulsion

ONE OF THE MORE UNSEEMLY ASPECTS of the Clinton character is his relentless sexual activity. Clinton's long-standing history of sexual liaisons throughout his marriage has resulted in scrutiny from a variety of sources. Prior to the presidential election of 1992, Gennifer Flowers's statements of a multiyear affair raised a firestorm of interest until Clinton and his wife appeared on television to respond to the allegations. As is typical of Clinton's ability to deny, his response was less than forthcoming and made allowance for ambiguity. Following the president's election, further allegations appeared. The *American Spectator* and the *Los Angeles Times* published articles which were the result of extensive background research by the authors. The articles disclosed reports from state troopers in Arkansas alleging that Clinton had the troopers arrange for sexual liaisons with women while he was governor of Arkansas. Clinton denied the allegations, and the media spin was that Clinton's sexual behavior does not matter and does not impact his presidential duties.

It is important to discuss Clinton's sexual liaisons because they exceed normal behavior and do affect his presidential activities. This sexual behavior most adequately can be described as pathological. It has been reported that Clinton's sexual activity was so extensive that he cannot recall all of his partners. The number of partners reportedly led Clinton's handlers to develop a list, known as the Doomsday List, to track this activity. The list was supposed to serve as preparation for anticipated revelations about sexual activity by the president. It would enable the handlers to have the upper hand vis-à-vis such accusations.

But what does all of this have to do with Clinton's functioning as president? To answer this question, it is important to understand the psychological functioning of someone engaging in obsessive thinking and compulsive behavior. In this case, the compulsion is being acted out in a sexual nature.

People who have such problems spend an inordinate amount of time thinking about sexuality and engaging in sexually related activities. Since it is a private activity which results in feeling bad and shameful, it is not one which is openly discussed by most people experiencing the problem. The thought process and behavior serve a particular purpose which more easily may be understood by comparing it to related obsessive or compulsive activity. The misunderstood goal of an individual engaging in such behavior is to avoid emotional conflict. When a person has stored up emotional pain, he seeks out the means either to resolve or to avoid his pain. In the case of the sexually compulsive individual, the activity is one of avoidance. If a considerable amount of the day is spent thinking about sexually related activities or engaging in such behavior, the emotional pain can be ignored. It serves as a diversion from what is truly important.

It is easier to understand this concept when one likens it to the cognitions and behavior of an individual compulsively engaged in drug activity. One of the truths about such behavior is that it increases over time. Another factor is that individuals engage in what is called drug-seeking behavior. They do not sit back passively and hope that drugs arrive at their doorstep. Instead, they engage in behavior designed to enable them to get drugs. Another factor to consider is that the drugs obtained are never enough. Even though a person has drugs for the immediate moment, future needs are not satisfied. Therefore, following the ingestion or injection of drugs in the present, the thought process almost immediately becomes consumed with thinking about drugs and how to obtain more of them.

Obviously, it is easier to identify the willingness of a compulsive drug user to engage in illicit activity to satisfy his need, since most drugs are illegal. The drug user will engage compulsively in behavior detrimental to personal relationships and business dealings. Most important, the compulsive drug user is utilizing a substance to "numb" emotional pain. Unfortunately for the abuser, the numbing is temporary, and the emotional pain continues once the high subsides. This is another reason why the thought process immediately returns to drugs. The activity itself is designed to help the person ignore his problems. When he realizes (to the extent that a drug abuser is self-aware) that the emotional pain is still present, he responds by obsessive thinking and compulsive behavior. Doing so becomes a mechanism to avoid his pain.

It would be difficult to comprehend press or public responses of indifference to a president's alleged repeated use of marijuana or cocaine. It is doubtful that the overriding belief would be that such prior behavior, without any known or observable resolution to the problem, is unimportant to the functioning of the president. It is my argument that the same consideration should be given to a president with sexually compulsive behavior as to one with drug compulsive behavior. The reason that such an argument is defensible is that the cognitive and emotional processes involved for both types of problems are quite similar. The only difference is in the possible effects from the addictive quality of drugs.

Many would argue that sexually compulsive behavior as alleged against the president has addictive qualities in and of itself. My experience as a therapist does not lead me to accept the addictive nature of sexual compulsion, but I do believe that such compulsions are difficult to correct. The reason for the therapeutic complications in treating sexual compulsion is that the behavior itself is self-reinforcing. The attempt at behavior change is designed to assist clients in discontinuing behavior from which they receive gratification each time they engage in it. The leverage a therapist holds is that although the behavior may be enjoyable, an honest, sexually compulsive client will admit that considerable emotional pain is involved. Consider the self-degradation, the high degree of risk to marriage and family, and the risk to one's employment if sexual activity outside marriage is revealed.

The relationship between sexual compulsiveness and the negative effect on personal relationships and employment is a therapeutic given. Clinton's brother, Roger, when arrested for cocaine-related charges, became a focal point of treatment within the Clinton family. If the president were capable of making an honest appraisal of his sexual behavior, he would conclude that he is just like his brother; only he engages in a different type of compulsive behavior.

Sexually compulsive activity is not likely to place a person behind bars, as does illicit cocaine activity. An intervention, a common technique utilized by therapists, could be employed in discussing the sexual behavior of the president. Imagine conducting an intervention with the expressed purpose of showing Clinton the connection between his sexual compulsion and the harm that it does to himself, his family, and the nation. An intervention is a process typically used by drug and alcohol specialists in which family members, employers, close friends, counselors, or clergy gather to surprise the loved one and help him see the self-destructive quality of his behavior. It often is a highly emotional meeting, with the expressed purpose of encouraging the person to seek treatment.

An intervention to address Clinton's sexually destructive behavior could focus on the following: the marital pain and embarrassment that has been caused to his spouse. Imagine what it must be like to appear before a national television audience and state that any marital problems that existed are between the two of them, with a vague attempt at accepting responsibility. This humiliation is followed by further allegations by the conservative media as well as liberal newspapers which the First Lady must respond to when making public appearances. Like it or not, the reality is that the sexual behavior of a presidential candidate, and certainly a president, is now open for discussion. The pain felt by the First Lady undoubtedly goes much deeper than that experienced on a public or political level. Assuming that she loves the president, her feelings would mirror those of any spouse pained by marital infidelity.

The next speaker in the intervention could be the president's daughter Chelsea, who would tell him what her experience related to the allegations has been. It can be presumed that a daughter is troubled when she hears rumors about her father's pathological sexual behavior. Undoubtedly, it is easy for Clinton to identify with the embarrassment felt at the schoolyard and the desire to hide from it. After all, as a child, he experienced similar feelings when attempting to hide his family's problems. A significant difference exists in that few people knew who Roger Clinton was, while nearly all Americans know who Bill Clinton is. The comparison between his childhood feelings and those felt by his daughter could greatly assist the intervention specialist in helping Clinton to seek treatment for sexual compulsion.

Following the exchange between daughter and Clinton, his minister could address the spiritual and religious factors related to the behavior. The minister could point out the duplicity between words and behavior in a way which could significantly lend itself to healing and forgiveness.

With the personal aspects of the sexual compulsion addressed, attention could turn to professional and legal situations. Staffers could discuss their need to have compiled a list tracking his sexual liaisons. The president could be told that such lists are quite unusual. In fact, most people do not have a history that would prevent them from remembering who their partners were. The staffers could demonstrate that his behavior has been detrimental to his political career because, despite their best efforts and his denial, allegations continue to be made repeatedly. In fact, legal action has been taken against the president for alleged sexual harassment. If, in fact, such an allegation is false, it should be condemned. If it is true, at some point the president would best serve himself, his family, and the nation by admitting it. The staffers could summarize their position by stating that his sexual behavior is not, in their opinion, normal or healthy.

With personal, spiritual, legal, and employment issues discussed, the intervention specialist could inform the president about the compulsive nature of his behavior and summarize the impact that it has had on all of those present. The counselor would emphasize that the people attending the intervention gathering love or care a great deal for him and his personal welfare. The counselor should encourage the president to seek the treatment available to him now. It is unfortunate that when his brother was being treated for his compulsion, the president did not expose his own problem. Perhaps he did not identify it as a problem, or perhaps he was too ashamed to tell the truth. It is time to be truthful.

The intervention scenario was presented for several reasons. First, it is important that readers or their family members who have compulsive problems receive effective treatment for their problems. Second, it is designed to help the reader understand the complex web woven by an individual with sexual compulsion and how it invades virtually every aspect of his life. The scenario hopefully clarified why the issue of sexual compulsion is a valid one for a discussion related to the president's functioning. His behavior forces him to lie. He must present himself to his family and to the public as something that he is not. It necessitates an inordinate amount of thinking to cover his tracks. Imagine having your co-workers attempting to track your sexual behavior to prevent future employment complications. Realize that Clinton needs to keep similar records mentally. It is not as important for him to keep track of who the partners were as it is to remember who has been told what. This requires a tremendous expenditure of emotional energy, energy that needs to be directed toward effective leadership.

Sexual compulsion detracts from an individual's true problems. Attention is focused on the symptom—the sexual behavior—as opposed to the problem that underlies the symptom, the ACOA. It is important to consider both. The feelings underlying the compulsive behavior have been discussed throughout this text. The failure on the part of the president to resolve those feelings necessitates his avoidance of them. He has elected to avoid them by this compulsive activity.

It is interesting to speculate why he became sexually compulsive instead of having some other form of compulsion. One of the characteristics of an individual seeking self-esteem is to question his prowess. It also is likely that since Clinton is a power figure, he has had plenty of opportunities to engage in aberrant sexual behavior. Unfortunately, once more his response to the opportunities is abnormal. His failure to accept responsibility for his response pattern, his questioning of normalcy, and his inability to maintain an effective intimate relationship all are likely factors contributing to the sexual behavior. Regardless of the underlying factors, the president needs to accept personal responsibility for his behavior.

Apologists for Clinton's behavior may still raise questions about whether his sexual activity really matters. Polls indicate that many Americans have not drawn a connection between the sexual issues and his presidency. I am suggesting that such a belief is held out of ignorance of sexual compulsion. We are not observing a man who had an affair and is remorseful for hurting his spouse. We are observing an individual who is consumed with thoughts and behavior related to sex in much the same way that a drug abuser is consumed with thoughts and behaviors about his compulsion. He seeks out fulfillment of his compulsion in much the same way the drug abuser engages in drug-seeking behavior. This is pathological behavior that requires effective treatment.

It also is pathological behavior which does not get better by itself. The drive to engage in the behavior did not discontinue when Clinton became president. A compulsive drive that is neither treated nor satisfied will continue to infect the individual's thinking. Either the president is satisfying his compulsive urges or he is thinking about satisfying them. Either way, such urges serve to avert his attention from the underlying conflicts of the compulsion and distract him from functioning fully as president. His sexual behavior prior to the presidency would solely be his and the First Lady's concern if the problem were not pathological. With relative ease, one can predict, from past behavior, that Clinton's sexual behavior will continue to produce problems for his presidency.

A rather distasteful admission must be made by Clinton as part of his healing process. That admission is that he is no different from his stepfather; neither was emotionally mature. Both Clinton and his stepfather used other means to avoid emotional pain. If a difference between the two exists, it lies in the fact that his stepfather used alcohol and Clinton used women.

CHAPTER FOURTEEN

What the Election of Clinton Says About Americans

WHAT DOES THE ELECTION OF BILL CLINTON say about Americans? More important, what does his continued strong approval by polled voters mean? And what does it mean when most polled adults do not think that Clinton's sex life is relevant to assessing his presidency?

Obviously, a certain percentage of respondents in such a poll will oppose or support Clinton for reasons of political expediency. That still leaves a remainder who support Clinton despite their awareness of his problems. After all, he has reneged on many promises made to his liberal allies as well. As a psychologist, I think that a parallel may be drawn between the attraction (for some) to Clinton and the attraction between an ACOA functioning with unresolved conflicts and an unaware partner.

A common question a partner of an ACOA will ask is: "Why do I feel that my partner has such a hold on me? I know that I don't like what he does, but I can't seem to get away and stay away from him."

Many people are attracted to an ACOA's problematic behavior. Ironically, the attraction frequently centers on the partner's desire not to believe that the ACOA's problems really exist. The partner prefers to remain in a "confused state" attempting to explain away the bizarre behavior of the ACOA. The partner is at a loss to explain why, when the relationship seemed to be developing and becoming increasingly intimate, the ACOA engaged in some behavior to create problems for the relationship. What seemed so positive turned into chaos. The partner struggles to deny that the problems exist and at the same time experiences significant energy to maintain any semblance of a quality relationship.

The parallel to Clinton is justifiable in that he is the ACOA who has unresolved conflicts. He is an ACOA who has engaged in bizarre behavior and has created unnecessary problems. His partners are the American people. Enough of the electorate selected Clinton so that all Americans are in a relationship with him. A large percentage of those Americans refuse to accept that he has significant behavioral problems. Some pundits have been asking questions about Clinton's character. For example, Rush Limbaugh questioned Clinton's character and exposed his lies. Following the release of Bob Woodward's book about the chaos in the Clinton White House, even Washington insiders are being forced to acknowledge that significant problems exist. It is as if the people now know that something is wrong with Clinton but they prefer not to believe that something is wrong.

In the course of a chaotic marriage to an ACOA, eventually the partner who willingly has refused to believe the obvious will wake up to the reality. This will be difficult for many Americans, as it will leave them with little choice but to examine the problem with Clinton. Understand that Clinton represents thousands of psychotherapy clients across the country. Many people in therapy are there precisely because of their ACOA problems. Unfortunately, their therapeutic process may fail them if the therapist does not understand the degree of importance that their family life played in their development. An additional large segment of the therapeutic population includes those affected by their ACOA behavior. The spouse or the children of the ACOA often feel just as confused by the behavior of the ACOA, and many Americans feel confused by the behavior of the president. The point is that a large number of Americans are affected by the behavior of ACOAs. Many of them are voters who would have to acknowledge not only Clinton's problems but also problems personal to themselves, as if they were to acknowledge their error in supporting him.

It is important to reiterate that an ACOA is not necessarily a poor partner. The test for such problems in relationships occurs when an ACOA has not resolved his problems. Bill Clinton is not a poor presidential leader because he is an ACOA. He is a poor leader because he has failed to resolve his problems. Do not end your relationship with an ACOA because Clinton is so affected. Instead, seek to improve your relationship by encouraging that partner or yourself to resolve the problems.

Psychologists often are decried correctly for overstating a case. One could read the information about Clinton's life as an ACOA and misconstrue that this psychologist believes that most people have the same problem. I want to be clear. Clinton reflects that group of Americans commonly seen in outpatient psychotherapy offices. He does not reflect the majority of Americans. Because therapists spend each day speaking with people who have problems, they often lose sight of how normal most people are. The majority of Americans have no need to go to a therapist. Most people who are in therapy are more appropriate for short-term therapy in which they rapidly learn to manage their lives more effectively.

The majority of Americans who do have problems are willing to receive help for those problems. I do not think Bill Clinton understands this. I state that emphatically, for it is exceedingly difficult for a person with significant personal problems to understand clearly how an emotionally mature person functions. When Clinton says, "I feel your pain," what he needs to do is feel his own. He has to stop hiding behind self-created chaos, outbursts of anger, and sexual compulsion.

Part Three

CHAPTER FIFTEEN

Bill Clinton's Little Rock

A VISIT TO LITTLE ROCK, ARKANSAS, leaves a favorable impression. While the physical environs of Little Rock are pleasant, perhaps the greatest resource of the community is its people. The citizens of the state capitol are friendly and good-natured, polite and cooperative, even to an out-of-town author inquiring about their most famous favorite son. They show an obvious pride in their city and in Arkansas as a whole.

They are are sharply divided in their assessment of their former governor. Almost everyone seems to have a well-defined opinion of President Clinton formed from experiences with him at the helm of their state for most of the previous twelve years. Those who oppose Clinton are vigorous in their negative characterizations. Supporters of the president passionately defend him but are more reticent about offering "on the record" information. The hesitancy to speak out apparently stems from their belief that the media have miscast the president into someone whom they do not recognize.

An example of such hesitancy occurred when I contacted a well-known Clinton supporter and requested an interview to discuss his personal style and the individual's experiences with him. The supporter expressed interest in the topic but prior to consenting to an interview wanted to know if the book was "White House approved." Certainly anyone has the freedom to accept or reject a request for an interview. It was disappointing, however, to learn that for some of Clinton's supporters a White House seal of approval is necessary to obtain an interview.

This was particularly disheartening because one of the objectives of traveling to Little Rock was to obtain interviews with supporters of the president so as to provide a balanced view. The president's supporters, particularly those who had known him for an extended period of time, undoubtedly would have been able to provide insights into his personal style which his opponents would have overlooked.

At the time, I had already been made privy to the fact that a White House aide had attempted to discourage another's cooperation with me. That person had the courage to speak with me "on the record" despite having information which did not cast the president in a positive light. Furthermore, I tended to doubt that my topic would receive White House approval.

I thought it important to speak with individuals who knew Clinton well. The interviews showed that, on the issue of Clinton's character, the city of Little Rock is a house divided. Identical Clinton behavior was given a positive appraisal by his supporters and a negative one by his detractors. Both groups seemed certain that they were portraying him accurately. The difference of opinion is not based on partisan politics, as many of Clinton's detractors are fellow Democrats. They were onetime friends of the president, and some would still consider themselves to be his friends. Supporters of Clinton were as sincere as his detractors. They were loyalists who would deny that they are being loyal to a fault. The disparity of opinion and the divergent characterization of Clinton's behavior leads me to accept one individual's description of the president when he stated that "Clinton is an enigma."

One longtime friend of the president not only was kind and cooperative but also went so far as to pick me up at my hotel and drive me to his office for a lengthy interview. What made such a gesture particularly notable was that he did so on exceedingly short notice on Father's Day, thus giving up a portion of that important day with his family. I was grateful to him for his generosity of time and information. Such a spirit of hospitality was typical of the people of Little Rock.

The focus of this book is the impact of Clinton's childhood on his personality. I was not expecting to stumble across financial information and campaign practices which might cause complications for the president. I am concerned that the financial information and campaign practices might overshadow the theme of this book, and I do not wish them to do so. As a psychologist, I will leave the determination and possible continued exploration of those dealings to those much more experienced at ferreting out the accuracy of that information. To that end, I will merely report what information came to me in an unexpected fashion.

With all this information as background to the interviews that were conducted in Little Rock and the opportunity to get a "feel" for the city, the following will present comments from interviews held with detractors and supporters of the president. Every attempt will be made to represent the comments as closely as possible to their perceived intent and meaning at the time of the interviews. Those who were supportive of the president were assured that readers of the book would be made aware that they hold the president in very high regard. Comments by the detractors of the president will show the intensity with which some think and feel negatively about Clinton.

On several occasions one person spoke of a scenario in one way and another person discussed the same situation in a completely different way. I will describe those situations and leave it to the reader to determine whose description of events is more believable. I do not think that any of the people interviewed were lying about their core thoughts and feelings about the president. It will serve as a good example of how one person can witness an event and report it in one way, while another can see the same event and report it in another. Everyone has heard of the dilemmas that face police officers in discerning the truth from witnesses to an accident. Even though the witnesses have seen the same accident, their reporting of it frequently differs significantly.

Why the viewpoints differ so significantly is, I think, due to the cognitive perception of each person. If one maintains a positive perception about someone, he is much more likely to view the behaviors of that person in a positive light. If, however, one views a person negatively, he is more likely to view that person's behavior negatively. When the opposite is true, when one views a person positively but considers behavior negatively, it places a person in what is known as cognitive dissonance. Since people are uncomfortable when they experience cognitive dissonance, they seek to reduce the incongruity either by reidentifying their beliefs about the person or by reframing their beliefs about the behavior. Therefore, a person who holds negative thoughts and feelings toward another is more likely to identify negatives with that person than positives, and vice versa. When cognitive dissonance occurs, a person attempts to rectify the incongruity by changing his perception of the person or event.

Those who have a negative perception of Clinton are more likely to view his behavior in a negative way. When he does something which generally would be considered a positive behavior, they might acknowledge positive behavior (after all, nobody can be all bad); or they might view the generally accepted positive behavior in a negative light.

Those who have a positive perception of Clinton are, similarly, more likely to view his behavior in a positive manner. When Clinton engaged in behavior that generally would be considered obviously negative, such as lying, the supporters would be placed into cognitive dissonance. It would be necessary, then, either to ascribe some negative quality to the president (nobody tells the truth *all* the time, even Bill) or to reframe the behavior. (He has not gone back on his word; he just was not committed to his position before.)

Hopefully, a rudimentary understanding of cognitive dissonance will assist the reader in forming an opinion about the responses and viewpoints in the interviews which follow. Some readers might tend to believe one side more than the other, while others might gravitate toward a middle point. It might be interesting to take stock of what your belief about the president is first and then consider whether any of the viewpoints support your position or whether they place you in cognitive dissonance. If you do experience dissonance, try to become aware of how you resolve the discrepancy mentally.

CHAPTER SIXTEEN

An Interview With
Bert German Dickey III

BERT GERMAN DICKEY III has been involved with the Democratic party in Arkansas for many years. He is listed in *Who's Who in the South and Southwest*, with emphasis placed on his political and educational accomplishments. He is referred to in that text as a "political advisor." He earned a doctorate degree in teaching and adult education from the University of Tennessee. He has served the Democratic party in the following capacities: the Arkansas state committee, the state executive committee, the finance council, an alternate delegate to the national convention in 1980, and a conference delegate in 1982. He also has served as a federal bankruptcy trustee for the Eastern District of Arkansas and as commissioner of housing for the city of Earle, Arkansas.

His affiliation with Clinton dates back to approximately 1978 or 1979. He had personal contact with Clinton while participating in Arkansas politics, and Dickey conducted fund raisers for Clinton at his own home. Dickey was a contributor to Clinton campaigns and traveled with Clinton in efforts to solidify support among voters in eastern Arkansas. As Dickey said about Clinton, "I've known him a long time."

Dickey's knowledge of the president's personality, style, and political maneuvering was revealed in an interview held on June 18, 1994, at Dickey's home. His opinion of Clinton obviously has soured, in part because of Clinton's failure to live up to his promises to appoint Dickey to commission posts. Dickey's willingness to speak with me revealed what some might call a personal resentment toward the president but probably is described more aptly as his desire to set the record straight. I asked him to discuss Clinton's impression of him at this time, and he said that Clinton probably would describe him as "a disgruntled campaign worker" speaking out "for some political reasons." He continued by stating that "they'll come up with something to discredit me. He'll come back with something." At the time of the interview, Dickey expressed his awareness that retributions for his comments were likely.

Not all the statements Dickey made about Clinton were negative. He had high praise for Clinton in some areas. For example, Dickey gave the president very high marks for his campaign skills, calling him "the master politician, the best I've ever seen. He gets out among the people." Most of what Dickey had to say about Clinton, however, was unfavorable.

TENDENCY TO LIE

Perhaps Dickey's primary complaint about the president was his propensity not to tell the truth. It was for that reason that the president lost his support. Dickey reported that Clinton repeatedly promised various political favors but failed to follow through on the promises. Dickey related several instances to bolster his contention that the president lies. It is important to understand that his belief is that Clinton's lying goes far beyond the norm. Dickey responded to my questioning about whether the president is aware that he is lying by stating, "No, I don't think he's aware, I think he's a habitual liar. He's done it all his life, and it's just the way, business as usual. I don't think he's got a conscience. He can be true blue one minute and then the next minute you're out of there."

He described the president's persuasiveness as well as his capacity to deny responsibility for negative actions. Dickey said, "I've sat in his office and he has told me—and I knew he was lying—and

I'll sit there thinking, I'm believing this guy and I knew he was going to lie to me when I came in here. I'll end up saying, 'Well, yeah, that's fine, I'll agree with you.' I'll step outside and say, 'Now, how did he do that?' I'm about two blocks away before I know my throat's cut. The blood doesn't start until you get out of there. He's good, he's real good."

Dickey stated that the president likes to accept credit for positive things, whether he has been responsible for them or not. He also said that, to the contrary, the president distances himself from anything negative and denies responsibility. "If he'd be offering it [a position] to you, he'd be the first to make the phone call. If it's good news, he makes the call and takes all the credit. If it's bad news, his underlings did it. He'd say, 'It's all political. I am innocent. I had nothing to do with it,' " explaining why he had to renege on positions he had offered.

Dickey recounted incidents in which Clinton lied to him. One took place in West Memphis, when the Democratic Central Committee was holding meetings. Dickey had made arrangements for the group to attend the afternoon dog races at the Kennel Club. He was uncertain whether the events of the day centered around fund-raising. He recalled talking with Clinton, who inquired about what position Dickey wanted. He responded by saying that he wanted to be appointed to the Fish and Game Commission. Clinton answered, "Bert, no problem, if that's all you want, you got it." Dickey turned to his wife, who was present, and asked her if she heard what Clinton said, and she affirmed that she had. Before their departure, Dickey thanked Clinton for agreeing to appoint him to the Fish and Game Commission. Dickey said that the reason he confirmed the conversation in the presence of his spouse was that previously Clinton had promised him positions when no one else was present. His wife had pointed out that no one was there to witness it but said, "He wouldn't lie to you. You're too good friends."

Clinton promised Dickey that the announcement would take place at 4:00 P.M. At 3:00 P.M., Dickey received a telephone call from someone representing Clinton. The caller said, "It had to go to someone else," and I said, "Hell, I knew he was lying when he told me."

Dickey said, "I guess I was taking him at face value. If he said something, I went to the bank with it." Conversely, throughout the process, there were times when suspicions about the president's veracity would surface inside Dickey. Others also questioned Dickey's acceptance of Clinton's promise.

Dickey recounted: "I did call on occasion to find out when the announcement would be and whether he'd want me in Little Rock. He'd say, 'Oh, we'll just make an announcement from the office, no big deal.'" Dickey stated, "In hindsight I should have thought, Well, those appointments are usually made in the governor's conference room with television." Dickey said that part of his acceptance of Clinton's promise—even though he had been lied to in the past—was: "He's the governor. I took him at his word."

Dickey also said that others tried to lead him to the truth about Clinton's promises. He said, "People would say, 'Bert, you know he's lying to you.' I'd say, 'No, he's not this time. I worked hard for him this time and raised a little money, spent a lot of hours, and I think he's going to come through.'" Dickey added, "He did not, and he's done a lot of people that way."

Not long after that particular letdown, Dickey moved to Vail, Colorado. He joined the Democratic Committee and made a telephone call to the governor's mansion, but Clinton was not home at the time. Dickey said that Clinton called him back from New Jersey. "I said, 'Well, I hear rumblings that you'll be running for the presidency and I want to help.' He said, 'Well, if it gets kicked off, I want you to be my western regional campaign manager.' I said, 'Yeah, I'd love to, and I know you. I'm on the committee out here, and I'll be glad to help.'" When Dickey hung up the telephone he said, "There he goes again. He did it again. I knew he was lying when he said it. He said he wasn't running, and then he was telling me, 'I'm going to,' and that I'll chair the commission. He's smooth, he's slick."

Dickey summarized his position about Clinton's lying in the following way: "I keep using the word, he's a liar. That's not a good word, but that describes him pretty well to everybody that knows him. One on one he's very personable, very likable. But sit with your back against the door 'cause that knife will go into you. It's not what did you do for me yesterday and today, it's what can you do for me tomorrow."

THE USE OF POWER

Dickey's concern about Clinton's failure to keep promises of commission positions has some additional ramifications. According to Dickey, one of the complications for Clinton in keeping his promises was that he would promise the same position to seven or eight people. Dickey said, "The one who gave him the most money got the slot. That turned a lot of people off." The interview revealed Dickey's belief that then governor Clinton used his position to appoint in a rather dubious fashion. Dickey described the process of being appointed to a commission. He said, "Say you wanted to be on any one of the commissions. There was a price you had to pay—fifty thousand for this one, fifteen thousand for that one, and the limit was fifteen hundred."

He recounted a story in which Dickey conveyed to Clinton the danger in treating people in such a way. He reported that the two of them were in east Arkansas and saw a picture of John F. Kennedy, Martin Luther King, Jr., and Robert Kennedy. Dickey said, "Bill, you're going to be the next one on everybody's table," and Clinton reportedly was not sure whether the comment was humorous or not. Clinton said, "Hell, I'd have to be dead to have my picture there."

Dickey spoke of other situations in which he thinks that Clinton used his position of power within the state. He recalled an instance in which a local activist was disseminating a flier which accused Clinton of having "sired a black baby." The flier was said to have surfaced at a time that would have been politically harmful to Clinton's presidential campaign. The activist's son was in jail for selling cocaine, and rumors about his parole coinciding with the activist's withdrawing the flier were discussed by knowledgeable Little Rock politicos. They speculated, according to Dickey, that Clinton used his influence to affect parole decisions.

Dickey said, "Tucker, the governor at the time, was going to be in D.C. So the speaker, Jerry Jewell, who is black, was going to be governor for the weekend, or whatever. So as soon as Tucker left, Jewell paroled [person's name's] son, and the talk around town was that it was all set up. They were going to let Jewell take the heat because Tucker wasn't going to be there." Dickey also believes that Clinton instructed the activist to stop disseminating the rumor about a black baby in exchange for arranging for the release of his son from jail.

According to Dickey, since the parole of the activist's son, "he's dropped it, he's been real quiet since he's been released, you don't hear a word from him, not a word out of him. He got real quiet, and he got his son out of jail, and I think that was the deal." Dickey speculated that the activist was told that if he resumed his allegations, arrangements would be made to have the son arrested on other charges. Dickey said of Clinton, "He's dangerous."

A view of Clinton as a power broker also was clear in comments that Dickey made regarding employment in the government and what happens to a person who confronts the power structure. In terms of obtaining a job, Dickey said, "He was the governor who controlled everything, almost like a, I wouldn't say benevolent dictator, but almost like a dictator. Say a state senator's girlfriend needs a summer job or a secretary's job— bam, it was done. You went through the office."

Similarly, individuals who worked for the government, according to Dickey, needed to be cautious in how they dealt with the power structure. "Maybe they wouldn't fire you, but they'd reassign you. Your job description will change; therefore, your salary will go in half, and then you have to quit, and no one will hire you because you're on that black list."

Subsequent to the interview with Dickey, I was informed that a state trooper allegedly had conducted an investigation into the state education department at the behest of his superiors. The resulting investigation reportedly uncovered significant flaws in the financial handling of the department. The asked-for investigation has been stalled, and the state trooper assigned to the investigation has been demoted to a position of traffic officer conducting radar scans.

Dickey likened the manner in which Clinton conducted business in Arkansas to that of Huey Long. "He's trying to be like a Huey Long, and he's as close to the Kingfish as I know of." When questioned as to whether Clinton's influence in the state remains great now that he has moved to Washington, D.C., Dickey said, "He keeps his hands on the different races. His machine is out there, and if you have his blessings, then you've got X number of votes from Bill's hand, the lion's share."

Dickey described Clinton's handling of a potential political adversary threatening his hold on the governor's office. According to Dickey, Steve Clark, then attorney general of the state of Arkansas, was gaining in strength and popularity and was thinking of challenging Clinton for the governorship. Dickey speculated that when Clinton reviewed the polls indicating that he would have a difficult time beating Clark, Clinton pushed for "somebody to take him down. What can we get that's real good?" The result of either Dickey's speculation or serendipity was that at the same time Clark was considering opposing Clinton, he was accused of using his state credit card for personal use. Clark was disbarred for this violation.

Several aspects of this situation are interesting. The average citizen undoubtedly would support the discovery of a politician's misusing a state credit card. What perhaps is less well known is the extent to which these cards were distributed and used. According to Dickey, "Many have one." To add credence to his statement, Dickey showed me a state credit card made out in his name. He told me that since Clark was disbarred, he, Dickey, immediately stopped using the card. Dickey said, "You look up and see him [Clark] jogging with the president a couple of years later." Dickey found it inconceivable for the two to be running together several years after what had happened to Clark. According to Dickey, "Clinton's people turned him in, because they knew, they all did it."

The Clark story follows a theme which Dickey maintains. That theme is that Clinton's use of power in the state of Arkansas was excessive. His characterization of the use of power can be considered in the light of his personality. Dickey said, "He wants to have his hand on your throat, and it's do it my way—or you're gone. If he can't have that [total control], you won't be there."

CAMPAIGN FINANCES

In a previous chapter I alluded to the fact that in the course of an interview some financial information was revealed which could have a considerable impact on the administration. It is information that, to the best of my knowledge, has not been revealed previously. While attempting to maintain the focus on the psychological factors, particularly ACOA issues, which affect Clinton, I would be remiss not to include the following information, given the possible ramifications. As previously mentioned, I am not an expert in campaign-financing law or Internal Revenue Service regulations.

The comments made regarding some of the campaign practices caught my attention, for obvious reasons. One of the reasons was that one of the practices sounds like those disclosed by Ed Rollins about the campaign of Christine Todd Whitman, a Republican. Rollins had said that Whitman's campaign had used "walking-around money" to suppress the black vote. He later retracted his statement and apologized. At the time, there was an uproar over such practices, and the Democrats were reviewing whether they would seek to have the results of that election overturned. The parallel between the two practices was too great to overlook.

In a preceding portion of text, it was discussed how various political commissions allegedly had a particular financial value. Some of the commission positions were said to have been obtained by donating campaign contributions anywhere from $50,000 to $1,500, at the bottom of the scale. The posts were said to have been promised to any number of individuals, with the one giving the greatest contribution receiving the position. But that was not the only scenario which Dickey revealed which was questionable from a legal and ethical standpoint.

From the outset, let me state clearly that Dickey was not willing to reveal for publication the names of the individuals who had assignments within the Clinton campaigns. Given the sensitivity of the disclosure, however, I do not believe that his lack of willingness to make the disclosure necessarily negates the seriousness of the allegations. Consider whether you would make such an allegation, assuming that it was true. In the atmosphere that Dickey described which exists in the state of Arkansas pertaining to the use of power, it was indeed a risk on his part to do so. Also, some of the information that he disclosed demonstrates his involvement in some of the dealings. Dickey is not someone who would make such allegations without the awareness of the possible ramifications of the information.

Dickey alleged that he was contacted by Clinton's campaign workers and was told, "We want you and your wife to give three thousand." Dickey reportedly declined to contribute that amount. "I said, 'No,' and they said, 'Well, will you give one hundred dollars apiece?' and I said, 'Well, yeah.' " Dickey continued by saying, "So they gave me twenty-eight hundred-dollar bills and said, 'Put this in your farm account and write two checks for fifteen hundred dollars.' " Furthermore, Dickey said he asked them, "well, what if the IRS checks me?" And they said, 'Well, just tell them you sold a piece of used farm equipment to somebody and they paid you cash.' "

The interview continued, with Dickey offering further disclosures about the campaign-financing process. He said, "If you wanted to sit on the Highway Commission or the Fish and Game Commission or another commission, well, it would cost, and that's how they laundered money, because he was really strong in the black community, and you have to go in and pay. We still do, they do it today, even on the county levels. You have to pay your drivers and the preachers to get in the black church and it's X number of dollars a vote. And that's how you got the so-called street money to go out and grease the skids, and that's what we would do. Ah, I say that's why he had such a big control over the black community."

Later, Dickey described a situation in which he and Clinton were at a black church in Earle, Arkansas. He said, "Of course, they're passing the plate, and he [Clinton] leaned over and said, 'I don't have any money, man.' I said, 'All I got's a couple of twenties.' He said, 'Well, give me a couple of those and I'll pay you back.' Of course, I never did see them. I got a picture of him and me at that church. The money didn't bother me. It's not the fact that he took it and never did pay me. It's just the principle behind it. He knew what he was at that church for. It was a fund raiser to get the black vote, and he should have known he'd have to put a little somethin' in the plate 'cause they were going to pay him a whole lot more after church out of the slush fund."

The results of such appearances and financial dealings, according to Dickey, had significant political returns. He described the voting behaviors which came from the black churches in which the drivers and preachers received campaign money. Dickey said, "Of course those boxes there would turn out 99.9 percent for Clinton, and the .1 percent that didn't just got confused and pulled the wrong button. We have palm cards printed, but after a while, you didn't need them for Clinton, but for whoever was riding his coattails in the county."

Dickey described a "palm card" as one which fit in the palm of a voter's hand and had a list of candidates to vote for. The voters would take the "palm card" into the voting booth and vote accordingly. He described it as follows: "Say you had a little list and you'd get into the voter's [booth] and when you picked them up, it'd say, 'Here's how you're voting.' " He continued, "I even heard that some areas where they had the machines they'd have a string in where it would hang down and where the knots were, that's what buttons you'd push out. That's hard to mess up."

THE IMPOSTOR SYNDROME

Portions of the interview provided insights into Clinton's behavior similar to the impostor syndrome discussed earlier. This syndrome means that ACOA do not believe that they truly are who they represent themselves to be. Dickey revealed that his observations of Clinton would support such a contention. Some of Dickey's descriptions of Clinton reflect an admiration for some of his skills but a lack of conviction or belief in what he says.

Dickey said, "He could go out and just regurgitate facts and numbers that were just phenomenal. But the nuts and bolts of all the things I don't think he even knew. He'd have to have someone come tell him, and they might be wrong, but he sounded good. Now, if you gave him enough time where someone could go in there, he has a brilliant mind, no doubt about it, and he can retain facts and figures and just spit them out. But you never know if they're right or wrong. I mean, you just take his word for it because he's such a good speaker."

Dickey's other comments further support the concept that Clinton is an impostor. As have other political observers, he said that Clinton follows the polls and formulates his opinions and actions based on the collected data. "What's good at the time, he's a big believer in polls. Whatever the poll says. If he was against it but the polls would be for it, he'd be for it. If the polls change, then he would change. It's just whatever is politically expedient at the time, that will help him look good. Then that's his role he's going to play. Then he can change the next day." (Earlier sections of the book discussed how the impostor syndrome lends itself to the chameleon approach to political action.)

Further demonstration of the impostor syndrome can be gleaned from the presentation which Clinton puts forth as one of the "common man," while reality tends to refute that presentation. During the presidential campaign the American public learned that Clinton's annual gubernatorial salary in Arkansas was a mere

$35,000. Yet the Clintons' combined annual income exceeded $200,000. According to Dickey, the lifestyle which Clinton led does not reflect that of the "common man" or someone getting by on an average annual salary. "He was making, what, $25,000 as governor but got almost one million dollars budget to live off of." The following comments could just as well have been included under the heading "use of power," but are included here to indicate the conflict between the appearance Clinton put forth and the reality.

Dickey said, "If he saw a suit that he liked,—I saw that happen —he'd say, 'Boy, I like that suit.' The next day it just happens to be sitting there in the governor's office. Somebody just dropped it off to him, just little things like that." Dickey conjectured that such conveniences might be common among governors of other states as well.

DECISION-MAKING

I asked Dickey to describe the president's decision-making process. His response was: "He takes forever. If he had to make a rational, quick decision, I don't think he could do it." His style was more, "sit down and have a conference, weigh the pros and cons. How are the people going to react? Regardless of whether it's right or wrong, how am I going to end up looking the best out of this deal?"

Dickey described a worst-case scenario about how Clinton might react to a situation. Dickey said, "There are missiles in flight over here now, what should we do? They'd be going off before he'd ever make a decision." Regarding the potential for Clinton's responsiveness to domestic unrest, Dickey said, "If there were a riot going on, I'm sure it'd take him awhile before he'd say, Well, how many votes do I have on this side versus this side that can harm us? I don't care about who's getting hurt out there. Should I send troops in or let them fight it out?" Dickey said that such a conversation would take place with his advisers about how a positive response would work to Clinton's benefit versus what was best for the situation. "That was the way he was here, just took forever to get something through."

OUTBURSTS OF ANGER

Recently, considerable attention has been directed toward the level of the president's anger. As discussed earlier, anger is defined as hurt feelings from the past. It is used to protect oneself from further hurt. Clinton's anger was recently discussed in *The Agenda* by Bob Woodward, who portrayed the president as someone who experienced periodic bouts of rage. This behavior is symptomatic of someone with an ACOA history. He overreacts to situations by lashing out with anger in ways that far exceed any rational response to a present situation. The following comments by Dickey about the president's displays of anger will add further credence to previous reports of Clinton's tendency to overreact.

Dickey said, "[Clinton's] got a violent temper. I mean, short fuse. It's either his way or no way, and if you crossed him, it was not good. I mean, he'd just go off in a heartbeat." I inquired as to whether Dickey was referring to yelling and cussing by the president, both traits reported in Woodward's book. Dickey said, "All of the above."

He had witnessed the president's verbal tantrums but said he had never seen the president become physically violent. Dickey described the president's physical response when his anger would get out of control: "Face would just turn beet red. You could see the muscles and veins in his neck. You could see it coming, and he would just go off. You know, how dare you challenge me?"

Personal styles in which pent-up emotions from the past are held in until the dam bursts are typical of individuals who control the people around them as well. Assuming that the descriptions by Woodward and Dickey are accurate, further credence is afforded to Dickey's contention about Clinton's need to "have his hand on your throat."

LEADERSHIP STYLE

Dickey mentioned a number of factors that offer insight into the president's leadership style. He said that the president would prefer to campaign for office rather than administer it. That was his style as governor, and it continues into his presidency. He also said that one of the primary problems which Clinton faced both as governor and as president is the people with whom he surrounds himself. He said that the president tends to surround himself with a small circle of friends. "They were the only ones he would listen to, and most of them didn't know what the hell they were doing." Dickey added, "He tried to have his fingers in all the pies and had just enough general knowledge to be dangerous."

Several months ago, when Hillary's father was seriously ill, Dickey encountered the president in the hallway of his building and rode in the elevator with the president. "I think everyone had a hard time calling him Mr. President instead of Bill, and I saw him in the hall and said, 'Hello, Mr. President'—I was going to be formal." Clinton reportedly responded, "Hello, how's my pal?" As the elevator descended, Dickey said, he started to say something about the women in D.C. but elected not to. Instead, he said to the president, "I'm praying for you, Bill, and I know you got your work cut out." Clinton responded, "Well, I'm surrounded by a good group." Dickey said he shook his head, saying, "My God, you're taking that same group up there with you. It's going to be bad."

Dickey made it evident that not all of the staffers that went with the president to Washington, D.C. were incompetent. He named several people who were particularly effective in their political skills while Clinton was governor. Foremost on that list was Betsey Wright, whom Dickey described as "politically competent, politically astute, a real power broker. She's about the best there is." He stated that he believes it was an error by Clinton not to utilize her more during the presidency. "She's the best one that he's got, and he doesn't use her, that's typical." Dickey did point out that whenever Clinton develops a crisis, Ms. Wright surfaces, "putting the spin on it."

CHAPTER SEVENTEEN

An Interview With Joseph Purvis, Attorney-at-Law

THE INTERVIEW WITH BERT DICKEY contrasts sharply with the impression of Clinton presented in this interview and the one that follows. (The results of the three interviews will be presented in detail and related to issues involving the ACOA.)

Joseph Purvis has been a close friend of President Clinton's since childhood. They grew up together in Hope, Arkansas, and have maintained their close bond throughout their adult lives. Purvis's mother was a good friend of Clinton's mother, Virginia Kelley. As a result, he has had the opportunity to attend school with Clinton as a child and to work with him as an adult. Their friendship enables Purvis to visit Clinton in Washington, D.C., despite the president's very busy schedule. He also is very close to Thomas "Mack" McLarty, former chief of staff, and was a good friend of the late Vincent Foster.

Purvis also had a professional relationship with the president, serving as head of the Criminal Division of the Arkansas state attorney general's office while Clinton was attorney general. That particular experience provided Purvis with additional knowledge about Clinton's leadership style and management approach.

A lifelong friend of the president's, Purvis was clear in stating that it was essential to him that this interview be presented in a manner in which the reader clearly understood his strong support for Clinton. He approached the interview cautiously and sought assurance that this book was not sponsored by any group attempting to harm the president. I assured him that I was entirely responsible for this work and that no group sponsorship was involved. When informed that the focus of this work centered on various psychological factors that I associated with Clinton, Purvis appropriately brought up the issue of confirmatory bias. Such bias occurs when a researcher has predetermined the outcome of the research and obtains information to confirm that outcome.

Although this response was not discussed with Purvis, I think it would be helpful for the reader to realize that the issue of Clinton's being a child growing up in an alcoholic home is an established fact which does not require formulation of a hypothesis to determine its accuracy. The impact of ACOA factors is more open to interpretation. It is obviously my contention that the impact was significant and has had a deleterious effect upon Clinton.

Purvis further questioned whether a psychological assessment of an individual can be conducted accurately without personal clinical interviews and psychological testing. I related to him that the type of psychological factors which I believed affected Clinton were behavioral problems rather than deep-seated psychological issues, such as personality disorders.

Given those assurances, Purvis granted an interview. Care has been taken to present his comments with accurate quotations and to cast them in light of his support and affection for the president. Purvis said, "He and I are lifelong friends. I have had a problem in the past with things that I have said to some individuals that have been taken out of context and misconstrued." The reader is assured that throughout the entire interview, Purvis said nothing in that was intended to reflect negatively on Clinton.

Purvis epitomized the genteel manners of many people whom I met in Little Rock. On very short notice, he agreed to meet with me. He gave up his Father's Day afternoon with his family. He even picked me up at my hotel. His automobile was adorned with a Clinton-Gore bumper sticker from the presidential campaign. The interview was conducted in his office, high above the city of Little Rock. The state capitol, where Clinton conducted the affairs of the state for the majority of the past decade, was a short distance away.

CHILDHOOD MEMORIES

As previously mentioned, Purvis grew up with Clinton, McLarty, and Foster in Hope, Arkansas. His childhood memories of Clinton's family are positive. He described them as "very middle class all the way through. Salt-of-the-earth folks." Clinton, he recalled, was "very much a peacemaker. The kind who was always sort of the arbiter if people were involved in altercations or fights. He was usually the peacemaker that stepped in, that made peace, that did the bridging, if you will, between the two parties."

Purvis recalled an event in which Clinton regrettably was ridiculed by his classmates. It was a kindergarten story in which Clinton was jumping rope. "He fell and hit the ground, and his cowboy-boot heel caught the high jump rope. My good friend, here in Little Rock, is the one who pulled the rope as he fell. He started crying and screaming. Everybody circled around and said, 'Billy's a sissy.' And it turned out he'd broken his leg in four places and spent about six weeks in traction with the leg up. We really felt horrible."

THE ATTORNEY GENERAL'S OFFICE

When Clinton was state attorney general, Purvis worked in that office as head of the criminal division. Purvis provided insight into Clinton's management and leadership. He said that Clinton operated the office on the "Do Right Rule." The "Do Right Rule," according to Purvis, was highlighted by former University of Arkansas football coach Lou Holtz. Approximately sixteen years ago, Holtz suspended two of the team's premier football players from an Orange Bowl game which potentially could have landed the university the national title. The players were suspended for an incident with a woman. A civil rights attorney filed suit to prevent Holtz from suspending the players from the game.

When Holtz appeared in federal court, he declared that the players "violated the 'Do Right Rule.' I don't ask much of these fellows, but I do expect them to do right. These twenty-plus-year-old men are certainly old enough to know the difference between right and wrong in this situation, and they may not have violated a law, but as far as I'm concerned, I'm the coach of this team, and they violated the 'Do Right Rule' and will not make the trip."

Purvis related the Holtz story to explain how Clinton ran the attorney general's office. He said, "There were a lot of highly intelligent people that were part of the administration that were all young, that did not mind working, did not mind putting in eighteen- to twenty-hour days."

Some of the issues which involved the office at that time included prison reform and consumer protection. According to Purvis, procedures employed by "the state penitentiary had been declared unconstitutional by the federal court." The action taken related to overcrowding and overall prison conditions. The current governor of Arkansas, Guy Tucker, was attorney general the four years preceding Clinton's election to that post. During that time, "there had been some rather extensive litigation over the conditions of the prison. It [the overcrowding and prison conditions] was struck down as unconstitutional or declared unconstitutional for a number of different reasons—the treatment of prisoners and the food that they served, just the general way the prison was operating." The litigation found its way to the U.S. Supreme Court. The language from the case described the prison "as a dark and bloody place." Purvis said that "Bill made that a real top priority, bringing that into constitutional compliance."

Purvis described the Clinton attorney-general years as "a real good, energetic time, 1976, really 1977 through 1979. It was just a good, very activist time." He credited Clinton with providing direction for actions taken while he was attorney general. "Bill obviously provided the leadership on all of that. There were no policy decisions really made without his input. He was very much involved in directing the leadership in all of those issues."

Purvis described Clinton as a man who worked long hours, and told of an instance in which a staffer did not share Clinton's work ethic. "My area was criminal law, and we might get a call from his office asking if we could meet at four-thirty, five. We had a meeting one day, early on, and several of the deputy AGs, talking about prisons, about a number of different things, almost like a staff meeting, and we would go in and bring up problems, and getting direction, how to proceed. One of the older deputies who'd been there for several years had a buzzer on his watch that went off at five. Clinton looked around and said, 'What the hell was that?' It was just five. This was a guy that walked out of there at five every day. He [Clinton] just kind of shook his head, and we kept going."

I asked Purvis about Clinton's reputation as a workaholic. He said, "He is. You know, normal people will take vacations, and he'll take a vacation, but the man is incredible in his stamina." He said Clinton has worked until two or three in the morning for years. "He's sort of famous for calling people at one in the morning, saying, 'Did I wake you?' I mean, he'll be wired, and he'll have something on his mind and be going through it. I think he's got a study area there on the second floor of the White House, and he'll go to that and use that at night. Although the job itself pretty much gives itself to fifteen-, twenty-hour days." He stated that Clinton "will run himself to exhaustion but pretty much subsists on about four hours sleep."

ARKANSAS POLITICS

I asked Purvis about the divided opinion about Clinton held by people of Little Rock. Purvis expressed a theory to explain why some people hold negative views. He said, "There are a hell of a lot of people that are envious. I think there are a hell of a lot of people who basically have such an inferiority complex about this state that they refuse to believe anything decent can come out of here. A lot of it is just flat out jealousy. Growing up to be president of the United States is literally the dream we tell kids. I mean, you can grow up to be president."

He continued his explanation of why people of Arkansas suffer from a feeling of inferiority. "There were so many skeptics when he announced for president. It's like people can't believe it. What is the old adage? 'A prophet in his own city is not appreciated.' I don't think that's fully true, but there are an awful lot of people that are jealous."

Purvis attributes part of the current rancor to Arkansas state political dealings. He detailed his perspective on some of the maneuvering that occurred prior to and during the 1990 gubernatorial election. One of the individuals involved, Sheffield Nelson, is a man of whom Purvis speaks well personally. Nelson is an influential member of the Arkansas political world and is an attorney in Little Rock. He is a Republican who was unsuccessful in his 1994 election bid challenging Governor Guy Tucker for the governorship. "He and I have a cordial relationship, but he really has a hang-up about Bill." According to Purvis, Nelson considered running for governor in 1990. "He wanted to run. You've got to understand that in 1990 Bill Clinton appeared to be dead politically." Clinton's motivation to be governor had apparently waned. "He, by his own admission, had lost the fire in his belly with the legislature. He had been governor for ten years. And it's like a ten-year affair, the thing, his relationship had grown old. The legislature was full of a bunch of good old boys in key positions that were anti-Clinton, and everybody sort of sensed that Clinton was not going to run for reelection in 1990, and he had all but announced that he would not run."

Purvis described how Clinton's long tenure as governor was one reason why the 1990 gubernatorial race resulted in division. "All of these people, after a ten-year period of time, there had been something of a void, this vacuum, whatever you want to call it, in leadership. There had been a bottleneck, so with everyone speculating that Clinton would not, indeed, run in 1990, folks really began scurrying." One of the hopefuls for the Democratic nomination for governor was then Attorney General Steve Clark. Purvis alleges: "Steve Clark, who was attorney general and a real mental and political lightweight, had been attorney general as long as Clinton had been governor. He began scurrying to get folks lined up to contribute to his campaign."

The other significant player in the Democratic nomination process was Sheffield Nelson. Purvis said he understood that a number of people had encouraged Nelson not to run. They were concerned about his having headed "one of the two largest utilities in the state of Arkansas." Nelson was president of ArklaGas, Inc. Purvis said, "But he really seemed intent on running. It appeared, however, that brother Clark was drying up most of the Democratic money." Purvis said that Nelson then changed his party affiliation to Republican.

According to Purvis, Nelson had made some political enemies along the way. He went on: "When Nelson became president of ArklaGas, he turned and bit the hand that fed him, the Stephens folks, who owned and controlled ArklaGas at that time." The Stephens family, Jackson T., Mary Anne, and Wilton R., is extremely influential in the state of Arkansas. They have contributed to Clinton's campaigns but do not have a history of always being supportive of the president. Purvis said that the Stephenses wanted Nelson to "continue doing some things that led to sweetheart deals for them. He didn't do it. He made an undying enemy in the whole Stephens family. They loathe Nelson to this day. And even now, the biggest contributors to his Republican opposition in the governorship were folks from the Stephenses."

According to Purvis, as a result of the Stephens-Nelson rift, the Stephens family encouraged a congressman, Tommy Robinson, to oppose Nelson in the Republican primary. Robinson also was a former Democrat who had become a Republican. Robinson had been a sheriff of Pulaski County and, Purvis said, was "involved in more litigation than any sheriff before. In fact, the bunch that I used to be with when I left the AG's office in 1980, we represented the insurance company that carried the sheriff's malpractice-insurance coverage. They wound up dropping Robinson as Pulaski county sheriff because they told us they had more open litigation files involving Robinson and his administration for alleged beating of prisoners, violations of civil rights, and that sort of stuff on him than on any other sheriff in the country, and probably any two or three combined." Purvis declared, "Robinson was a wise, redneck cracker."

During the primary campaign, he said, "Nelson and Robinson go at it hammer and tongs, with Robinson accusing Nelson and his buddy, Jerry Jones, who owns the Dallas Cowboys, of making a number of sweetheart deals that padded each of their pockets. Although, ostensibly, it was padding Jones's pocket—and there's no question Jones's pocket was padded. Anyway, Robinson and Nelson wind up literally assassinating, killing, themselves in the Republican primary."

Clinton surveyed the political landscape. The Republican candidates were fighting each other. The Democratic hopeful, Steve Clark, "gets involved in a scandal that winds up with him being convicted of misapplication of public funds." This was a reference to the credit-card problem. Purvis related the scandal as "the credit card deal; shoots himself in foot, blows himself up, gets a felony conviction." So Purvis thinks Clinton examined the field for governor and reflected, "I may be tired of being governor, but I really don't have any place to go politically. If I step out, there is no senate seat coming open. Where will I go?" So Clinton "reluctantly files at that point for reelection."

The impact of Clinton's reentering the gubernatorial race proved significant. "It did two things. It put a screeching halt on Clark's campaign money from the Democratic side, and Clark's problems literally took him out. So Clinton really had token Democratic opposition. Nelson wins a very bloody Republican primary and runs against Clinton."

The result of the 1990 election was that "Sheffield (Nelson) gets beat real good. Clinton wins in a walkaway, and not only does he win, but Clinton's primary obstacles in the legislature also get upset. The end result is that in the span of about seven to eight months, Clinton goes from being in political limbo, almost never-never land, to being governor and with a legislature that's ready and willing to do whatever he wants to do. And Clinton himself gets invigorated. But I think, Sheffield, it really stuck in his craw that he got beat."

I contacted Nelson for an interview. He was unavailable because at the time he was running for governor.

The political scenery in Arkansas is important because it describes how Clinton's rise to the presidency is indeed remarkable considering that in 1990 even his loyal friends thought that his political options were coming to an end. Purvis attributed Clinton's rejuvenation as governor and politician to the political climate and the legislative upsets.

Included in the 1990 campaign was Clinton's famous promise to his Arkansas constituents that he would not leave office to seek the presidency prior to the conclusion of his term. I asked Purvis about that pledge, since some cite it as an example of Clinton's looseness with the truth. Purvis responded, "It's almost like, gee, Billy Bob, if we name you captain of our Babe Ruth or our American Legion team, will you promise not to go to the major leagues?" Basically, then, it was an opportunity not to be refused. "Sure, you get the opportunity, what are you going to do? The state of Arkansas really didn't suffer as a result of it, in fact, benefited, if anything. But, so the people who resented that statement and thought it shows a deep character flaw were the people that really didn't care for Clinton in the first place."

I mentioned to Purvis that this is one of the points related to credibility issues. His response was to describe the national political climate at the time and the inner workings of Clinton. "In 1990 I don't think anybody in their right mind thought George Bush would be denied a second term. In 1990, we've got Gulf Storm. George Bush is a guy that has what? A ninety-one percent approval rating, the highest of all time, probably, by the American public. And you know, by the tail end of 1991, Clinton had obviously decided to run for it. He wouldn't have made a run had he not thought there was a chance to win."

Purvis said that at the time of Clinton's decision to seek the presidential nomination, "there were a lot of folks that felt he ought to wait until 1996, when Bush's term is up. Whoever runs will just be cannon fodder, and it was obvious to people like Gephardt, Nunn, others who were prominently mentioned as potential Democratic candidates, felt the same way and they backed off." Interestingly, much like Clinton's assessment of the political opposition in the Arkansas gubernatorial race in 1990, he sized up the opposition for the Democratic nomination for president.

"The first guy, I guess, to announce was probably Tsongas, a very nice man but certainly never been accused of being a guy that inspired. He talked, bless his heart, like Elmer Fudd." Purvis's point is that Clinton's decision to run was due, in part, to the declared field of opposition. "There were a number of factors that entered, that played, into this. In the intervening year between the time he's elected in 1990 and October of 1991 when he decides, 'I'm going to get into the race.' "

He again rejected the contention that Clinton's response indicated a character flaw. "Is it anymore than the parent who says, 'You're not going to do such and such,' and then a year and a half later says, 'Well, I think we will do such and such.' "

For Purvis, the change in Clinton's mind came about because of changing circumstances. "Circumstances change, and Clinton was pretty forthright at the time. I mean, he didn't make any secret of it. It was pretty well known and rumored for a good while that he was thinking seriously about the run, and he obviously conferred with a number of people, and he came out and talked when he made the public speech."

Purvis said that the political insiders were privy to Clinton's decision only shortly before it was made public. "I don't think anybody was really aware that he was giving it serious consideration until, say, the last month to six weeks before he announced. Probably September, August, or September of 1991. There were rumors, but, I mean, who from Arkansas had ever run for president? Nobody's going to do that."

He was referring to the inferiority complex which he believes inhibits Arkansans. "I mean, it's not as though the world was beating down Arkansas' door at that point in time. Clinton had certainly been viewed in a number of national publications as one of the potential rising stars of the Democratic party. And it was one of those things that, I'm assuming, he looks around and sees nobody else is going to step up and announce, and there were a ton of people that literally said, discounting the so-called pledge that 'I'm not going to run', that said, 'Man, you're crazy. What in the world do you want to do this for? You're listening to people who are going to take money for giving political advice and the election is over and you will have spent or indebted yourself several million bucks. These people will have their money. They'll skip back to Boston, Chicago, New York, Los Angeles, wherever, and you'll be back here at the statehouse in Arkansas after having your tail whipped.' "

Purvis disclosed further thoughts about the political decision making involved in Clinton's decision to run for the nomination. "In this day and age of media electronics you get really one run at the presidency. And a lot of people figure, 'Okay, if you get the nomination, but then what?' You know, it's like the gift nobody wants because of Bush's popularity." Purvis mentioned such national figures as Sen. Sam Nunn and Rep. Richard Gephardt as probable challengers in 1996. "And the other thing, I guess from a strategy standpoint, if people that arguably have a lot greater name recognition than you do are going to be in the run in 1996, you know, you're going to spend a ton of money just trying to get your name known. Much tougher to win, for anybody to win." Purvis concluded, "There were probably a lot more people that just thought he was crazy for making the attempt in 1991 than castigated him for changing his mind, going back on his word."

The small population of the state of Arkansas affects the manner in which business dealings occur. Arkansas has a population of 2 million people, about one-quarter the population of the city of Los

Angeles. The major business dealings, therefore, take place between "the same people over and over again. In any given state you have people who are powerful people, the Golden Rule still applies. The gold generally rules. We'd like to delude ourselves into believing that people with huge sums of money don't influence government wherever you are. But it's just a fact of life. Anywhere you are, people with money are going to have influence and clout." The powerful people in a state with the population of Arkansas are comparatively few.

"Money talks, that's exactly right, and it's in any jurisdiction where you are, power is going to be concentrated. The only difference is, in Los Angeles and California, what, a state with fifty million [approximately thirty-one million] people, it's going to be spread more than it is in a state of two million people." Despite the smaller concentration of wealth and power, Purvis strongly defended the people of Arkansas and their character. "There has been an intimation that everybody down here is either the biggest bunch of lying, cheating sons of bitches or that we're all married to our first cousin. This state's no different than anywhere else."

DECISION MAKING AND INTELLECT

Purvis speaks with admiration of Clinton's intellectual abilities. He declares, "The guy's got a brilliant mind, a brilliant mind." He said that not only his supporters but his detractors as well realize Clinton's intellect. "A fellow that I talked to that I've known for a long time, never liked him [Clinton], never voted for him, said, 'I'll tell you in all candor, I've never seen anybody like him. He's brilliant, he's resilient, he's just unlike anybody I've even known. I mean, I've known people who were good in some areas, but it's like, in so many ways, it's like there's a computer up there, up top. That stuff is running through, and it's constantly being analyzed.' "

Purvis has visited Clinton in Washington, D.C., several times since the election. He attended the inauguration ceremonies and returned to visit his friend in April 1993 and April 1994. He gave an example of Clinton's tremendous capacity to remember detail. During the latest visit to Washington, D.C., "he and I had not had a talk about my family in, I don't know how long, probably ten years. And yet he knew my brother was still in [a particular town in Arkansas]. My brother's been down there probably five or six years, a little longer than that. But I mean, he knew."

He also described Clinton's decision making style. "I heard somebody the other day talking about Clinton's style of making a decision. He's incredible. I never knew anybody that tried to get more information on a topic before he will make a decision. If we were doing something when we were at the AG's office in a criminal area, he might talk to me two or three times and then question me about specific areas, and he'd talk out loud. And it would take him awhile to make up his mind. But usually when he made it up, he was pretty firm."

It was fascinating to hear Purvis's analysis of the decision-making process, because it revealed Purvis's explanation for some of the difficulties the president is experiencing. He said, "The thing that I think he's getting some flak for now is maybe thinking out loud before the final decision is made. And you know, maybe he shouldn't do that." I questioned him about whether he meant that some of the questions of credibility for the president are because of his "thinking out loud" before formulating his true opinion. He responded, "Yeah, I think so."

SEXUALITY

I asked Purvis to comment on Clinton's sexual notoriety. He first mentioned the president's handling of the Gennifer Flowers situation during the primaries. Purvis said, "I think he dealt with it about as well as it could be dealt with. If you come out and you say, 'I have had,' and you know, I'm not saying that he has or he hasn't, but the fact is that if you come out and say, 'Yes, ladies and gentlemen of the press, I had a prior affair,' then you invite and beg the next question. Which is, 'How many? Who? When?' And at some point, you simply draw the line."

Purvis considered the president's privacy versus the public's right to know. "If you say, well, the public has a right to know as to whether or not my officials are pure and chaste. Part of the problem that we're looking at is that people tend to forget, we don't elect a saint, we're not electing God or Jesus or something like that. We're electing politicians. We're electing leaders and none of us are perfect. I think he handled it really about as well as he could have handled it in simply saying, 'We [Bill and Hillary have] had problems in the past. The main thing is, our marriage is stronger than ever right now, and we're together.' "

He took a similar position in response to a question about the number of affairs that Clinton has had. "You know, I don't know. I remember a story that a fellow told me several years ago. He was talking about the press and how it changed." The press at the time of the Kennedy administration was more willing to overlook indiscretions than the press is today. "This fellow is hanging around the lobby, and he's watching, and my friend goes back to his editor and says, 'Boss, it's incredible. There are all kinds of people going in and out of that suite. A ton of them are women. This guy, Kennedy, is having some affairs.' The editor reportedly responded, 'I couldn't give a rip about this guy's personal life. What I want to know is who are the deal makers that are going in there, that are cutting deals that are affecting the future of this country. I want to know who he's meeting with and doing what.' "

Purvis related the story to point out how the interest level has changed from when reporters were willing to overlook presidential foibles to now, when journalists report them. He said, "I think it goes back, again to the fact that, if we're looking for saints, if we're looking for perfection . . ." He then compared some of the more recent presidents to Clinton. About Reagan, Purvis said, "I think he was too old to have any kind of affair and wouldn't know if he did unless Nancy told him." He recalled the "pretty hot rumor" about Bush which surfaced during the presidential campaign. He said that

Bush "got extremely testy in a hurry. And it did strike me now, in the light of what we're looking at, that the press backed off. But I think they did the right thing, whether he did or he didn't." He then referred to Eisenhower's affair, Carter's lusting of the heart, and Nixon as "asexual."

Further comment about presidential sexual behavior included his belief that one would find "the same thing if you look over in business. I'm sure that there are a number of corporate executives in the business world that have had their affairs of the heart. I don't know whether the president has had any or not. Whether he has or he hasn't really is no matter to me now."

He did comment about both Gennifer Flowers and Paula Corbin Jones. Regarding Flowers, Purvis said, "Gennifer Flowers never did say who . . . She admitted there were some people who had paid her an awful lot of money, but she never did say who they were." This was in reference to Flowers's decision to speak publicly about the alleged long-term affair.

Purvis discredits some of the allegations as political fireballing by the Republicans. "The Republicans, I think, have just done a terrific job of trying to run a smear campaign to take focus off legitimate issues that are facing this country, by trying to bring up a scandal a day and all this." He included Paula Corbin Jones as an example of scandal mongering. He made a comment that was not complimentary about Jones's sexual history.

I had a telephone conversation with Joseph Cammarata, Ms. Jones's attorney, on July 26, 1994. Cammarata flatly denied the allegation: "It is a bald-faced lie. It is irresponsible and totally untrue." He expressed concern about the inclusion of the derogatory comment about his client. "Even though it is completely untrue, when unsubstantiated things like that are printed, they take on a life of their own." I did not include the specifics of the allegation, since I was unable to substantiate it.

Purvis's contention is that much of the sexual concerns exposed about Clinton are attempts to detract from important issues. "If we can't derail him with a smear based on personal attacks, then what we'll try to do is bring up enough of these little things to trivialize him. That people brush him off and don't give him any consequence. They think of scandal, oh, God, not again. Well, in that sense, it may have worked. And how do you fight that? How do you take the high road and say, 'Look, these are problems, these are issues confronting our country, not just us but our children. We need to deal with now.' "

A fair characterization of Purvis's position regarding the sexual issue would be: He does not know whether the allegations of sexual affairs are true or false. Regardless, he thinks they are not an important issue for press or public concern, and the Republican party is utilizing the sexual innuendoes as a means to discredit the president and sway public focus from the "real issues."

POLICIES AND LIMBAUGH

Some of the "real issues" have been addressed by Clinton and enumerated by Purvis. He also made comment about one particular observer of the Clinton White House. Purvis's statements about Rush Limbaugh were made several days before President Clinton's well-publicized comments about Limbaugh. While aboard *Air Force One*, the president complained to a St. Louis radio station of a lack of opportunity to respond to the three hours that Limbaugh discoursed on the radio. Therefore, I will include Purvis's comments about Limbaugh.

Purvis thinks Clinton went to the White House with a strong agenda. He contrasted this position with his perception of Bush in the White House. "Bush, I think, wanted to be president, but he didn't really have any agenda. And Bush, I think, was caught in the in-between. I think, philosophically, in a lot of ways, he was much closer to Clinton than he was to Ronald Reagan. But he was trapped by the Republican party and these conservatives who put him there as Reagan's logical successor. I mean, he didn't have a clue. He was marching in place for four years. You can't do that."

In contrast to Bush, Purvis said, "Clinton may have faults, but a lack of vision isn't one of them. The health care, crime legislation, and some other things." He reported about someone who had complained about Clinton not pushing further for gays in the military, but Purvis defended Clinton's position. "For the first time in the history of this country, you had somebody who brought the issues of gays in the service to the table and proposed a resolution of it. And he promptly got it shoved up his nose at the cost of a good deal of political capital early on by Sam Nunn and a number of members of Congress. It was obvious that it would not have passed. It was obvious that he could have signed the order but it would not have flown. What did you expect him to do? He got an improvement."

Purvis mentioned gun-control legislation as an example of good policy in the Clinton agenda. "For all the criticism that he's gotten —and he's gotten criticism from the good old boys—and I can't figure out how the NRA or anybody would mind banning semiautomatic weapons." Purvis thinks the policy should not have been so harshly attacked, particularly "when you've got the chiefs of police of the country that are asking for the bill to be done and James Brady, Reagan's press secretary, begging for the bill."

Purvis described Clinton as a very caring individual. "The thing that's incredible about Clinton, he really, really, has a love for people. And a real sense of the future and of things that he believes needs to happen to better society. He really cares, and it sounds so trite, it sounds so corny." Purvis hopes that the "core of about forty-two or forty-three percent" will hold and continue to support Clinton, indicating that they are the people who "see through all the crap, and the slime, and the innuendo, the Flush [sic] Limbaugh and those people, and see what's there at the core is somebody who cares very much about the country and about the people. Who has an agenda of things we ought to be doing and wants to move ahead."

He contended that critics of Clinton have some credibility problems of their own. He cited Senator Alphonse D'Amato of New York as someone who was critical of Clinton's financial dealings. "Give me a break. D'Amato admits he makes thirty-seven grand in a one-day transaction." He did not speak negatively about Congressman Jim Leach but downplayed the legitimacy of a Whitewater investigation. "There isn't anything to Whitewater. We're spending millions and millions of dollars and wasting all kinds of time to give somebody a political issue. There's nothing there."

A discussion of Vincent Foster, which follows shortly, included an additional salvo directed at Limbaugh. Purvis was angry with Limbaugh for his handling of the Foster story. He said, "I got really angry over a lot of that. Rush Limbaugh's on a tape delay here of one hour and I had been somewhere and this was a couple of days after Vince's death and Limbaugh is really a master of innuendo and slime. He would characterize himself, I think, as a political satirist. But he raises specious innuendo and smears slime over really one of the best fellows that I've ever known." Purvis became so agitated over Limbaugh's comment on Vince Foster that he " started to call him up and say, 'You know, you grew up about two hundred miles from here up at Cape Girardeau, Missouri. Same part of the country, so you know what I'm speaking of. When you—if your mother knew that you were doing just a slanderous character assassination of a fellow who was dead with no basis and like this, she would probably wash your mouth out with soap and kick your fat ass and send you to bed.' " He concluded, "And that's probably what should have been done."

VINCENT FOSTER

The source of Purvis's ire was his perception that reporters from the *New York Post* "were working in concert with Limbaugh on this rumor that there was a love shack. Vince Foster was killed in a love shack and was there with Hillary and all that. I just said, 'That's just garbage.' " According to Purvis, the *Post* reporters said they "have talked to some of the federal investigators in all this, and they have told me that there is no way that this could be a suicide." Purvis told the reporters that having served in his position in the attorney general's office, he was aware that any investigators who revealed such information about an ongoing investigation would and should lose their jobs. He told the reporters that he had no knowledge of a love shack. "I said, as far as I know, the little bit I have learned, the investigators are pretty conclusive that he did, indeed, kill himself."

Following the telephone conversation with the *Post* reporters, Purvis received information that Limbaugh was on the radio interviewing the *Post* reporter with whom he had just spoken. The reporter was informing Limbaugh's listeners that his "sources tell me that there was an apartment." Purvis said, "It's the same clown I've been talking to. I became the source."

Foster was a close friend of Purvis's, and it was with obvious sadness that he recounted his thoughts about his friend. He said, "Put the pieces together and there are a whole lot of reasons, but the bottom line is that Vince was obviously suffering from clinical depression that no one realized until it was too late to do anything about it. And that's a good deal of a pressure cooker."

Upon reflection, he said, "Vince could have probably been helped. Vince probably could have come home earlier than he did and would have been [helped], but he couldn't have done that because he was a perfectionist. He was working in a vital position for two of his best friends in the world, a position that he thought really mattered. He thought they really needed him, and Vince couldn't admit failure. Vince couldn't have come back to Little Rock three months after having gone to Washington because he would have believed people would say behind his back that he couldn't cut it." Purvis described aspects of Foster's personality which offer insight into the development of the depression. He also spoke with him not long before his death.

"He had never failed at anything in his life. I talked with him several times in the six months that he was there, the last time probably about six weeks before he died. And it was amazing. He was low, and I just said, 'You need to come on home. Take a long weekend off and just come home. There's a bunch of us that love you, that would like to see you and have a beer with you.' And he said, 'Well, I'm coming home for the bar.' And then he couldn't come home and sent Hubbel home to pick up the award. That was in mid-June. But what a tragedy."

The impact of clinical depression is significant and certainly can result in the suicidal action that Purvis believes Foster took. Having been pained by the death of his friend, Purvis was willing to reveal this personal information, partially in the hope that others who feel depressed will seek help.

THOMAS "MACK" MCLARTY

Purvis also defended his other childhood friend, Mack McLarty, who was Clinton's chief of staff and currently is a counselor to the president. At the time of the interview, McLarty was still chief of staff but was facing criticism for his style.

Purvis described McLarty as "very courtly, but there's steel underneath. And Mack is one of those people who will be extremely friendly, but you don't get anything out of Mack that he doesn't want to give you." He thinks McLarty was misunderstood because of his style. "That's been one of the problems that people have had with McLarty, as opposed to his predecessors. In Woodward's book he is portrayed as being disorganized. I just said, 'That's garbage.' Because I've known him all my life, too, and he was born forty-five years ago making lists and working on a timetable and a schedule that he adheres to very, very strictly."

Purvis questioned the knowledge of those who informed Woodward otherwise. "I don't know who Woodward talked to, but the people he talked to that indicated they thought he was disorganized are obviously a bunch of people who have never had any experience in dealing at that level and are obviously not very mature people."

He commented on the dedication that McLarty and his coworkers exhibited. "Think of how many issues cross your desk every day. I've got some friends that are deputies working under him, and I don't know how they do it. He probably has four or five deputy chiefs of staff, and they're all working on a thirteen- to fifteen-hour day, five days a week. And then probably a six- to seven-hour day on the sixth day. If you've got a family, it doesn't leave much time." He summarized his position by saying, "That's a bum rap. I know him, and I've known him all my life, and it's a bum rap."

HILLARY CLINTON

Purvis described the First Lady as a "really nice lady, sharp lady." He gives one of the reasons that she faces such strong opposition: "It's amazing how many people, most of them male, can't accept a sharp, tough woman." He said that some men think that politics is "the last area other than baseball safe for men to be an exclusive men's club" and that they are, therefore, resistant to women such as Hillary Clinton when they encroach upon their playing field.

He also related information about the personal relationship of the president and the First Lady. I asked him about questions why the First Lady remained in the marriage despite Clinton's alleged affairs. Was it because he was her means to obtain political power?

He replied, "I really don't think that. I have been around them in about as private a moment [as a couple can have], and I know the affection that's there. I know the hand holding and the hugging and the kissing that goes on when no cameras and press are present." He continued by confirming that there have been difficult times in the Clinton marriage. "They've had some tough times, but they're going to weather it out. It isn't a marriage of convenience. It's really one of love."

Purvis agreed that questions about her role as chair of the health-care committee without an appointment or election was worthy of study. The lack of oversight, according to Purvis, "is a fair question to ask. I think you can't have it both ways. If you're going to take that on, in all fairness, I think you've got to be answerable to some people. I think you ought to come before Congress or whomever and make a full explanation."

CLINTON AS AN ADULT CHILD
OF AN ALCOHOLIC

The interview with Purvis provided considerable insight into the political atmosphere in Arkansas and his personal relationships with many of the key people in the administration. He also was forthcoming in a discussion of Clinton's ACOA background and adult issues common to ACOA. What made the discussion particularly interesting was that Purvis revealed that he himself had grown up in a home with an alcoholic parent. Although they were close friends and grew up in similar circumstances, Purvis and Clinton did not discuss this background as an issue in their lives until very recently.

Purvis considers their childhood an "interesting situation." He said, "There's a whole lot that goes on that affects you as a child of an alcoholic. A lot of the time you don't even realize you're being affected by it."

That was an interesting point because so often ACOA are unaware of the impact of their childhood on their day-to-day lives. He described the different reactions people have who come from such homes. "Different people react in different ways. People react sometimes with violence." He related the previously mentioned story about Clinton's interceding on behalf of his mother when his stepfather was behaving in a violent way. "His dad's drunk, or stepdad's drunk. He starts hitting Virginia. And he [Clinton] pops the door down." Clinton confronted his stepfather and said, "You'll never do that again." Purvis said, "And, I mean, I've been there, I know of what he speaks."

Purvis previously had described young Clinton as a peacemaker. When describing a child's life in an alcoholic home, he said, "Generally, I think that there's probably a yearning for peace. Because you don't have peace in your home." He said most children do not experience such conflict in their homes. "Most of the open conflict we have, at least when we're that age, occurs at school or in

our relations with others. When we come home, home is suppos-
edly a safe haven. Or at least it was viewed that way in the fifties
and sixties." He pointed out the difference for the child of the alcoholic. "With an alcoholic there isn't peace at home."

He reinforced my comment that the alcoholic's home is chaotic.
"It's worse than chaotic, because you can't carry on a normal relationship; because you can't bring anybody home. You literally never
know what you are going to find at home."

The lack of stability is particularly unsettling. "You can walk in
and everything will be fine. In his [Clinton's] case, either dad will
not be there, or if dad is there, dad may be sober and everything is
fine. Or you can walk in and find Dad passed out on the floor. Or
you can walk in and find Dad passed out in the carport or the
garage. Or you can walk in and Dad's half drunk and getting
drunker and getting mean. You just can't, you can't depend on a
stable home." Purvis said that Clinton's mother offered him some
love and stability to an otherwise worse than chaotic setting. "She
was there, she was strong, and she gave him love. But the fact is he
didn't have [stability] you know."

Purvis believes Clinton's time in Hot Springs, during his school-
age years, was spent away from his home. He assumes that in Hot
Springs Clinton spent "probably the majority of his free time at the
house of his friends." Most children growing up in such homes
attempt to minimize their home life to others.

This speculation is likely because the two friends did not discuss their dilemmas during their youth. "Several people who did not
grow up in alcoholic homes said, 'Why didn't you tell somebody?' "
Purvis indicated that such a question shows a lack of understanding
of the severity of the child's dilemma. "What do you tell, and who
do you tell? I mean, in a relatively small town most of your neighbors, and most people, are going to know anyway."

He described the embarrassment. People would know that
"Roger's a drunk. You know, he's drunk again, he's doing such and
such." For a child to disclose the information openly would be "like
standing on the street yelling, 'I'm sexually impotent' or something

like that." He indicated that such a revelation would leave the child raw and vulnerable. "Why would you want to reveal these deep inner things about your family that are family things?" he said, referring to the child's thought process.

Despite their close relationship, the two friends first discussed their mutual ACOA problems when Purvis visited Washington, D.C., in April 1994. He said of the president, "We talked a little bit about that [the ACOA experiences] for the first time, probably, this April [1994], and he was intrigued by that."

Clinton was also intrigued by the ACOA issues and with Purvis's similar family background. "His mother and my mother were very good friends." He believes that Clinton might have been aware of Purvis's family problems through information that Clinton's mother could have given him. Purvis himself has begun to address the ACOA issues "Only in the last year or two, I think, that I've been able to talk about a lot of the stuff that went on."

We discussed that opportunities now are available to resolve conflicts that remain from such childhood experiences. He said, "I think a lot of that comes from just getting it out, from talking with people about it." I told him that many of the problems occur as a result of withholding the pain from the childhood traumas. He replied, "That's exactly what it is, and you tend to hold a lot of things in that maybe otherwise you wouldn't." I mentioned that emotions are one of the primary things that are withheld and that such an approach negatively impacts personal relationships. He agreed that "very often that can happen."

Purvis concluded the discussion of the topic of ACOAs by responding to my comment about how he and Clinton were close in many ways and yet had secret lives that they kept to themselves. He said, "My dear grandmother used to say, 'No one knows what demons play in each of our minds.' "

CHAPTER EIGHTEEN

An Interview With Cpl. David Donham

Cpl. David Donham is an Arkansas state trooper. He has served as an officer for twenty-three years. He was assigned to the security detail of then governor Clinton during the first two years of his governorship. Experiences with Clinton left Donham with a very favorable impression. He kindly conveyed his thoughts about the president during an interview on June 20, 1994. The interview was held outside the state capitol in Little Rock.

Donham's assignment provided him with some unique opportunities to view Clinton in a variety of situations. It enabled him to know Clinton and see him during the best times and during some very trying times. As Donham said regarding his assignment, "You live with him, you're around him all the time, you get to know him." The time he spent with the governor led to a relationship which Donham still cherishes. "He and I were real good friends, real, real close friends. He and Hillary both, they were very, very close friends, and I have all the respect in the world for him." The trooper repeatedly mentioned the respect he has for the president and his family. It was a respect that developed from the kind way Clinton treated Donham as well as his observation of Clinton's handling of difficult circumstances.

Donham, who described himself at the time of his assignment to the security detail as a "seasoned officer," was with Clinton a significant amount of time. He said he was with the governor "in his first two years probably more than any other agent, any other of-

183

ficer out there." It was this personal contact which enables Donham to speak authoritatively about Clinton's personality.

He related the governor's capacity to take a tremendous amount of pressure and responsibility. "Sometimes I'd see things happen. He would take total blame and carry it on his shoulders, where a lot of times I don't know if I could have done it that way." Donham said that when Clinton would be struggling with an emotionally laden issue, his tendency was to direct the responsibility inwardly, although at times he also tended to get quite angry. Donham believes that the anger was justified and would surface after a relatively long time.

Donham said, "He's no different than any other man that walks this earth. He had his ups and he had his downs. Things disturbed him, and he'd get a little ticked off about it, but at no time did he ever take it out on anybody. In fact, a lot of times he took too much out on himself." The officer identified Clinton's fault: "He let a lot of things worry him that he shouldn't have." But Donham even considers this "fault" to be somewhat of an admirable quality. He believes the president functions in such a fashion because of his concern for the person involved with the particular issue in question.

For example, Donham described a side of Clinton that displayed compassion for the troopers assigned to the security detail. If a member of "the security force was having a problem, it was part of his [Clinton's] problem." Donham's picture of the president is that of a concerned, compassionate man.

He also considered Clinton to be someone who would bear the crosses of others. "The majority of the time he's that kind of person, and I don't see how in the world he does it, and I don't know very many men that could, but a lot of times he would take issues or problems and just bear them until they couldn't be carried anymore."

Donham described the president's behavior analyzing and expressing his emotions. According to Donham, Clinton "would get disturbed about things if he felt something wasn't going right. You could tell when he was down." But Donham also viewed the president during moments of anger. "I've seen times he'd get so mad at things fire would fly from his eyes." The trooper believes that the anger Clinton expressed usually was quite justified. He noted that Clinton's fury came after a tremendous amount of patience. "He would take, God he would take, so much. He was so unbelievable about how much he could take."

The trooper revealed that Clinton often appeared contrite following his outbursts of anger. "Yeah, he got mad about things. He's a human being. He'd blow his stack, and I mean, blow it. And you'd know it, but a lot of times when he would, five minutes later he would say, 'I was wrong.' "

Donham said that there were times following the governor's apologetic response that Donham would indicate to Clinton that he thought the governor was justified in his anger. "I'd say, 'How much can you take then?' " Donham indicated that Clinton's outbursts of anger were not as common as inward reflection. "He would always have the ability to work it out within his own mind, and he'd just keep going."

Donham described the president as a tireless worker. He said, "One thing people cannot take away from Bill Clinton when he was governor here was he put in the hours. I mean, the man very seldom slept. I don't see how he made it." The trooper recalled that the governor worked into the early hours of the morning. "You'd see him working at, until two-thirty, three, four, in the morning. And then, when the sun would come up, he's ready to roll again."

Donham said that Clinton was able to function on a very limited amount of rest. "He'd catch a fifteen- or twenty-minute nap and then it was like he'd been full of energy and had been reenergized. Like somebody charged a battery, full of just energy and raring to go again." Donham said that Clinton's energy was so great that "a lot of times that I worked with him, he'd work me into the ground."

He went on to say that long hours did not seem to affect Clinton's abilities. "You could never see any indication in the way he talked, the way he acted, the way he would think about things."

Donham also described how impressed he was with Clinton's

intellectual abilities. He described the president as having a tremendous capacity to remember even small details. "He had one of the most unbelievable memories of any human being I've ever seen. He'd be out here in one of the smallest towns in the state, someone would introduce themselves. You could go back six months from then, maybe there might be an occasion for us to go back to that location, and he'd call them by their first name."

I asked Donham about his response to published comments made by other state troopers that do not flatter the president, particularly regarding extramarital sex. He defended the president, based on his observation of Clinton's behavior. He said, "The whole time I was around the then governor, now president, Clinton, I didn't see anything wrong. And I was with him a lot."

He did say that he had not personally spoken with the other troopers that were quoted. He expressed his displeasure with "other people talking about other people." It is Donham's contention that such issues should be dealt with directly between the parties involved. "I believe if you've got a complaint or a gripe about somebody, you should go to them."

Donham's contention is that naysayers have not given him an ample opportunity. "I personally feel that some of the people that might be having the problems with him didn't give him the opportunity, or maybe they closed their minds to maybe something he was trying to say, or maybe something he was trying to do, and they took it wrong." Donham pointed out that he worked closely with many politicians over a number of years. He said that the majority of the politicians are "good, honest, hardworking people; and that's the way then governor Clinton was."

The trooper was assigned to Clinton during the time that his brother, Roger, was under suspicion for cocaine-related offenses. He said, "I was in his security unit when his brother, Roger, got in his first little stump with the narcotics and the then governor, now president, Clinton, said, 'Hey, you guys, do what you got to do. If he's wrong, he's wrong. And you do your job, the way it's supposed to be done, not because he's my brother.' "

It was a situation that had significant impact on the trooper's view of Clinton. It meant that Clinton would do the right thing even if it was at a cost of personal and family pain. Donham said, "You could tell it hurt him. I mean, you could look in his eyes and tell that it was the hardest thing for him to say. That happened right after his first term, and from that day on, you know, a man that does that, he stands tall in my book."

Donham also offered his observation of Clinton's decision-making process. He viewed Clinton as someone who took many opinions into consideration before deciding on an issue. It was a process that Donham considered admirable and one that he has sought to utilize in his own life. Donham said, "He was not the type, if he saw A and B, he'd say A is right, and B is totally wrong. He would sit there, and I think that is where the man would spend many, many hours at the mansion. He thought through things, or he would contact people and see what they would think. He took a majority of what different people thought, you know, before he would make a decision, and I respected him for that."

Donham further stated that Clinton would arrive at a decision even if it pained him. He said that Clinton would make decisions that "personally would tear him up inside. But at the time, he would make the decision because it's the way it had to be done."

A summation of the admiration and respect which Corporal Donham holds for the president may be found in the following comment. Regarding Clinton's character, Donham said, "I wish I had one like it." Donham holds the president in high esteem and is not pleased with those who attack him, particularly without having firsthand experience with him. He is thankful to the president for having taught him many of life's lessons and cherishes their friendship.

CHAPTER NINETEEN

What the Interviews Tell Us

THESE INTERVIEWS PROVIDE many insights into the personality and character of President Clinton. The following is an analysis of the interviews in light of ACOA issues and topics. Note that Purvis and Donham desired the reader to consider their interviews in the context of their support of the president.

INTELLECTUAL ABILITIES

The interviewees agreed that Clinton is a highly intelligent man. Some of them described him as "brilliant." All noted the president's capacity to remember information. Memory capabilities are an aspect of intellectual functioning and are elements of psychological testing of intelligence. The interviewees cited specific examples of Clinton's ability that amazed them.

Consider these reports of Clinton's ability to remember information and events in the context of the theme of this book. It is interesting to note that Clinton has the ability to remember facts and figures, locations of friends' family residences, and names of individuals whom he casually met six months previously. That is, indeed, a tremendous capability. What is of just as much interest, however, is how someone with such effective memory for detail can also be so "forgetful."

Is it reasonable to conclude that he was able to recall the name of someone whom he had met on a campaign trail six months earlier but that he was unable to recall providing his mother with $20,000 in assistance? According to Clinton, his recall of this information was triggered while he was reading a manuscript copy of his mother's book. Does this sound credible in someone with such an effective memory?

Other examples of Clinton's faulty memory range from his "forgetfulness" of being at the hotel in question related to the Paula Jones story to scrutinized financial dealings. Related to the financial matters, how does the president, who has a "hands-on" approach, allow someone else to be involved with the financial matters of Whitewater, particularly in the light of the possible personal financial gain involved?

The president's memory may be described as "selective." It is obvious that he is intelligent. Those who know him have acknowledged his effective memory. It therefore is reasonable to conclude that the explanation that Clinton frequently offers when in a pinch —"I forgot"—is not viable. Undoubtedly, it has its basis in the rudimentary defense mechanism of denial.

TENDENCY TO LIE

An interesting disparity of opinion relating to the charge that the president lies was put forth in the interviews. By specific examples, Dickey was explicit in his charges that not only does the president lie but that he has done so repeatedly.

Clinton's friend Purvis contended that some of the misunderstanding about Clinton's veracity may be due to his propensity to make statements prior to formulating his final opinion. He did say that doing so might not be in the president's best interests.

My belief as a psychologist and observer of the president is that there is no question but that he is an inveterate liar. I think that the rationale for such behavior has its foundation in Clinton's ACOA background. I consider the behavior to be a part of the Clinton personality that will not change without intensive therapy. The therapy would necessarily require a deep analysis of Clinton's denial about his past and the effect on him. Until that occurs, the president will continue to lie.

OUTBURSTS OF ANGER

Several people interviewed addressed questions about Clinton's reported temperamental nature. Dickey described the president's anger as violent in nature. Donham pointed out that Clinton has the ability to let you know that he is angry. Donham contended that Clinton had a tremendous capacity to "take it." He meant that the president appeared to have a higher than typical tolerance for unpleasant comments or situations.

These two descriptions of Clinton's anger are consistent. Consider Clinton's life as a child and the high tolerance of unpleasant circumstances that was required of him. A child growing up in an alcoholic home commonly learns to tolerate far more than what another person would accept. This does not mean that such tolerance is necessarily healthy to the development of one's personality. Being slow to anger is virtuous, but a violent outburst of anger is not. A high tolerance may be misconstrued by an observer who thinks that the person is not being affected. In truth, unless one frees himself from the emotional buildup, an outburst of anger is expected. Clinton's outbursts take on the extreme tone that they do because of his present frustration and the forty-odd years of pain that he has kept hidden from himself and his friends. Again, it is time for the president to free himself of his childhood pain so that he can be a happier person. This would enable him to reduce the number of inappropriate emotional outbursts and his need to control.

SEXUALITY

Donham reported that he had not seen any inappropriate behaviors while he was assigned to Clinton's security detail during his first term as governor. Purvis said he could not say whether the allegations about the president were true because he did not personally have such knowledge. Dickey portrayed the president as someone with an active extramarital sexual life. Dickey's comments provided support for my contention that the president's sexual behaviors are of consequence to the nation if they are of an obsessive or compulsive nature.

ADULT CHILD OF AN ALCOHOLIC BACKGROUND

The information obtained in the interviews that was most relevant to the topic of this book was provided by Purvis regarding Clinton's childhood. Purvis was forthcoming about his and the president's upbringing. It served as additional confirmation that Clinton's childhood was being portrayed accurately. It was indeed a childhood fraught with a problematic family life.

When speaking of ACOAs in general, Purvis mentioned that individuals may reflect the impact of their childhood in differing ways and that at times they even may be unaware of how their disruptive childhoods are affecting their adult behaviors. He is correct in such an assessment. There are times when it is necessary for an outside party to bring such information to light. That is what I considered my role to be.

I was interested particularly in Purvis's statement that the first time the president had spoken with him about his ACOA background was in April 1994. As mentioned previously, it is common for a child in an alcoholic home not only to avoid talking about the topic but also to attempt to keep the family turmoil secret from neighbors and friends. This was and has been Clinton's approach. I am not condemning this secrecy, but it is exceedingly important, since it is the center of his problem. Obviously, only recently is he beginning to talk about the topic. Therefore, it is impossible for him to have resolved the ACOA issues. That he has begun to mention it to his friends signals, it is hoped, that he is beginning to take the issue seriously. It was a positive step that the president took by opening discussions about their childhoods with his close friend. I hope Clinton will continue to seize upon such opportunities.

Although the president is now beginning to acknowledge his past, I contend that he lacks a clear awareness of how it affects him in the present. This book has addressed a number of ways in which I know that the president has been affected. It is quite likely that it will be some time before Clinton is able to acknowledge the truth of this book's thesis. One of the reasons that many people elect to enter psychotherapy is to receive an "outside" opinion of their problems. If the president had walked through my door for such an "outside" opinion, he would have received the information that has been presented in this book. It is hoped that his close friend Purvis, who is much further ahead of the president on this question, will be of great assistance to him in resolving some of the conflicts inherent to his ACOA issues. It is comforting when seeking resolution to such problems to be able to talk with someone who has a personal understanding of the problem. It undoubtedly would serve to make a close friendship even stronger.

Part Four

CHAPTER TWENTY

Does the President Have a Personality Disorder?

I HAVE READ HUNDREDS OF ARTICLES and scores of books while researching *The Dysfunctional President* in the past two years. The literature was devoid of a substantial analysis of the psychological functioning of President Bill Clinton until an article was published in the November 1994 edition of *Reason* magazine. The author of the article "Can the President Think" is journalist and contributing editor Edith Efron.

Efron considered a number of compelling factors in her article. Consideration was given to the appropriateness of examining the psychological status of a sitting president. The conclusion drawn was that, yes, such an examination is worthy in situations in which a president's performance is impacted negatively by a psychological or emotional disorder. The author wrote that in the case of Clinton, references detailing the existence of a possible emotional problem were already plentiful in the press during the primaries. Following the election, Clinton exhibited further examples of emotional and behavioral patterns which were noted by the press. What was lacking in the analyses by the press was the use of the word "psychological" and the declaration of exactly what was wrong with the president.

Efron's article and this book detail many of the writings which indicate that the president exhibits an emotional disturbance. One of the paradoxes in the press commentary about Clinton which Efron points out is that while the press has been alluding to difficulties in Clinton's functioning, it has done so at the same time that journalists are declaring Clinton's character to be off limits to review. Her summation: "It is, of course, Clinton's character which has caused the wave of psychological thinking." My contention is that Clinton's character became the catchall phrase for the behavioral expression of his emotional difficulties.

In the *Reason* article, Efron's emphasis is on Clinton's cognitive functioning as opposed to some of the behavioral evidence (such as his sexuality) that evidences an emotional disturbance. The author of the article considered Clinton's mental process to be significantly more important. I contend that both his mental process and his behavioral expression are mechanisms to avoid the emotional pain from his childhood.

Efron believes that Clinton's cognitive impairment is, in part, masked by the inclusion of Hillary into the decision making process. The author contends that Hillary's role in enhancing Clinton's thought process is "the only reason for which Hillary Clinton is a significant American figure. Her actual importance lies in one realm alone. She is known to be a prop to her husband's mind, and her husband is president of the United States. To an inordinate degree Hillary Clinton *thinks* for Bill Clinton."

The contention that Hillary thinks for the president may appear extreme. It is central to the theme of Efron's thesis, however. Her belief is that Hillary compensates for Clinton's cognitive deficiencies. Efron reported that Bob Woodward said during a C-SPAN interview, "I'd go so far as to say she's a part of Bill Clinton's brain," when referring to Hillary's role with the president. Eleanor Clift had written in June 1993 that many of Clinton's staffers believed that his failure to be decisive on significant issues, such as Bosnia and the BTU tax, were due to Hillary's attention to health care, which resulted in her decreased attention to Clinton. Efron wrote that Hillary's role with the president exceeds that of an assistant. She provides an intellectual and logical analysis of material. She contends that Hillary's role is essential to the president because "in a particular and important way, Bill Clinton is cognitively disabled."

The author feels that one of Clinton's strengths, his capacity to memorize, is evidence of his cognitive disability. Examples abound in literature detailing Clinton's ability to remember even the most minute details. The interviews presented in this book offer similar examples, such as Clinton's remembering the name of a person on the campaign trail six months after he had last been to that town. The photographic memory, according to Efron, is as natural to Clinton as breathing. However, she wrote: "But he finds thinking—analysis, evaluation, reaching conclusions—intensely difficult. And that is the essence of Bill Clinton's cognitive disability, and the reason for his dependence on his wife."

The cognitive disability which the author was referring to is an obsessive-compulsive personality disorder. The author cited the following six points to support her contention that Clinton has such a personality disorder. After reporting her contentions, I will explain what an obsessive compulsive personality disorder is and offer my comments as it relates to Clinton as an ACOA. Efron's six points about Clinton's cognitive functioning are: perfectionism, preoccupation with detail, inability to establish priorities, avoidance or postponement of decision making, poor time allocation, and an insistence that he be in control. Each of her points was supported by examples.

What is of particular interest is that Efron draws the conclusion that Clinton's cognitive disability has produced chaos. She writes, "Clinton's cognitive paralysis does not exist in a void. It exists in a context, and is not static. It affects others, it affects Clinton himself, and ultimately it affects his presidency. The most visible effect, which has appalled the political-media establishment, is the disorder that reigns at the White House. In the course of the publicity debut of *The Agenda* on *60 Minutes*, Mike Wallace said incredulously to Woodward, 'Chaos?' And Woodward replied unsmilingly, 'Chaos. Absolute chaos.' " Efron contended that Hillary's function was and is to manage the chaos that Clinton's cognitive disability develops.

President Clinton has not released his medical records. Efron speculated that "there is no reason to doubt that Clinton was diagnosed as being 'compulsive and obsessive,' since that is what journalists have been documenting since Clinton entered the White House." She believed that Clinton received such a diagnosis when he was in family counseling following his brother Roger's conviction for the sale of cocaine. The arrest and family counseling occurred in 1984. The following might help to clarify my position on this matter as a clinical psychologist.

A distinction needs to be drawn between two very different diagnoses. They are obsessive-compulsive disorder and obsessive-compulsive personality disorder. Obsessive-compulsive disorder is an anxiety disorder in which someone exhibits thoughts of an obsessive nature and behaviors of a compulsive nature. Obsessive-compulsive personality disorder is a diagnosis utilized for patients with long-standing personality traits, as will be defined below.

One of the diagnoses indicated by Efron is obsessive-compulsive disorder. Efron wrote that in a *New York Times Magazine* article by Peter Applebome on March 8, 1992, Clinton said, "I finally realized how my compulsive and obsessive ambition got in the way." This statement by Clinton is cited by Efron to bolster her contention that Clinton was likely given a diagnosis related to obsession and compulsion when the family sought therapy following Roger's arrest.

A diagnosis of obsessive-compulsive disorder, according to the *Diagnostic and Statistical Manual of Mental Disorders* (DSM-IIIR), is given to a client who exhibits obsessions, "recurrent and persistent ideas, thoughts, impulses, or images" in accordance with an attempt to curtail such thoughts and an understanding that those thoughts are self-created. The obsessive thoughts occur in association with compulsive behavior. Compulsions are "repetitive, purposeful, and intentional behaviors that are performed in response to an obsession, or according to certain rules or in a stereotyped fashion." The compulsive behavior is "excessive or unreasonable" and "is designed to neutralize or to prevent discomfort or some dreaded event or situation." The occurrence of the obsessions or compulsions creates significant discomfort for the individual and impacts his life in a negative fashion.

Efron cited several factors that would indicate that Clinton exhibits compulsive behaviors. She claimed that he "seems to have had sleeping and eating disorders since he was young." One of my areas of expertise is in eating disorders. I wrote a doctoral dissertation on anorexia nervosa, designed the psychology program for an eating disorder program for a Southern California hospital, and have treated hundreds of clients with anorexia, bulimia, and overeating problems. There is an absence of clinical data to make the claim that Clinton exhibits an eating disorder. In fact, even if he did, it would serve as a differential diagnosis for the diagnosis of obsessive-compulsive disorder. In another chapter of this book, the discussion centers on the "compulsive" quality of Clinton's sexual behavior. Activities such as eating and sexual behavior "when engaged in excessively may be referred to as 'compulsive.' However, the activities are not true compulsions because the person derives pleasure from the particular activity, and may wish to resist it only because of its secondary deleterious consequences."

In other words, Clinton's sexual behavior can be considered compulsive but would not be classified as an obsessive-compulsive disorder. Similarly, Clinton may utilize overeating as a means to avoid unpleasant feelings, but it would not allow for such a diagnosis.

Efron concluded that Clinton meets the criteria established by the American Psychiatric Association for a diagnosis of obsessive-compulsive personality disorder.

A personality disorder must be differentiated from other types of mental disorders. According to the American Psychiatric Association, "personality *traits* are enduring patterns of perceiving, relating to, and thinking about the environment and oneself, and are exhibited in a wide range of important social and personal contexts.

It is only when *personality traits* are inflexible and maladaptive and cause either significant functional impairment or subjective distress that they constitute *Personality Disorders.*" Personality-disorder diagnoses are given when particular diagnostic criteria are met as relates to a person's functioning over the past year and long-term functioning since early adulthood.

The criteria for making a diagnosis of obsessive-compulsive personality disorder are as follows:

A pervasive pattern of perfectionism and inflexibility, beginning by early adulthood and present in a variety of contexts, as indicated by at least *five* of the following:

(1)   perfectionism that interferes with task completion, e.g., inability to complete a project because overly strict standards are not met

(2)   preoccupation with details, rules, lists, order, organization, or schedules to the extent that the major point of the activity is lost

(3)   unreasonable insistence that others submit to exactly his or her way of doing things, or unreasonable reluctance to allow others to do things because of the conviction that they will not do them correctly

(4)   excessive devotion to work and productivity to the exclusion of leisure activities and friendships (not accounted for by obvious economic necessity)

(5)   indecisiveness: decision making is either avoided, postponed, or protracted, e.g., the person cannot get assignments done on time because of ruminating about priorities (do not include if indecisiveness is due to excessive need for advice or reassurance from others)

(6)   overconscientiousness, scrupulousness, and inflexibility about matters of morality, ethics, or values (not accounted for by cultural or religious identification)

(7)   restricted expression of affection

(8)   lack of generosity in giving time, money, or gifts when no personal gain is likely to result

(9)   inability to discard worn-out or worthless objects even when they have no sentimental value

Note that of the aforementioned nine guidelines, a diagnosis of obsessive-compulsive personality disorder cannot be given unless at least five of the nine criteria are met. Efron contended that Clinton met the first five criteria It is indeed plausible to make the argument that she has made. My judgment is that despite its plausibility, it would be unwise for me to make such a diagnostic assessment for the following reasons:

An example of the complexity of diagnosing a personality disorder without concrete clinical data is the caveat inherent in the fifth criterion. There is no question that the president exhibits indecisiveness in which decision making is postponed or avoided. However, this criterion is not met if excessive advice seeking or reassurance seeking is the rationale for the indecisiveness.

There is indication that Clinton's indecisiveness is because of his perceived need to obtain information from an inordinate number of sources before reaching decisions. The interview with Joe Purvis revealed that Clinton had such a tendency when he was serving as attorney general for the state of Arkansas. He displayed that tendency by calling for the opinion of associates at all hours of the day and night. Clinton has been described as a meetings-oriented person. He likes to have many people present at meetings so that he can obtain a variety of viewpoints. He also has been criticized for leaving each person attending a meeting with the impression that he is in agreement with each viewpoint when in fact he still is in the stage of gathering advice.

If, in fact, Clinton is indecisive primarily because of his tendency to seek advice and reassurance inordinately, then only four of the criteria are met. This would not allow for a diagnosis of obsessive-compulsive personality disorder. A more thorough evaluation of the president would be necessary to determine whether or not he met the fifth criterion.

The basis for *The Dysfunctional President* is that Bill Clinton exhibits behaviors consistent with that of an untreated ACOA. As a clinical psychologist, I make that statement with absolute certainty based on Clinton's own words and behavior, interviews with his friends, supporting documentation, and my clinical experience. There is no disputing the fact that Clinton's stepfather was a violent alcoholic. It is unnecessary to conduct a clinical interview with the president or to subject him to psychological testing to ascertain what is self-evident.

Efron wrote that since Clinton had referred to his obsessive and compulsive behavior following his brother's arrest and that journalists had documented thought and behavior patterns characteristic of an obsessive and compulsive nature, he likely had been diagnosed as an obsessive-compulsive. This diagnosis was to have been given by a psychotherapist who treated the Clintons for family therapy following Roger's arrest.

My experience with family therapists is that they would probably not make such a diagnosis. Family therapists tend to consider the family as a system and family members as integral parts of that system. There is less of an emphasis on individual diagnoses than a layperson might believe.

Also, consider some additional factors. The psychotherapist treating the Clintons would have been practicing in the state of Arkansas and would have been giving the governor of the state a diagnosis of a personality disorder. Even if the diagnosis were legitimate, my experience with family therapists is that they would not necessarily be so likely to make such a diagnosis. Furthermore, Clinton probably used "obsessive and compulsive" in everyday terms rather than according to their clinical meaning.

The reason I doubt that Clinton was given such a diagnosis is that he spoke about being an ACOA after family therapy. He is known to read books on the ACOA topic. He spoke with his friend Joe Purvis in April 1994 about his life as an ACOA. Betsey Wright, his chief of staff when he was governor and at the time of Roger's arrest, said, "Bill became very introspective, did a lot of reading about codependence." Donnie Radcliffe, author of *Hillary Rodham Clinton: Making Her Mark* wrote, "Together, Bill and Hillary undertook an intensive study of drug addiction. Later, in family counseling sessions, Bill looked at how his own childhood experiences had shaped his life." Betsey Wright drew another parallel which would lead one to believe that the treatment focus was on ACOA issues. She said, "Bill felt in a lot of ways there was a fine line between what happened to Roger and what happened to him." Donnie Radcliffe, in his book about Hillary, wrote, " 'People say my number one weakness is that I'm conflict averse,' Clinton told David Maraniss of the *Washington Post*. 'I think part of that is I'm always trying to work things out because that's the role I played for a long time.' "

All of the aforementioned comments indicate that if a diagnosis was given at the time of the family therapy, it was not a diagnosis related to an obsessive-compulsive personality but to Clinton's being an ACOA. If one had to speculate on the matter, it is of higher probability that Clinton's therapy as an ACOA was either too focused on his brother's drug problem or was discontinued too soon to resolve Clinton's emotional problems than that he was given another diagnosis. This speculation has some validity, since Clinton's behavior continues to demonstrate characteristics of an ACOA.

It is possible that giving Clinton a diagnosis of a personality disorder is meritorious. I would hesitate to make such a diagnosis without conducting clinical interviews and possibly performing psychological testing. The diagnosis that Efron suggested may indeed be correct, but it is a complex one to make. In order to consider the difficulty in accurately making such a diagnosis without adequate clinical data, analyze the four diagnostic criteria of an obsessive-compulsive personality disorder which were not identified by Efron, and compare them with Clinton's personality.

For example, has Clinton ever been accused of being overconscientious about morality or ethics? While his rhetoric may have made such claims, his behavior has been suspect in both the moral and ethical areas. Recall that he is presently seeking to delay the Paula Jones court case and that the Whitewater investigation continues.

Also, does Clinton exhibit a restricted capacity to display affection? I know of no evidence which would lead one to such a conclusion. Joe Purvis, Clinton's friend, indicated that Clinton and Hillary exhibit affection for one another when they have private moments. It is apparent from other accounts, including their *60 Minutes* interview, that they have had marital difficulties related to Clinton's affairs. Clinton's problems seem to stem from an overly affectionate behavior pattern.

Psychiatrist Dr. David Viscott, in his book *Emotionally Free*, wrote about infidelity: "Being unfaithful is not being willing to work out the problems between you and your loved one in an open manner. Besides reflecting commitment, being unfaithful is almost always the sign of both a lack of communication and a fear of what needs to be communicated. Whatever argument you had before you were unfaithful loses its legitimacy to you. Your guilt keeps you from finding the best solution because you don't feel you deserve to be happy."

What is interesting about the Viscott quote as it relates to Clinton is that it further demonstrates Clinton's inclination not to be straightforward. Note that Viscott wrote about the failure to resolve the marital problems in "an open manner." While this is descriptive of Clinton's tendency not to be honest, it does not mean that he lacks the capacity to be affectionate.

Is there any indication that Clinton is not generous with his time, money, or gifts? One of the individuals interviewed for this book indicated that Clinton is "tight" with his money, but I think that it would be taking his comment out of context to apply it to this criterion. Also, one of the concerns of Clinton's staff is that he is overly generous with his time. One of the reasons given for his being late frequently is that it is difficult to get him to discontinue conversations.

Clinton's inability to discard worn-out objects offers a little humor. Recall the laughter that occurred when the Clintons released their tax returns and it was discovered that they had taken tax deductions for his used underwear. He could part with his used underwear, but at taxpayers' expense.

Diagnosing a personality disorder is difficult with or without ample clinical data. Gerald C. Davison of the University of Southern California and John M. Neale of the State University of New York at Stony Brook wrote a textbook entitled *Abnormal Psychology*, which is widely used for graduate-level psychology courses in the nation's universities. The authors wrote about the complexities involved in making a personality-disorder diagnosis.

"Problems still remain with this diagnostic category, however. In *DSM-IIIR* it is noted that it is often difficult to diagnose someone with a single, specific personality disorder. The reason is that many people exhibit a wide range of traits that make several diagnoses applicable."

The authors cited studies which for certain pairs of personality disorders place the dual diagnosis for clients at between 47 and 57 percent. This indicates a crossover of many of these characteristics of the personality disorders.

The authors continued: "These data suggest that the categorical diagnostic system of *DSM-IIIR* may not be ideal for classifying personality disorders. The personality traits that comprise the data for classification form a continuum; that is, most of the relevant characteristics are present in varying degrees in most people.

"The personality disorders make up what many researchers regard as an unreliable, cluttered grab bag of a category. Ironically, the descriptions of them may seem to fit some of the members of our own families and some of our acquaintances, not to mention ourselves!"

I have some additional thoughts which caution me from making a diagnosis of obsessive-compulsive personality disorder in relation to President Clinton. It changes the president's intellectual strength to cognitive weakness. Memory is one of the intellectual components tested in assessing an individual's intelligence on such measures as the Wechsler Adult Intelligence Scale-Revised. Interpretations of cognitive difficulties drawn from scores of the various subscales of the test are typically based on significantly divergent scores between particular subscales. Additional information regarding Clinton's scores on subscales of intelligence measures would be needed before concluding that his high aptitude for memory was indicative of a cognitive disability.

Another concern that I have with such a diagnosis is that while it accounts for the problem areas, such as lack of achievement of some goals, it does not account for his achievements. It is plausible to conclude that Hillary compensates for some of the president's weaknesses, as Efron postulated. However, that conclusion does not account for the president's achievements prior to his relationship with Hillary. He was an academic high achiever throughout his schooling, attended Georgetown University, obtained a law degree, received a Rhodes scholarship, and was a university law professor without her help.

The diagnosis of the obsessive-compulsive personality disorder also fails to account for one of Clinton's most significant character traits. His tendency to lie has been well documented in this book. The personality-disorder diagnosis does not include a criterion for a tendency to lie. Supporters of the personality-disorder theory related to Clinton would have to argue that the tendency to lie is based on his desire to cover up his cognitive deficiencies. Since Clinton is supposed to have thought problems in the areas of analysis, evaluation, and drawing conclusions, these deficiencies would have to be masked by lying about them. That fails to account for his successes at analysis, evaluation, and drawing conclusions. Clinton is an intelligent man, and it would be inaccurate to portray him as anything less than that.

By far the more plausible explanation is that of the ACOA hero. The hero role accounts for Clinton's being a high achiever, as intelligence is not a factor in the ACOA syndrome. In fact, in the hero role his accomplishments would be expected. In addition to the accomplishments, however, the failures are accounted for, since the hero seeks to undermine himself by self-sabotaging behavior. This also is evident in the Clinton style. Finally, the tendency to lie is one of the characteristics of the ACOA syndrome.

I agree with Efron that Clinton exhibits characteristics of a controlling individual. However, he also exhibits the personality weakness of a dependent person, demonstrated by the defense of denial. David Viscott identifies various defense forms as a "range of the defense of denial." These defense forms help to explain many of the concerns that Efron wrote about as they pertain to the president's cognitive deficiencies.

Efron identified Clinton as "a spectacular procrastinator." Viscott wrote that procrastination is a defense form in which the person is "postponing facing unpleasant or difficult tasks." This book has placed much emphasis on Clinton's waffling. My experience in treating males who procrastinate is that they often developed their tendency to avoid tasks because of unresolved hostility toward their fathers. This may be due to having received criticism for the manner in which they undertook or resolved tasks in their youth. President Clinton's mother described the actions of his stepfather toward Clinton as being emotionally abusive. Clinton's procrastination today is likely a representation of his unresolved anger from that emotional abuse.

A related form of denial identified by Viscott and evidenced by Clinton is being late. Viscott describes the dynamics of that characteristic as "resenting where you find yourself in life." This description fits Clinton as the ACOA hero. It typifies how denial of Clinton's childhood emotional pain is the basis for his self-sabotaging behaviors. Clinton resents the role that he adopted as the hero of the family in an effort to cover up the problems of his childhood family. In turn, he resents his role as the national hero today and has done many things to undermine himself.

Efron also pointed out Clinton's tendency to lose focus. This is the defense form of denial described by Viscott. Viscott wrote that losing focus is "inattention to anything that might lead to a painful truth." If Clinton were to maintain his focus and accomplish his goals, he would be unable to self-sabotage. Without the capability to undermine himself, he would have to face the truth of his pain. Instead, the focus is placed on what is going wrong in the present, such as the lack of cohesion in policy making.

A similar form of denial, lying, is described by Viscott as "misstating reality to avoid pain." Clinton's misstatements have been chronicled in this book. Recall the many instances in which he lied as a means to avoid pain. Looking at his life as a whole, one easily concludes that he has lied for so long in his life that it has become second nature to him. A related form of denial, being confused, is described by Viscott thusly, "The obvious facts don't make sense, because their painful meaning is too frightening." The creation of chaos is noted in this book and is also central to Efron's description of Clinton. Regardless of the diagnosis, Clinton develops chaos as a mechanism to protect himself from the truth of his pain. It is this extension of his childhood chaos to the White House that is particularly alarming to me.

Viscott also identified forgetting as a form of denial. Forgetting, according to Viscott, is the "interruption in the recollection of a specific painful memory or anything symbolizing it or leading to it, ranging from a momentary lapse to a total inability to recall." This form of denial evidences one of the clear examples of the paradox that is Clinton. On the one hand, his memory capability is touted to be phenomenal. On the other hand, he manages to forget particular events when they are related to unpleasant situations. An example is his forgetfulness of a sizable loan to his mother when he was being questioned about his financial records.

The second-to-last defense in Viscott's range of denial is blocking. This is the "broad disruption of the thought process to avoid pain so that not only the specific painful event but also much benign reality is shut out." This is a form of denial second in severity only to global denial, which Viscott identifies as being of psychotic proportions. It also tells us something of tremendous significance about Clinton, since he engages in this form of denial. Recall that Clinton's mother rather proudly proclaimed that she and her son, Bill, had the ability to block out unpleasant segments of time, in addition to which was the blocking of related information. For example, Clinton and his mother both were unaware of his comments in a deposition taken relative to the abusive household in which he grew up.

I contend that Clinton's far-reaching use of many forms of denial that were identified by Viscott is the reason Clinton exhibits many of the lapses Efron identified as cognitive deficiencies. The denial stems from Clinton's long-standing avoidance of his childhood pain. Anxiety, masking that pain, inhibits his potential to be an effective leader and administrator.

Before Clinton could receive proper treatment, a correct diagnosis would be necessary. My suggestions for him to be treated as an ACOA are presented at the conclusion of this book. In my professional opinion, any other course of treatment would be flawed.

CHAPTER TWENTY-ONE

A Second Opinion

AN IMPORTANT ASPECT OF MY RESEARCH regarding the president and his unresolved ACOA issues was to speak with another professional involved in the field of addiction treatment. The research itself had led me to the unmistakable conclusion that this problem did plague the president. Speaking with a mental health professional schooled in this field provided a sounding board for some of my perceptions and also offered interesting information regarding addiction, ACOA problems, and the treatment process.

The comments made in the interview must be seen in the light that the physician did not review clinical data related to the president. In the absence of such data, his comments on Clinton and his family are based on observations of the president in his public life. I am grateful to him for personalizing some of his comments about the president based on his observations.

Michael Meyers is a physician who is board certified in family practice in the state of California. Dr. Meyers's subspecialty is addiction medicine. I became aware of his work while attending a lecture that he presented on chemical dependency several years ago. His expertise in the field was impressive. I was confident that his insights would be helpful to the reader in gaining understanding of addiction and ACOA problems.

Dr. Meyers is the medical director of Choices at Brotman Chemical Dependency Treatment Centers in Culver City, California. He is committed to increasing the knowledge of individuals and professionals about addiction and its impact on society. He is a faculty member at the University of California, Los Angeles, Department of Family Medicine. His position as a clinical instructor at the university enables him to educate medical students and residents about addiction. He also serves as an instructor in the UCLA extension program. In this capacity he is able to educate "his peers, as physicians, about addictive disease, how pervasive it is and how poorly trained most physicians are in this area."

In addition to his professional expertise in the area of addiction medicine and family systems, Dr. Meyers has a personal interest in this area. He described himself as a recovering addict-alcoholic who had over twelve and one-half years of sobriety. This personal experience serves to further "qualify [him] as someone who knows about addictive disease because I have it and because my whole professional and personal life now revolves around taking care of people with addictive diseases which include those people with the disease, itself, those people who have the genetic predisposition to go on to use psychoactive substances to their detriment." Dr. Meyers said he uses a family systems approach in treating addiction "because it is a family-system problem." The scenario that he described relating to symptoms developed by family members of an alcoholic or addict underscores the impact that the disease has upon the family structure.

One of the reasons for writing this book was to have an opportunity to show how alcoholism can affect family members. The unfortunate example in this instance is the president. It also is of value to consider some of the factors that contribute to the continuance of addiction in America. One of those factors is the defensive process of denial, both individually and collectively.

Dr. Meyers considers denial to be "one of the core problems that this country and society has that they don't want to deal with, be it on the chemical-dependency level and on a lot of other levels." To assist in combating such denial, Dr. Meyers works with adolescents and spouses of alcoholics as well as the alcoholics themselves. He conducts interventions to "break through the denial of the individuals and the microcosm and macrocosm of the world they live in because denial is an incredibly powerful, pervasive element."

Dr. Meyers cited another factor in the problem of addiction: "the stigmatization of addiction and alcoholism that this country is still very much involved with." He pointed out that such stigmatization makes it "very difficult to talk about this as dispassionately as a medical illness because of the stigma that it is still considered by many, many individuals to be a moral failure, a weakness." He said that such a viewpoint results in a belief that "alcoholics and addicts, even in recovery, are somehow inferior human beings." This position may, in fact, hamper the recovery of an alcoholic who is truly desirous of a life free from the chemical. "There are a great deal of individuals who still feel that way about themselves even in recovery."

Dr. Meyers stressed that addiction should be considered in terms separate from moral failure. "Addiction is not about those things. But it is about illness, and it is a disease that has very effective treatment for people." One concern is that alcoholism is the result of moral failure and therefore could perpetuate an alcoholic's resistance to seeking treatment because of a fear of being stigmatized. Dr. Meyers was clear that treatment is not successful for all people, just as nothing is successful for everyone.

Dr. Meyers commented on the dysfunctional family structure as it relates to his knowledge of President Clinton's childhood upbringing. The firstborn child in such a family system "often is thrust the mantle of hero." The family hero exists to counteract, or deny, the actual addiction problems and family systems problems inherent to the family. When such a marvelous child is present in the family, how can the family have problems? The emergence of the hero belies the fact that this father, in this case the stepfather, is "a failure in a lot of areas in his life."

If ever there was an example of the hero role within a dysfunctional family, it is President Clinton. He emerged as the hero from the alcoholic, violent family and was the star student, the Rhodes scholar. He achieved the pinnacle of success, the presidency of the United States. Some might question how such a hero role could have a negative effect and how a childhood family situation could have relevance to him today. His alcoholic stepfather is dead, and his mother died recently. Yet, according to Dr. Meyers, the role that a person develops to cope with the family dysfunction persists. He declared: "Even if the family has dissolved by then, Dad is not even in the picture as the drunk, or the codependent mother isn't giving these [hero] messages, that script, however, was there from the beginning. So there is a pronounced need for that child to be an overachiever, someone who has to rescue that family from the social stigma of the failure of the parents continues."

A key point made by Dr. Meyers serves to explain why such a circumstance can have, and I strongly contend, has had, negative effects on the president in his adult life. He said, "Oftentimes, that hero is begrudgingly taking that role. They resent it, and they don't want to have to be perfect. They don't want to have to be the star, but this family so desperately needs it that the person must go out there and be the superstar."

Note that when people fail to express their hurt, that pain results in feelings of anger. One form of anger is resentment. A hero who begrudgingly accepts the role of stardom would develop feelings of resentment over time. I asked Dr. Meyers to explain how such an individual, as he grows older, would typically act out his resentment over begrudgingly accepting the role of hero. His response was telling.

Dr. Meyers said, "Oftentimes the untreated heroes will sabotage themselves. The untreated hero is not cognizant of the fact that he harbors intense resentment from his childhood. The resentment is therefore not communicated in a direct fashion. Instead, the resentment is displayed behaviorally. The behavior is evidenced by creating a mechanism to ultimately fail."

Consider the untreated hero in relation to President Clinton. He was an intelligent, talented child from a dysfunctional home. His success figuratively counteracted the failure of his stepfather and the turbulent home life. It was a burden placed on the president because of his circumstances and self-imposed expectations. The resentment grew commensurate with the achievements. Since the source of the resentment was not clearly identified, the resentment would on such occasion surface in the form of outbursts of anger. Such resentment would result in personal behaviors destined to overturn the heroic achievements. It is also possible that the fiasco involving Clinton's financial affairs may demonstrate another example of self-sabotage.

I asked Dr. Meyers whether a begrudgingly accepted role with denial would result in the untreated hero's denying his responsibility for his problems. In other words, is the untreated hero likely to accept responsibility for the mess created by his sabotage, or would it be blamed on external, situational forces?

He answered that "the whole point is to not have to take responsibility for your life." A little knowledge about the subject is not enough to be able to break through the denial and see that a person is causing his own problems through sabotage. It is often easier to continue to blame the problems on Dad's drunken behavior and Mom's codependency rather than accepting responsibility for one's own sabotaging behavior.

Dr. Meyers's generic commentary on the untreated hero's denial of responsibility for self-created chaos or sabotage supports my contention that the president employs denial and denial of responsibility. This model demonstrates that the president's denial of responsibility has its roots in his failure to accept or receive treatment to resolve his childhood problems. Blaming others for one's actions is very problematic because until the person is willing to accept responsibility for his actions, no resolution of the problem will occur.

Dr. Meyers continued his explanation of his observations of the Clinton dysfunctional family. He said, "We know that there is often the second child in this situation who realizes they can't compete with the hero but they need some sort of attention and interaction. They become the scapegoat. They start creating havoc because at least it gets attention and then the family thrives on having somebody else to blame." He mentioned that the scapegoat's behavior often serves as a mechanism for the family to further their denial.

The person who acts out (Roger Clinton in this situation) gets blamed for Dad's drinking. The deflection of family problems to the scapegoat means that the family does not deal with the severe problems in the family that caused the outlandish behavior. Dr. Meyers summarized his commentary about the Clinton family system by saying, "And so, in that generic, oversimplified family system, we've got the president as the hero and the scapegoat, ne'er do well brother."

Dr. Meyers believes "after AA [Alcoholics Anonymous], the ACA [adult child of an alcoholic] movement has been one of the largest social movements of greatest value of the twentieth century." The benefit is that "the individuals who have grown up and gone on with their lives and have no clue as to why they're living their lives the way they are, are now being able to find out why." Once the ACOA becomes aware of the source of his behavior, it is his responsibility to seek treatment to resolve the problems.

I told Dr. Meyers that the president has some awareness of his ACOA problem. The president mentioned that role to Joe Purvis in April 1994 and friends said that the president reviews ACOA materials to better understand his behavior. I also told Dr. Meyers that it was clear to me that any treatment Clinton sought was incomplete.

Dr. Meyers cited several possible reasons why, in the president's case, treatment was not completed. First, a social stigma is attached to seeking such treatment. Clinton was in a position of prominence, governor of Arkansas, when he became aware of his ACOA difficulties. People assume that someone with such capability should be able to resolve the problem himself. Second, adverse political ramifications would occur if a governor or president entered psychotherapy. Recall that Sen. Thomas Eagleton removed himself as the vice presidential nominee on the ticket with George McGovern following the revelation that he had received treatment for depression. Clinton worked for the McGovern campaign. Dr.

Meyers stated that despite the political ramifications, an effective treatment system exists for those seeking assistance.

I asked Dr. Meyers to speculate on what the future might hold for an untreated hero who has reached the pinnacle of success that one day will be passed. Either the president will sabotage himself to such an extent that he is removed from office, or he will fulfill his term or terms and become an ex-president. His speculation was that continued sabotage of success will occur until "there isn't any more success to sabotage."

All of his life Clinton has been treated as someone who is special. It is time to relieve the president of that pressure and allow him to acknowledge his ACOA problems and to obtain adequate treatment for them. No one would want to have the president continue with self-created chaos or act out sexually. This would be an undue humiliation to the president and to the nation, given the atmosphere of moralism to which Dr. Meyers alluded. The comments by Dr. Meyers and the remainder of this book should provide greater insight into our personal issues related to these problems, the obvious ACOA problems faced by the president, and finally the national attitude toward addiction.

CHAPTER TWENTY-TWO

A Presidential Profile

WHEN A CLIENT ENTERS OUTPATIENT psychotherapy or an inpatient psychiatric program, information is gathered to provide the therapists and staff with a condensed profile so that the client may be treated effectively. This profile enables those involved in the treatment to gain insight into the client's psychological history and current needs. Recommendations for treatment are offered so that therapists may be consistent in their approach in assisting the client. In a hospital setting this is referred to as the treatment or care plan.

I have completed such a profile of President Clinton based on my observations and research. It is designed to serve as a summation of what I believe to be relevant history of the president's emotional problems and what would be a reasonable means for him to attempt to resolve those problems.

IDENTIFYING CHARACTERISTICS

The client, Bill Clinton, is a middle-aged Caucasian male. His birthdate is August 19, 1946. He is the president of the United States. Clinton is married to Hillary Rodham Clinton and has one daughter, Chelsea Clinton. He was born in Arkansas and currently resides in Washington, D.C.

CHIEF COMPLAINT/PRECIPITATING FACTORS

Clinton entered therapy in response to growing awareness of personal problems related to family history. These problems have resulted in various dysfunctional behaviors, including lying, excessive use of denial, denial of personal responsibility, self-sabotaging behaviors, and alleged sexual misconduct. Significant sources of stress currently exist which have precipitated an increase in the use of the dysfunctional behaviors to avoid resolution of underlying unpleasant emotions related to family history. Precipitating factors include a sharply dropping approval rating, a failure to convince the populace that a health care crisis exists, a lawsuit filed alleging sexual misconduct, ongoing inquiries into financial matters related to Whitewater and Madison Guaranty and Loan, and an upsurge in Americans' awareness that he fails to be truthful. The accumulation of sources of stress with the underlying, long-standing personal conflict has resulted in a decreased effectiveness.

FAMILY HISTORY

The client's family history is the source of many of his current conflicts. His father died from drowning following ejection from his automobile in a one-vehicle accident. The father's death occurred prior to the client's birth. The client's mother pursued further education and left Clinton with his grandparents during his initial years of life. He grew up in Hope, Arkansas, and later moved to Hot Springs, Arkansas. His mother married Roger Clinton Sr. He was an alcoholic who exhibited violence within the home directed at the client and his mother. This marriage resulted in the birth of a half brother, Roger. The half brother had subsequent chemical dependency problems.

His mother and stepfather divorced. They remarried over the client's objection during his teen years. Following the remarriage, the client changed his name to Clinton. The client left home for a college education. The stepfather died when the client was in college. His mother married two additional times. Within the past two years, other half siblings from his biological father have become known to Clinton. The client's mother died recently. Family history is replete with unusual circumstances that resulted in a clearly dysfunctional upbringing. The client publicly describes his childhood as "happy."

EMPLOYMENT HISTORY

The client currently is employed as the president of the United States. He previously has worked as governor of the state of Arkansas and as attorney general for the same state.

EDUCATIONAL HISTORY

Clinton has a strong educational background. He has completed a law degree. He also received a scholarship to Oxford but did not complete the Rhodes scholarship program.

FINANCIAL HISTORY

The client reported a maximum income of $35,000 prior to his current position. His wife also was employed as an attorney in the state of Arkansas. Despite his moderate salary, assets greater than $1 million were placed into a blind trust several months after he became president. Finances are currently causing stress for the client, as inquiries into various investments, notably Whitewater, are ongoing. Also, questions have been raised about his spouse's capacity to earn approximately $100,000 in cattle-futures trading. This occurred during her initial venture. Allegations about possible campaign-finance improprieties also have surfaced. Current litigation costs have caused the client to seek public donations of up to $1,000 per person. An accounting for the total sum collected is not available at this time.

LEGAL ISSUES

Legal problems are an ongoing source of stress for the client. A legal defense fund was previously mentioned. The fund was established to pay for legal expenses related to possible financial inquiries and a sexual-misconduct lawsuit. Attempts are being made by the client's counsel to delay a hearing of the sexual misconduct lawsuit until his term as president has been completed.

SEXUAL HISTORY

The client also has experienced significant sources of stress in his sexual history. During the presidential campaign, allegations of a longstanding marital affair surfaced. The initial response by the client was to deny the allegations. Later, he appeared with his spouse on television to state that they had had past marital problems but that their relationship presently was intact. Other women also have claimed to have had sexual relationships with the client during his marriage. Another party has filed a lawsuit alleging sexual impropriety. This allegation involves an unwelcomed sexual advance by the client.

MILITARY HISTORY

The client did not serve in the military. His statements about R.O.T.C. obligations and draft deferments have been found to be conflictory.

MEDICATIONS/MEDICAL HISTORY

The client has not released his medical records. He is the first president who has not made these records public.

ALCOHOL/CHEMICAL DEPENDENCY

The client acknowledged past use of marijuana but maintains that he "did not inhale." A family history exists for chemical-dependency issues.

STRENGTHS AND WEAKNESSES

A person's strengths and weaknesses are polar opposites. This client's weakness is a tendency to lie. Emphasis should be placed upon his need to be honest, which can be developed to be his strength. A second weakness is his proclivity to create chaos. This weakness should be alleviated following treatment, which will decrease the need to re-create his childhood dysfunction.

DIAGNOSIS

The client is an adult child of an alcoholic stepfather. He adopted the role of hero within the dysfunctional family system. He utilizes denial as a primary defense mechanism. His present behavior and problems indicate that the client has very little insight into the impact of his childhood problems as it relates to his current difficulties. He denies responsibility and blames others. He exhibits periodic outbursts of anger because of the long-standing nature of his pain. His anger becomes confused with present situations and appears bizarre to others. His begrudging acceptance of the hero role has resulted in repeated behavior of self-sabotage and self-created chaos. It appears that sexually acting out behavior is likely and would be consistent for this individual, given his diagnosis and lack of insight into the problem.

RECOMMENDATIONS AND TREATMENT PLAN

This client requires intensive, directive psychotherapy to break through the established walls of denial. He should be under the care of a licensed clinician familiar with the concepts of ACOA treatment. Recommendation is made for the therapist, at least initially, to be a male to defuse the potential for sexually acting out. If a female therapist is the primary therapist for this client, the possibility of sexual acting out should be considered and confronted if it occurs. Initial treatment should focus on the enhanced awareness of the client and insight into the impact of his childhood. The therapist should confront the client's use of disingenuousness. This client has a strong need for approval, and the clinician may utilize that need to assist in the development of motivation.

The client, however, is a workaholic, and the therapist should be attentive to his potential of "working too hard" at his treatment. He may utilize this strategy as a means to avoid his unpleasant feelings and place too much of an emphasis on "how well he is completing his treatment plan." The client is personable, and the therapist should be able to develop an effective rapport with him. He tends to desire control, and the therapist should be cautioned about this tendency at it relates to the therapeutic relationship.

The treatment plan outlined for this client is as follows:

    1. Individual psychotherapy with a licensed clinician focused on the underlying ACOA issues.
    2. Peer-group psychotherapy led by the client's clinician.
    3. Twelve step ACOA self-help group.
    4. Family therapy to address existing family systems problems.

The above treatment methods should be conducted on an outpatient psychotherapy basis. Each of the four modalities should be made available to the client on a one-session-per-week basis. The client has a responsible position and will need to be reminded that the treatment program is a necessity for him. The treatment plan will be reviewed after six months. It is anticipated that treatment will take considerably longer than that period of time because of the client's level of denial and the duration of the problem.

The President Responds

ON JULY 25, 1995, approximately four months after *The Dysfunctional President* was first published, journalist Nancy Collins interviewed President Clinton in the Oval Office. The purpose of the interview was to inquire about the president's reflections on the life of his mother, Virginia Kelley, who died on January 6, 1994. The interview expanded to a discussion about growing up in an alcoholic home and the impact of being an ACOA. Collins's article, "A Legacy of Strength and Love," was published in the November 1995 issue of *Good Housekeeping* Magazine.

Collins's article is an important contribution to the analysis of the ACOA syndrome as it affects the president's personal life and his presidency. The interview provided the most extensive comments to date by the president about his troubled childhood. The president recalled the time when Roger Clinton Sr. shot a gun inside the home, the bullet narrowly missing the president's mother. "I remember that incident vividly, like it was yesterday. That bullet could have ricocheted and done anything. It could have killed me."

Imagine the feeling of terror that would arise in a five-year-old child witnessing such an incident.

The president recalled that his stepfather threatened to kill his mother on two other occasions. President Clinton claimed that as he grew older, he attempted to protect his mother and brother from his stepfather's alcoholic rages. The president said he called the

224

police to arrest his stepfather, or he took the family to motels when violence ensued.

Because he felt responsible for protecting his mother, he considered attending the University of Arkansas instead of an out-of-state university. His mother strongly encouraged him to go out of state, convincing him that he would not be able to protect her even if he attended the University of Arkansas, which was two hundred miles from their home.

Despite the chaos caused by Roger Clinton Sr.'s alcoholism and anger, the president's assessment of his stepfather was charitable: "Roger wasn't a bad man, and he didn't want to hurt anybody. He was just an alcoholic, full of self-loathing and anxiety, with no way to deal with it. He had problems before we ever came into his life."

While Clinton's stepfather may not have been motivated to hurt others, the reality is that he did cause considerable harm. A fine line exists between explaining someone's behavior because of alcoholism and excusing that behavior. Whether someone is an alcoholic or not, the individual must accept responsibility for his behavior. Surely it is entirely inexcusable to fire a bullet at one's spouse, beat her up, and emotionally abuse children. If one is an alcoholic or suffering from self-hatred or anxiety, it is that person's responsibility to seek help so that he does not hurt others. Having the motivation to do good, in and of itself, is inadequate if one's behavior belies that motivation.

Collins wrote that, as a youth, Clinton "redeemed the family honor with his own successes. He learned to put on one face to the world, while privately feeling something totally different."

Recall this is the genesis of Clinton's impostor syndrome and why the president is so aptly accused of lacking conviction. Often his true beliefs and feelings are suppressed in favor of thoughts and feelings he thinks others want to hear. A child growing up in an alcoholic home is not encouraged or allowed to express his thoughts and feelings. As a result, intellectual and emotional development is stunted. Convictions are either not formed or, if formed, the willingness to "put on one face to the world" in order to receive approval transcends the conviction.

Collins's observation also demonstrates the paradoxical nature of an existence in an alcoholic household. On the one hand, Clinton did not reveal to friends the turmoil inside his home because of a sense of shame. On the other hand, Clinton was motivated to redeem family honor, which friends were unaware was tarnished. This is the role assumed by the hero of the family who holds the false belief that his personal overachievement compensates for the embarrassing family life. Evidence of the isolating effect of this disparate existence is found in Clinton's comments to Collins: "The violence and dysfunction in our home made me a loner, which is contrary to the way people view me because I'm gregarious, happy, all of that. But I had to construct a whole life inside my own mind, my own space."

Noting that assessing the impact of a violent, alcoholic home can be a lengthy process, Collins asked the president what he thought were the effects of his youth upon his adult life. The president identified "three bad things" that were consequences of his youth. He cited the failure to have a male role model as one of the "bad things." The president recounted the death of his biological father three months prior to Clinton's birth. He also pointed out that his stepfather's involvement in his life was so limited that he recalls each of the very few times that the two of them did something special. Clinton stated that despite this lack of involvement, "I loved my stepfather very much." ACOAs will identify with the president's statement, as it demonstrates the intense craving that exists for love from the alcoholic who is physically and emotionally unavailable to provide the love. It is important for the president to acknowledge not only feelings of love that he had for his stepfather but also the feelings of hurt, resentment, anger, and guilt that accompany such relationships. The negative feelings are often difficult to admit because of the fear that others will think one is a bad person for feeling that way.

The president expressed to Collins that he was also concerned with how his childhood might affect his ability to have a successful marriage. Clinton raised a concern common to ACOAs. Often a fear exists that since they have not witnessed a functional marital relationship as children, they will be inadequate in a relationship as adults. The ACOA is left to guess at what normal adult relationships are like. Often the ACOA "performs" in a relationship as he or she imagines is required in a normal relationship. There frequently is great anxiety that the partner will discover this shortcoming. The president revealed his self-doubt in this area to Collins:

"I wanted it desperately, but I did not know if I could do it. When I was twenty-one, I put down the things I really wanted in my life—and having a good family and a child was one of them. But I just didn't know if I could ever get there, because if your model of a marriage has been bad, it has a subconscious drag on you."

The truth is that Clinton's marital relationship has been fraught with difficulty. In the chapter called Sexual Compulsion, I wrote about the similarity between Clinton's sexual compulsion and his stepfather's alcoholism. Clinton's compulsive behavior has caused great hurt to the family despite Clinton's obvious motivation since age twenty-one to be an effective marital partner. According to Clinton, just as his stepfather did not want to hurt anyone, the truth is that he did harm. The hurt and embarrassment to family members caused by Clinton's sexual compulsion is why it is essential that the president's treatment include family conseling. Family counseling, perhaps, will provide the president with the tools not only to long for a successful marriage but also to have one.

The third "bad thing" that the president acknowledged to Collins was: "When you grow up in a dysfunctional home, inadvertently you send mixed signals to people. You learn that other people, in the outside world, didn't live in this same context as you. I see this as president."

This startling admission by the president, that he sends mixed signals to people, is at the crux of much of his dysfunctional behavior. In considering the president's comment, one must first determine what he means by "mixed signals." The president's position is that people who have not had life experiences similar to his will misinterpret the meaning of his communications. Clinton's position enables him to hold others responsible for his miscommunication. The "mixed signals," in actuality, are not a result of misinterpretation by others but are caused by inconsistent communications by the president. What the president terms "mixed signals," I have called the tendency to lie unnecessarily. While many examples of this behavior have been presented in *The Dysfunctional President*, the following example demonstrates the "mixed signals" and also provides some insight into the underlying motivation for the behavior.

In the aftermath of the Oklahoma City bombing tragedy, the president was garnering approval ratings for his handling of the crisis in the range of 85 percent. News analysts described the president as "appearing presidential." The president, however, becomes uncomfortable when he is perceived to be doing well for an extended period of time. When this occurs, it becomes necessary for Bill Clinton to focus attention elsewhere by cultivating self-created chaos.

After several days of "appearing presidential," Clinton made a speech in Minneapolis, Minnesota, in which he declared that talk radio hosts were spewing hate over the airwaves. According to the president, such hate stimulated individuals such as the Oklahoma City bombers to engage in acts of terrorism against government employees. His speech created significant turmoil, as speculation in the press centered attention upon successful conservative talk radio hosts such as Rush Limbaugh, G. Gordon Liddy, and Oliver North.

The evening of the president's speech, I was interviewed by Peter Schofield, WCCO radio, in Minneapolis. I said that the president had brought up this issue as a way to divert attention from his recent success and to create chaos. I predicted that within two days his aides would come forward to disavow that the president was speaking about any radio host in particular. The next morning, news reports included statements from White House aides that the president was not referring to any host in particular, including Rush Limbaugh and G. Gordon Liddy. In order to cultivate the chaos he created, the president came forward two days following his aides' denial, and specifically mentioned G. Gordon Liddy as one of the talk radio hosts he considered dangerous.

This example demonstrates that the president creates chaos when a sense of normalcy exists for even a relatively brief period of time, because chaos is what he knows. The example also demonstrates the "mixed signals" or dysfunctional communication that the president presents and which he believes others misinterpret. Also, and very importantly, the talk radio example demonstrates that the president's dysfunctional behavior is predictable when viewed in the context of Clinton as an ACOA.

The president himself, in his interview with Collins, cited an alarming example of how sending "mixed signals" affects his presidential decision making. In discussing his decision to formulate plans to invade Haiti, the president told Collins, "When you are president, and go the extra mile, others will interpret it as weakness. In Haiti, I pretty much had to invade the country because people didn't believe me. When I finally had the planes in the air, they believed me and got out of there. That's happened all my life, from the time I was in school. People underestimate your resolve because you go out of your way to accommodate them before you drop the hammer."

In describing himself as the peacemaker "going the extra mile," the president disavowed responsibility for the misinterpretation of his intentions by the Haitian junta leaders. The president failed to include other information in his analysis of the Haiti confrontation. As documented in earlier chapters, Clinton's policy toward Haiti wavered not because of misinterpretation but because of stated policy changes. Examples are Clinton's criticism of President Bush's policy not to allow Haitian refugees free access to American shores. After Clinton's election, he adopted the same policy. However, the Haitians who believed the new president's assertions attempted to travel to America in droves, with as many as four hundred people losing their lives. The president's policy then shifted to housing the Haitian refugees in camps in Cuba. Subsequently some of the refugees were granted resident status in America while others returned to Haiti. Thousands of Haitians, believing the word of the new president of the United States, did not misinterpret Clinton, they were responding to his "mixed signals."

The junta leaders in Haiti, similarly, had good cause to question the president's resolve. Recall Vice President Quayle's comment that because of a lack of credibility, President Clinton had lost leverage in dealing with foreign dignitaries. It is clear from Clinton's remarks that America was poised for an invasion of Haiti, not because it was necessary, but "because people didn't believe" the president of the United States. Quayle's comment, months before the president's invasion plans, demonstrates once more the predictability of Clinton's dysfuntion. It is alarming to accept that Clinton's foreign policy was driven by psychological factors. Yet Clinton's own words make it indisputable that the psychological factors creating his lack of credibility and his long-standing desire to be believed were the driving forces behind the planned invasion. Military need or American interest should be the driving forces in which invasion plans are formulated, not lack of presidential credibility.

It is also important to note that it was not only the Haitian junta leaders who questioned the president's credibility. According to an article in *U.S. News & World Report* concerning the Haitian invasion plans, "When military planners put together the aborted plan for invading Haiti, among the major factors taken into account: Bill Clinton's indecisiveness. The mission was constructed so that if—as happened—Clinton canceled or postponed the invasion, all the units could be recalled right up to H-hour." In his interview with Collins, the president did not address the military planners' similar disbelief in Clinton's word.

In the chapter on foreign policy, I asserted that Clinton's dysfunction would affect his foreign policy decision making. Clinton directly tied his ACOA behavior to his decision making on matters related to Haiti. Fortunately no American lives were lost, as the invasion was averted. But what if other military measures are considered by the president to make up for his psychological shortcomings and "mixed signals"?

The president's motivation to invade Haiti to prove the value of his word is strikingly similar to his claim that America's integrity is at stake in his formulation of Bosnian policy. The president claims that, since American troops have been promised, America would lose credibility if there is a retreat from his commitment. American credibility is not at stake, as the president's Haitian policy indicates. It is his credibility that is lacking. Because of a lack of credibility, how do we know what the president's true motivation is behind the Bosnian proposal? Also, how confident can Americans be in standing behind President Clinton when it is known that his foreign policy decisions are driven, at least in part, by personal psychological factors?

The president told Collins: "I don't believe in psychobabble, but I think I have to be acutely aware that I grew up as a peacemaker, always trying to minimize the disruption."

When one tries too hard to minimize a flaw, all too often that flaw becomes painfully evident. I share the president's lack of confidence in psychobabble. I have appeared on television and talk radio programs nationwide, and delivered numerous lectures on *The Dysfunctional President*. I have had the opportunity to receive feedback on my thesis from many people. To date, not one mental health professional has disputed my findings. While I am certain that there are some who disagree with my theory, they would have to do so in light of the president's own admissions.

While I was on the radio in Little Rock, Arkansas, a caller identifying herself as a licensed clinical social worker informed me that she had been writing then-Governor Clinton since the mid-1980s urging him to seek psychological assistance for the ACOA syndrome. Other therapists have informed me that prior to the publication of *The Dysfunctional President*, they had contemplated writing letters to the editors of national magazines to explain Clinton's behavior in light of the ACOA syndrome. A reporter for the *Wash-*

ington Post who interviewed me for an article that did not appear in the newspaper told me that the reporters in Washington D.C., who cover the president, are well aware of his psychological problem but they have been precluded from writing about it.

The Collins interview provided the most revealing public disclosure to date of the president's thoughts about how his alcoholic stepfather and dysfunctional family system affected his adult life. Noticeably missing from the president's statements was an acknowledgment of any therapeutic treatment he has received to resolve this problem. I have been asked, "If the president knows that he has this problem and reads books about it, what is the problem?"

Merely having an intellectual understanding that the problem exists is not sufficient to resolve it. If a person had a strep throat and knew he had strep throat, even read books about strep throat, but did not seek treatment, he would still have strep throat. He would be contagious, and others could be affected by his disease. Similarly, the president would not only help himself and his family but would minimize the effect of the ACOA syndrome on his presidential office if he would seek appropriate psychological treatment. The failure to do so, I believe, is a valid point of discussion as the two-term presidency of Bill Clinton winds down.

Source Notes

Chapter 1

Robert J. Samuelson, "Please Tell the Truth, Mr. President," *Washington Post*, June 9, 1993.

Michael Kelly, "Why the President Is in Trouble," *New York Times Magazine*, July 31, 1994.

Chapter 2

Meredith L. Oakley, *On the Make—The Rise of Bill Clinton* (Washington, D.C.: Regnery Publishing, 1994).

Arkansas Gazette, July 24, 1991.

New York Times, March 30, 1992.

Donald Lambro, *Washington Times*, October 8, 1992.

New York Times, September 19, 1992.

Paul Greenberg, *Washington Times*, February 16, 1992.

Martin L. Gross, *The Great Whitewater Fiasco* (New York: Ballantine Books, 1994).

Gary Wills, "Clinton's Forgotten Childhood," *Time*, June 8, 1992.

Matthew Cooper, "Bill Clinton's Hidden Life," *U.S. News & World Report*, July 20, 1992.

Chapter 3

Meredith L. Oakley, *On the Make—The Rise of Bill Clinton* (Washington, D.C.: Regnery Publishing, 1994).

Washington Times, January 16, 1993.

Edward P. Moser, *Willy Nilly: Bill Clinton Speaks Out* (Nashville: Caliban Books, 1994).

Orange County Register, September 15, 1994.

Thomas McArdle, "Can Clinton Come Back Again? Or Has President's 'Trust Gap' Grown Too Large?" *Investor's Business Daily*, August 31, 1994.

Dan Quayle, *Standing Firm* (New York: Harper/Collins, 1994).

John McLaughlin, *One on One* interview with Robert Dole, September 25, 1994.

Harrison Rainie, "But Do They Believe?" *U.S. News & World Report*, March 14, 1994.

Michael Kramer, "It Is a Time for Cunning," *Time*, March 1, 1993.

Carl Bernstein, "A Matter of Honesty: Bill Clinton and Whitewater," *Los Angeles Times*, July 17, 1994.

Mona Charen, "The Draft-Dodgers' War," *Orange County Register*, September 16, 1994.

Patrick J. Buchanan, "Liberalism's Jim and Tammy Faye," *Orange County Register*, March 25, 1994.

Thomas L. Friedman, "Clinton's Foreign-Policy Agenda Reaches Across Broad Spectrum," *New York Times*, October 4, 1992.

Walter Isaacson, "A Time for Courage," *Time*, November 16, 1992.

Michael Barone, "Once Again, It's the 'Vision Thing,'" *U.S. News & World Report*, January 31, 1994.

William F. Buckley Jr., "A Foreign-Policy Vacuum at the Top," *Orange County Register*, April 21, 1994.

Thomas L. Friedman, "With a Bow to Economics, Clinton Eats Crow on Rights," *New York Times*, May 1994.

Dana Rohrabacher, "Voices," *Orange County Register*, October 1994.

"Vote on Haiti Could Embarrass Clinton," *New York Times*, September 14, 1994.

David S. Broder, "Hostage to Haiti," *Washington Post*, September 20, 1994.

William Safire, "Jimmy Reduces Bill to Carteresque Stature," *New York Times*, September 22, 1994.

Lance Morrow, "Evil Is Not Impressed for Very Long," *Time*, October 3, 1994.

Michael Kramer, "The Carter Connection," *Time*, October 3, 1994.

Charles Fenyvesi, ed. *U.S. News & World Report*, October 3, 1994.

Gary Wills, "Clinton's Forgotten Childhood," *Time*, June 8, 1992.

Joel Connelly, "Panetta: White House Shakeup Not Done," *Orange County Register*.

Lance Morrow, "Day of Reckoning," *Time*, February 22, 1993.

Joel Klein, "What's Wrong?" *Newsweek*, June 7, 1993.

Michael Nelson, "The Press and the President: How the Press Views the President," *Current*, October 1994.

Chapter 4

William A. DeGregorie, *The Complete Book of U. S. Presidents*, 2d ed. (New York: Dembner Books, 1989).

Ronald Reagan, with Richard G. Hubler, *Where's the Rest of Me? The Ronald Reagan Story* (New York: Duell, Sloan, and Pearce, 1965).

Anne Edwards, *Early Reagan: The Rise to Power* (New York: William Morrow and Company, 1987).

Ronald Reagan, *An American Life: Ronald Reagan, the Autobiography* (New York: Simon and Schuster, 1990).

Meredith L. Oakley, *On the Make—The Rise of Bill Clinton* (Washington, D.C.: Regnery Publishing, 1994).

Chapter 5

Robert E. Levin, *Bill Clinton: The Inside Story* (New York: SPI Books, 1992).

Charles F. Allen and Jonathan Portis, *The Comeback Kid—The Life and Career of Bill Clinton* (New York: Birch Lane Press, 1992).

William A. DeGregorie, *The Complete Book of U.S. Presidents*, 2d ed. (New York: Dembner Books, 1989).

Richard J. Gelles and Murray A. Strauss, *Intimate Violence* (New York: Simon and Schuster, 1988).

Judith S. Seixas and Geraldine Youcha, *Children of Alcoholism: A Survivor's Manual* (New York: Crown Publishers, 1985).

David Viscott, M.D., *Emotionally Free* (Chicago: Contemporary Books, 1992).

Chapter 6

Dennis Wholey et al., *The Courage to Change* (Boston: Houghton Mifflin Co., 1984).

Ronald W. Goodman, "Adult Children of Alcoholics," *Journal of Counseling and Development* 66 (1987): 162.

Bernadette Mathews and Michael Halbrook, "Adult Children of Alcoholics: Implications for Career Development," *Journal of Career Development* 16 (1990): 261–68.

Judith S. Seixas and Geraldine Youcha, *Children of Alcoholism: A Survivor's Manual* (New York: Crown Publishers, 1985), pp. 63–64.

Sheryl L. Robinson and Shona K. Goodpaster, "The Effects of Parental Alcoholism on Perception of Control and Impostor Phenomenon," *Current Psychology Research and Reviews* 10 (1991): 113–19.

Nat Hentoff, "A President's Principles: 'There Is No Bill Clinton,' " Syndicated Column, June 6, 1993.

Lisa D. Hinz, "College Student Adult Children of Alcoholics: Psychological Resilience or Emotional Distance?" *Journal of Substance Abuse* 2 (1990): 449–57.

Sandra H. Tweed and Carol D. Ryff, "Adult Children of Alcoholics: Profiles of Wellness Amidst Distress," *Journal of Studies on Alcohol* 52 (1991): 113–41.

Howard Protinsky and Steven Ecker, "Intergenerational Family Relationships as Perceived by Adult Children of Alcoholics," *Family Therapy* 17 (1990): 217–22.

L. G. Bradley and H. G. Schneider, "Interpersonal Trust, Self Disclosure, and Control in Adult Children of Alcoholics," *Psychological Reports* 67 (1990): 731–37.

Tarpley M. Richards, "Recovery for Adult Children of Alcoholics: Education, Support, Psychotherapy," Special Issue: Co-dependency: Issues in Treatment and Recovery, *Alcoholism Treatment Quarterly* 6 (1989): 87–110.

Charles F. Allen and Jonathan Portis, *The Comeback Kid—The Life and Career of Bill Clinton* (New York: Birch Lane Press, 1992).

Elizabeth Stark, "Forgotten Victims: Children of Alcoholics," *Psychology Today* 21 (1987) 58–62.

David Gergen, "Give Clinton a Chance," *U.S. News & World Report*, May 10, 1993.

Bick Wanck, "Treatment of Adult Children of Alcoholics," *Carrier Foundation Letter* 109 (1985): 6.

Barry S. Tuchfeld, "Adult Children of Alcoholics" *Hospital and Community Psychiatry* 37 (1986): 235–37.

Chapter 7

Robert E. Levin, *Bill Clinton: The Inside Story* (New York: SPI Books, 1992).

Bernadette Mathews and Michael Halbrook, "Adult Children of Alcoholics: Implications for Career Development," *Journal of Career Development* 10 (1991): 261–68.

D. R. Segal, "Honesty Lies in the Eyes of the Officeholder," *Orange County Register*, April 11, 1993.

William F. Buckley Jr., "The Con Man in Clinton Slowly Emerges," Syndicated Column, February 26, 1993.

Janet Geringer Woititz, *Adult Children of Alcoholics* (Deerfield Beach, Fla: Health Communications, Inc., 1990).

Charles F. Allen and Jonathan Portis, *The Comeback Kid—The Life and Career of Bill Clinton* (New York: Birch Lane Press, 1992).

James Risen, "Clinton Aides: No More Budget Cuts on the Way," *Sacramento Bee Final*, February 27, 1993.

Charles Green, "Perot Tossing Verbal Barbs at Clinton," *Orange County Register*, April 3, 1993.

"The Clintonometer," *Orange County Register*, March 1, 1993.

William F. Buckley Jr., "Clinton Squanders the Taxpayers' Trust," Syndicated Column, June 9, 1993.

Anne Wilson Schaef and Diane Fassel, *The Addictive Organization* (San Francisco: Harper & Row, 1988).

Bob Deans, "Remarks by Clinton Put White House on Defensive," Cox News Service, April 6, 1993.

Chapter 10

Georgie Anne Geyer, "Clinton's Dangerous 'Pay-Off' Foreign Policy," *Orange County Register*, October 25, 1994.

Michael Elliott, "Something to Salute," *Newsweek*, October 24, 1994.

"Foreign Policy, Stupid," *National Review*, November 7, 1994.

David C. Hendrickson, "The Recovery of Internationalism," *Foreign Affairs*, September-October, 1994.

" 'No' to Clinton's Foreign Policy," *World Press Review*, August 1994.

World Press Review, July 1994.

Swapan Dasgupta, "Clinton's Sanctimonious Diplomacy," *World Free Press*, June 1994.

"Clinton's First Year," *Economist*, January 15, 1994.

"Cornered by His Past," *Economist*, June 4, 1994.

Chapter 11

Eric Alterman, "So, Comeback, Kid," *Mother Jones*, November-December 1994.

Jeffrey Klein, "Editor's Note," *Mother Jones*, November-December 1994.

Michael Krasny, "Let's Talk Clinton," *Mother Jones*, November-December 1994.

William Greider, "What Went Wrong?" *Rolling Stone*, November 3, 1994.

Chapter 12

Mary Matalin and James Carville, *All's Fair*, (New York: Random House, 1994).

Bob Woodward, *The Agenda* (New York: Simon and Schuster, 1994).

Elizabeth Drew, *On the Edge* (New York: Simon and Schuster, 1994).

Chapter 20

Edith Efron, "Can the President Think," *Reason*, November 1994.

Diagnostic and Statistical Manual of Mental Disorder, 3d ed. rev. (Washington, D.C.: American Psychiatric Association, 1987.

Donnie Radcliffe, *Hillary Rodham Clinton: Making Her Mark* (New York: Warner Books, 1993).

David Viscott, *Emotionally Free* (Chicago: Contemporary Books, 1992).

Gerald C. Davison and John M. Neale, *Abnormal Psychology*, 5th ed. (New York: John Wiley & Sons, 1990).

Afterword

Charles Fenyvesi, ed. *U.S. News & World Report*, October 3, 1994.

Nancy Collins, "A Legacy of Strength and Love," *Good Housekeeping*, November 1995.

Index